TODDLER TAMING

To the caring and compassionate staff who
make the New Children's Hospital, Westmead
one of the great children's hospitals

TODDLER TAMING

The guide to your child from one to four

Dr Christopher Green

with illustrations by Roger Roberts

DOUBLEDAY

Sydney   Auckland   New York   Toronto   London

TODDLER TAMING

This new edition first published in Australasia in 1990 by Doubleday,
a division of Transworld Publishers (Aust.) Pty Limited, 15-25 Helles
Avenue, Moorebank NSW 2170 and Transworld Publishers (NZ) Ltd.
3 William Pickering Drive, Albany, Auckland.

Original edition first published in 1984 by Doubleday Australia
Pty Limited
Reprinted twelve times between 1984 and 1986
First revised edition published initially in 1987
Reprinted seven times between 1987 and 1990
Reprinted 1991 (Three times), 1992

This edition reprinted 1993 (twice), 1994 (twice), 1995 (twice), 1996 (twice), 1997, 1998 (twice), 1999

National Library of Australia.
Cataloguing-in-Publication data

Green, Christopher.
    Toddler taming: the guide to your child from one to four.

    New ed.
    Bibliography.
    Includes index.
    ISBN 0 86824 434 1.

    1. Child care. 2. Child rearing. 3. Parenting. 4. Discipline of
    children. 5. Toddlers. 1. Title

646.12

Edited by Ann Kern
Designed by Lizard-esque
Printed by Griffin Press Pty Ltd, South Australia
Computer Typeset by Global Graphics, Sydney

Contents

Introduction

I used to think I was a real expert on child care, but that was before I had children myself. When my boisterous boys arrived I discovered how little I knew, and how out of touch and impractical was the vast majority of child care information of the day.

That was fifteen years ago, and from there I set out to find some more appropriate ways of managing and enjoying our young. I started by bouncing my own amateur ideas off the parents I saw each day in my practice. Some returned a week later amazed with the success of my suggestions, while others told me I was crazy.

As the months and years went by the ineffective techniques were dumped while the good ones were built on, refined and tested by the hundreds of parents I saw. After eight years I realised that I had been given a unique education, thanks to the thousands of parents who showed me the realities of child care.

This was when *Toddler Taming* was written, a book that surprised my wife and me with its immediate success. What made the book work were not just the practical ideas it contained, but also the way it demystified child care, brought fun back to parenting, boosted confidence and reassured parents that they were normal and not on their own. I am sure the key to effective parenting is knowing what to expect and having the self-confidence to see the various stages through.

With the present edition of *Toddler Taming* still in such demand, it took some courage to undertake this major revision, but child care must keep moving with the times.

We are now in the 1990s and my ideas have become much stronger, clearer and more effective. So they should as I have talked to over 50 000 parents since *Toddler Taming* was first published.

The *Toddler Taming* message in the new edition may be more finely tuned, but it is still essentially the same. The important things in child care will always remain: love, consistency, example, tension-free homes, sensible expectations and confident parents at the helm.

In the 1990s we will all have to come to terms with a number of inevitable hurdles. I believe our economic situation may well continue to deteriorate—leading to greater financial pressures on parents. This will further stress families and that will affect our children. A greater number of mothers with young children will return to paid employment as a matter of necessity rather than choice. With this, the present limited provision of quality child care must be addressed. Husbands must accept a more equal share of child care. After all they are equal partners in the decision to have children. I worry that we will follow the American trend with an ever increasing number of broken relationships. While this happens, parents and professionals must continually be reminded of the emotional vulnerability of the innocent bystanders—the children. Then there are all those difficult problems which are in danger of being swept under the carpet for another decade. These include issues such as teenage pregnancy and the rights of the child with alcoholic or addicted parents.

I believe the time has come to filter out all those impractical academic theories (that do nothing but confuse) and concentrate on the values that really matter. It seems pointless to me to philosophise about the evils of an occasional smack if our children are brought up with such ineffectual discipline that they are too insecure to know where they stand. It is useless playing classical music to the unborn foetus to soothe its nerves, if the home we provide for our children feels as tense and troubled as downtown Beirut.

Toddler Taming for the 1990s stresses a commonsense approach to child care, but one that fully recognises the importance of relationships, and protecting children from uncertainty and tension in the home environment. In reconsidering discipline, I believe this should be based on love and clearly defined limits, with parents put firmly back in charge.

It is all too easy to believe that child care is a complex science, when in fact it is very natural. Parents have been doing it well for years without authors interfering. It is now time to loosen up a bit, to take yourself and experts like me less seriously. Time with our children passes all too quickly. Children are fun—enjoy them!

Author's Note

Thanks to:

My wife Dr Hilary Green for researching, editing, encouraging and being a very special person.

James and Tim, without whose help this book would have been completed much earlier but would have contained less practical wisdom.

Jon Attenborough, the publisher whose vision and encouragement made the first *Toddler Taming* possible.

Roger Roberts, a talented illustrator with a wonderfully warped sense of humour.

Michael Morton Evans, who turned my dyslexic ramblings into a form of English.

Kate Watson, Joye Downes, Paul Hutchins, Pamela Joy, Lorraine Partington and Neralie Cocks—the Child Development Unit team I have the privilege to work with.

Numbers throughout the text refer to references I have used in my research. Details are given on page 289.

I do apologise for the consistent use of the pronouns 'he' and 'his' when referring to a toddler. I realise this may offend or irritate some readers. I have used these words for practical reasons and in no way is it an indictment of boy toddlers! Little girls are equally responsible for the characteristics I describe in this book.

Confidence is the Key

As I look back on twenty years of my work with children, I often wonder what, of all the fads and fashions I have seen, was really important. Certainly it was not the huff and puff over diets, ways to wean, breast versus bottle, bonding, early education of infants or the banning of corporal punishment.

Most of what has come and gone was little more than an orgy of academic nitpicking, but behind this glitzy window dressing of child care there are hidden some solid and vitally important ideas. It is these which provide the foundation for strong and emotionally secure children.

I see five ingredients in this important recipe, which were just as important to past generations as they are today. There is no doubt that our children thrive best when they:

● feel loved and wanted;
● live in a happy, tension-free home;

- are given a good adult example;
- receive clear, consistent child care; and
- are brought up by parents who are confident.

This book has not been written for 'head in the clouds' dreamers. It is for parents with feet firmly on the ground who want practical ideas to make their child-rearing both successful and enjoyable. With this aim in mind, where better to start than with the mainstay of successful parenting—confidence.

Confident parenting

Confidence is what makes parents positive, powerful and puts them firmly in charge. When confidence is high the trivial hassles of our day-to-day lives seem like molehills. But as soon as confidence crumbles, we quickly lose all perspective for what's important and those same molehills become as towering as Mount Everest. Confidence has a spin-off in almost everything we do. It promotes effective discipline, which improves children's behaviour and, in the long term, forms much of the basis for the child's own self-confidence.

Some years ago, when addressing a large gathering of good parents, I asked one simple question: 'How confident are you in your own parenting abilities?' Seventy-seven per cent of those who responded to this secret ballot said that they had serious doubts about what they were doing.

It seems strange to me that in these days when there is almost an epidemic of child care gurus, and bookshops are overloaded with how-to-do-it manuals, parental confidence appears to be sinking rather than rising. There are some good reasons for this slide.

Confidence busters

The breakdown of the extended family has left many new parents isolated and uncertain. Many have never experienced a behaviour problem or even held a child before their own. It also seems that the more complicated that child care theory becomes, the less we are prepared to trust our natural instincts. This leaves us very vulnerable to a predictable group of factors that erode our confidence.

Not knowing what's normal

When our first child blasts in on the scene, few of us are prepared for the onslaught that follows. As most of us now live away from our close family, we suffer one of the penalties of this, that we cannot get easy access to advice on the common problems of behaviour and management. Often we feel we are the only ones with troubles when, if only we knew it, everyone else is in the same boat.

With the toddler, some behavioural concerns are so common, they must be seen as a normal part of parenthood. Toddlers have fiddly fingers, don't think of the future, like constant attention, and often ignore much of what you say. It is said of normal 2-year-olds that 44 per cent attack their younger or older brother or sister, 50 per cent eat too little, 70 per cent resist going to bed, 83 per cent whinge and nag, 94 per cent constantly seek attention, 95 per cent are stubborn and 100 per cent are active and rarely still. Some children show these characteristics to a minor degree while others hold in their hand a full house.

That's life! There are quite enough genuine worries in the world without making ourselves feel inadequate by believing we are to blame for the normal non-problems around us.

Ground down by competition

We live in a very competitive world and we can't help noticing how other people manage their homes, relationships and children. Soon our lives are lived constantly looking over our shoulder to see that we are performing up to scratch.

This is made worse by the media which presents a strange slant on reality. Many popular magazines overtly promote the everyday endeavour to find perfection. 'The Perfect Marriage', 'Perfect Sex', 'The Perfectly White Business Shirt', 'The Perfectly Balanced Breakfast Cereal', 'The Perfect Child Rearing Method'. Needless to say nothing is perfect and most of what we are striving for are unattainable myth-like goals.

Those who appear regularly on television talk-back or soap operas are just actors, with impressive public faces, who may seem controlled and in charge on the screen but privately get just as confused, tired and unhappy as the rest of us. When one of Australia's trendy women's magazines recently celebrated its tenth anniversary, a cynical reviewer commented... 'The typical girl they feature needs—a career, a husband, children, a home, jewels, clothes, excitement and travel.' Faced with this picture it is

little wonder that so many women feel they have been cheated. For many of the super mums I look after, the only excitement and travel they get is the train trip down to the hospital to seek help with their far from perfect child.

In the past, children spent most of their first six years at home, but now we parade them in public from their earliest days and with this comes competition and embarrassment.

As you wait in the baby clinic, you may wonder why all the other children seem bigger, stronger, toothier and more advanced than your meagre scrap. You love playgroup but are aware that others watch you and your children. 'Look at that child over there, she's 13 months and not yet walking. I think there is something wrong with her.' 'Look, that one just bit the other, he's a potential juvenile delinquent, and he is barely 1 year old.' At pre-school you may feel the pressure when your little one fails at cutting-out or romps around when the core of children are pasting, painting and listening to stories.

Parents can feel extremely vulnerable when their children do not achieve at school. This is made worse by those painful people who boost their own inadequate egos by boasting about their children's brilliance. As you sit at a parent/teacher night, some opinionated adult makes it clear that 'My boy is 5 and he reads Shakespeare sonnets like Laurence Olivier'. Before you can catch your breath this is trumped by another painful parent who says, 'My girl is 4 years and plays the violin perfectly by the Suzuki method'. All you can think is 'My little one is 5 years old and wets the bed every night'.

Bed wetting is quite common, affecting one in ten of all at the start of school. In fact there would be three children in your child's class with the same problem, but competitive parents tend to cloud the perspective by boasting about the rare and clever while keeping quiet about those common things that make us feel ashamed.

Overwhelmed by experts

In my more sombre moments I often wonder if all us experts were to be blown from the face of the earth, would parents be any the worse off. As I set out to demystify child care and boost confidence, it seems that a hundred others are out there hell bent on making it all much more difficult. Confidence is fragile enough without being confused by some of the way-out and incorrect ideas I hear, such as:

- Working mothers do great harm to their children. Not true.

- Every mother should want to be a 24-hour-a-day parent. If she does not, she should feel ashamed. Rubbish. Few fathers want to be 24-hour-a-day fathers and some time to ourselves is a help to both parent and child.

- Infants placed in a baby walker strain their legs which then become bandy. All infants at the age of 1 have bandy legs, not through weight-bearing and baby walkers, but because it is the way God made them.

- The toddler who wakes often every night must be comforted by its parent. An impractical, out-of-touch theory. This is a sleep problem which should be cured quickly. Sleep deprivation is a form of torture, and parents who chronically lack sleep become a little deranged, which is not good for their children.

- If a baby is not breast-fed it is severely disadvantaged. While the breast is strongly recommended, it is never obligatory for the average Australian or New Zealand child.

- Parents who use occasional corporal punishment on their children cause emotional damage. This is a complete misreading of the facts.

- The toddlers who play occasionally with their private parts do this as a sign of sexual abuse. Nonsense. Little children do this because it feels pleasant and they are bored.

Books that give impractical, out-of-touch ideas which set unattainably high goals, do nothing but generate fears and create feelings of parental inadequacy. These should be pulped and recycled to save some of the world's trees. Life is tough enough without some smart philosopher producing learned writings to make us feel as though we are second class citizens.

Being unaware of individuality

Every child is born an individual with unique talents and temperament which can be adjusted but not rebuilt by the warmth and skill of the parents. One of the quickest ways to crush confidence is when parents try to force their children to be something they were never designed to be. The child with an active temperament will never sit still long enough to learn to read at the age of 3, any more than the gentle boy with the temperament of St Francis will ever be suitable for the front row of the State of Origin footy team.

No matter what I say there is still an archaic view, held by many who should know better, that all children are born with an identical clean slate, and every difference, fault and misdemeanour is caused by the actions of their parents.

We all have to learn to accept the child we have been given, and then do our best. Remember that as parents, we too are individuals, with our own temperaments and styles of parenting. We must have the confidence to do our own thing and not be brainwashed by those who do things differently.

Hindrance from the helping professionals

Some of us professionals can make parents feel pretty inadequate. It is easy to shatter a parent's confidence by implying that we know how to bring up our own children perfectly and that behaviour problems only occur in your child. Even worse, some of us are still steeped in the prehistoric ideas of the 1950s and find it impossible to give any practical advice on behaviour without psychoanalysing the parents.

I call this psychodynamic approach 'the Irish weather forecaster technique'. They can tell you every detail of what happened yesterday, the day before and right to the day you were born, but when it comes to helping with today, tomorrow and the future, they turn mute. Choose your professional well. The helping professions should be good at helping, but unfortunately this is not always the case.

Watch for the school of thought that says that unless you bring up your children 'the one and only right way', some form of permanent, psychological damage will ensue. There is no one right way to bring up children. Child care fashions come and go with the regularity of Parisian hemlines. As we chop and change the children look on bemused, showing how well they survive despite our professional interference.

Conclusion

Life is tough for parents today, due to our frantic lifestyles, competition, isolation and unreasonable expectations. There is also an oversupply of unimaginative and impractical information. Most parents are doing an amazingly good job, but many do not realise this. Parents don't need criticism but do need words of encouragement and support.

Parenting is a compromise. We all start out with incredibly high ideals but as tension and tiredness take their toll, we tend to lower our sights to a more middle-of-the-road position, a state of peaceful equilibrium. It is not for others to criticise and compare. What feels right and works for you is as good a way to bring up children as any. If you love them, enjoy them and do what feels right and works for you; no-one can do better.

The foundation for happy, secure children

Love Being wanted and welcome. Love may be a vague term but it is a very important word.

Consistency Children need to know where they stand and that what stands today will still be standing tomorrow.

Tackle tension Tension is probably the most common destructive influence in today's child-rearing. There is no point in bringing up your child by the book, if home feels like a war zone. Friction in adult relationships can never be hidden from children. The most considerate thing we as parents can do for our children is to be kinder to one another.

Good example Children cannot behave better than those whose example they follow.

Reasonable expectations Parents need to know what is normal and what to expect. Unrealistic expectations cause non-problems which undermine parents unnecessarily.

Fun and enjoyment Children should be brought up as apprentices to fun-loving parents who enjoy having them around. Some

parents take child-rearing so seriously that it becomes an interesting scientific experiment. You cannot fall in love with some laboratory animal.

Confidence Here is the key to effective parenting. Confident parents are positive and positive parents are very powerful people.

2

What Makes Toddlers Tick

TICK
TICK
TICK

Toddlers are those interesting little people aged between 1 and 4 years who suddenly discover that they have an immense amount of power to make their parents jump. Some pass through this stage with hardly a ripple, whilst many others surge through making waves so large that all is swamped in their wake.

Toddlerhood starts at around the first birthday. You are in no doubt of its arrival when one day you put the dinner down and instead of the usual appreciation, your littlie takes one look and says 'Yuk!' You take this badly, jump up and down and in fact have a tantrum of your own. Toddler looks up, likes it and thinks 'Wow! Me do this again'. Now you have a problem.

Don't let me depress you. I know that as you look back some years down the track, you will see this as one of the most enjoyable stages of childhood. Toddlers are so alive, so full of fun and what's more they seem to see life with innocent eyes and the most vivid of vivid imaginations. To enjoy toddlerhood, you need to know what to expect, then tuck some toddler taming techniques up your sleeve and go for it. First let's see what makes toddlers tick.

Behavioural development—the overview

In simple terms, we can expect our children to go through three very different stages of psychological development between birth and 8 years of age. The first stage is from birth up to 1 year—the baby. Stage 2 goes from 1 to 4 years—the toddler. Stage 3 moves on up to about the age of 8 years—the early school-age child. Within this framework, as our children grow in size and cleverness, their behaviour will alter, but not necessarily for the better.

The baby: birth to 1 year

The baby from birth to 1 year is a cuddly little article who spends most of the time getting to know mum and dad, while they get to know him. This is the important process of bonding. The aim of the first year is to develop a secure and trusting child who has a secure and trusting relationship with his parents. The views of child care change regularly, but the current belief is that babies cannot be spoilt in the first year of life. When hungry, they should be fed; when frightened they should be comforted; when crying they should be cuddled, and when just being a nuisance, they should be given the benefit of the doubt anyway.

Babies do not need discipline—they need to be taught regular routines and then enjoyed. There are times when it is not so easy and this is when parents must drop the theory and change the ground rules.

The toddler: 1 to 4 years

At this age, little ones discover that they have the muscle to manipulate and challenge and are not backward about flexing it. This stage starts gradually after the first birthday with senseless and unthinking acts predominant up to the age of 2 years, when more considered forms of manipulation take over. Toddlerhood hits a peak at about 2 to 2$\frac{1}{2}$ years and then gradually eases. I say it eases but the behaviour challenges do not disappear, they just take on a more artistic form.

Unlike babies, toddlers need to know exactly where they stand and how far they can push the limits. The toddler needs discipline.

Many parents find toddlerhood a trying time and in fact it has been shown that toddler mums have triple the trouble with their nerves[1]. This should not be the case if you know what is normal, are confident and in charge—which you should be by the time you finish this book.

The early school-age child: 4 to 8 years

Somewhere around the fourth birthday the child gradually slips out of toddlerhood to become an early school-age child. There is no firm developmental age for this. With some it may be as early as 3 years, and others $4^{1}/2$. This third behavioural stage is once again quite different from all that has gone before. We now have a child who thinks of the repercussions of his actions, exhibits quite a bit of sense, is interested in rules and, what is more, will often obey them. It is thought that at this stage, some of our best bureaucrats are born.

Many 5-year-olds at school will sit at their desk, not only obeying the class rules themselves but seeing that the laws are applied equally to all. They take on the role of the class policeman, reporting the slightest transgression to their teacher. This is the age when it is fashionable to 'dob on your mates', an activity which becomes unpopular after the age of 8 years.

Parents can cash in on this obsession with rules, now at last being able to lay down 'laws of the house' that have a fair chance of being obeyed. At this stage of psychological development, the child can be treated more like a little adult, with more trust, democracy and reason.

The toddler—his goals

As children move from being babies to being toddlers, they are amazed at the unbelievable acceleration of freedoms that appear. Suddenly they can stand, walk, climb and run. They have the ability to manipulate objects, touch, take things apart and fiddle. They are amazed and overawed at their behavioural power. It is almost as if someone had left open the door of a mighty arsenal of behavioural weapons, but unfortunately they don't know how to use them wisely.

This is an exciting time for toddlers, but not without its fair share of confusion and frustration. They find that by using their new-found behavioural weapons they may get lots of attention, but this often backfires as the angry reaction they may provoke can rob them of the closeness and love they enjoyed as babies. They are frustrated as their little brains run hot with good ideas, which the immaturity of their bodily co-ordination prevents them from seeing through.

For the parents, toddlerhood is a time of introducing controls, guiding gently, setting limits, avoiding confrontation and being 100 per cent firm when needed. For the children, toddlerhood is all about control—learning to control their bodies and behaviours.

- *Control of bodily functions* Becoming toilet trained.

- *Control of impulses* Learning that their demands cannot be met immediately.

- *Controlling the frustration of failure* Knowing they want to feed themselves but accepting that they can't do it successfully.

- *Control of behaviour* Learning that tantrums are not an appropriate way to influence people.

- *Control of separation anxiety* Moving from the close clinginess usual at 1 year to be able to separate for pre-school and later for school.

- *Control over selfishness* Sharing attention, sharing belongings, not interrupting and realising that others also have rights.

The toddler will learn these controls and even take on board a smattering of commonsense and something that vaguely resembles a conscience.

The toddler—trademark traits

Whether you think of your bundle of joy as 'a little treasure', 'an ankle biter', 'a midget mafiosa', or 'the terrible 2-year-old', all toddlers have one thing in common and that is an interesting collection of behavioural traits that are their trademark.

Plenty of power

Small toddlers can exert an amazing amount of power over adults. If they don't get what they want, such is their protest that parents often buckle under the onslaught. Toddlerhood may be an age when children show little self-control but it doesn't stop them trying to control those around them.

It is not the power that causes the problem but rather how it is used. Toddlers are negative, show little sense and totally lack appreciation of the rights of others. With such a strong hand, all they have to do is to dig in their heels and shout, and adults jump.

Power without sense is a combination popularised by Idi Amin. This man carried the reputation as one who was hard to live with.

Little sense

If you were to list the attributes of the toddler, it is unlikely that sense would immediately spring to mind. It is my belief that between the ages of 1 and 2 years most toddlers have zero sense. From 2 to 2$\frac{1}{2}$ years a delicately calibrated instrument might raise a flicker of a reading, but it is often hard for us parents to see this with the naked eye. Fortunately, from this time on sense starts to grow with a significant amount present by 3 years. By the time they have reached their fourth birthday, most little ones are reasonably reliable.

When people talk of the 'terrible twos' I believe it is really the 'terrible 1$\frac{1}{2}$ to 2$\frac{1}{2}$-year-olds' that they refer to. This short period is the time of minimum sense with the maximum of mobility and militancy. You don't need to be called Sigmund to know that this combination is going to be psychologically upsetting for someone, and that someone is likely to be you, the parent.

This is the age of unthinking behaviours (e.g. head-banging) and complete disregard for danger, in the interests of the moment.

Young toddlers can argue, fight and get into no-win situations but they don't have the sense to know when to stop. For effective discipline, parents need to know when it is best to back down. Unfortunately some parents find this impossible as they possess even less sense than their offspring.

Wanting attention 25 hours a day

Toddlers love to be centre stage at all times. They resent it if others steal the limelight, whether it is a friend dropping in for a chat, a lengthy phone call, or when husbands come home from work.

Toddlers want attention 24 hours a day and if you give this, then they will want 25 hours. Attention is important but it does take its toll. After a day of play, answering incessant questions, arguing and trying to keep one jump ahead of such inventive and imaginative little people, mothers are exhausted. This is not physical exhaustion but a special sort of tiredness that leaves you numb from the neck upwards. Now dad swans in exclaiming 'Gosh I had a tiring day at work'. He knows nothing of that numbness that leaves you in a state closely resembling brain death.

Self-centredness

Most toddlers have tunnel vision, which focuses only on their own needs and happiness. It never occurs to them that other people may have rights too. When a child is playing and wants a particular toy, it is unlikely that he will ask politely for it when 'smash and grab' is more effective. The idea of taking turns and thinking of another's point of view and sharing is quite foreign. Although toddlers enjoy being with other children, they tend to play beside them rather than with them. This self-centred behaviour is normal for most toddlers, although it has been known to extend into adulthood! Some of the world's most notable dictators have shown skills that leave the toddler looking an absolute amateur.

Ten-minute time frame

The young toddler lives only for the here and now with an interest in time that extends little past the last ten minutes and the ten to come. At this age praise and rewards must be immediate, while discipline must happen now or not at all. It is pointless punishing the 2-year-old hours after the event once dad has returned home in the evening. It is equally foolish to expect the toddler to understand that being good today will be rewarded by going to the zoo next week.

Negativity

Children learn to say 'No' long before they learn to say 'Yes' and at the age of 3 this simple little word flows out with the clearest articulation, due mainly to two years of non-stop practice. Some experts say that toddlers only copy their negative parents who say 'No', 'No', 'No' constantly from the child's earliest age. This is an interesting explanation, but I think the trait is inbuilt and can also be seen in the children of the most positive parents.

Conclusion

The toddler is that little person aged between 1 and 4 years who demonstrates some interesting behavioural traits. Early toddlerhood is a time of flexing muscles and exhibiting minimal sense, while the older toddler conducts a more considered form of assault on powerless parents.

The trademarks of the toddler are; more power than sense, living for the moment, demanding centre stage position. Philosophical, religious and philanthropic ideals are not conspicuous.

Parents should know this is normal, use commonsense and cunning, not blame themselves, then go with the flow.

3

Behaviour: What is Normal?

The more I work with toddlers, the less surprised I become with the extremes of behaviour that I see. The truth is that there is an immense breadth of behaviour that can be confidently classed as normal. I am less certain of what could be considered average, but when it comes to what is tolerable, I am in no doubt that this decision is in the eye of the beholder.

If you put a busy, noisy toddler in with a busy, noisy family, he will not be noticed, whilst a quiet, violin-playing, well-mannered child would stand out like a vegetarian at a butcher's picnic.

Tolerance depends on the individual make-up of the parents and how the world is treating us. It varies from day to day. When life is going well we can take a lot but on those bad days, a little toddlerhood goes a very long way.

We know that all toddlers have a tendency to be negative and stubborn, to have more power than sense, to live for today and to be short on the humanitarian skills. All toddlers will have a smattering of these. Some will have been dealt a weak hand, others will present with all the trump cards. Over the years there have been a number of studies that have looked at the incidence of toddler behaviour.

The studies—the incidence

If you look at what has been published in overseas literature[2], it would seem that nine out of ten parents experience some behaviour difficulties with their toddlers while one in four find toddlerhood quite tough. These figures echo our experience in Australia where, in addition, we have found that of parents who attend our education programmes, 77 per cent say they have serious doubts about their parenting abilities, 98 per cent say they will smack their children at some time whilst about 15 per cent find that shopping and toddlers don't mix.

For further figures it is best to look at some old but good studies.

The New York longitudinal study

A study begun in New York in 1956 followed up 133 children from birth to adulthood[3]. During this time researchers were most interested in temperament and behaviour. This study showed children to have individual temperamental traits at birth. When results were analysed, 40 per cent of the group fitted into the 'easy child' category, being a joy to look after as babies and usually during childhood. Parents, teachers and paediatricians all found this group easy. Whether the mother was competent or hopeless and the father a saint or Jack the Ripper, children of this 40 per cent would probably do quite well.

More than half of the 133 children, however, were not so easy to handle. Ten per cent of the study group were little terrorists from the word go. They were difficult as babies, often difficult as toddlers with their difficulties frequently accompanying them into school. Parents, paediatricians and teachers all suffered under the strain. These children tended to be particularly negative, extremely loud in both voice and crying, and easily frustrated; they had irregular sleeping and feeding habits and showed great difficulty adjusting to any change. They were hard to handle, disputed decisions and had tantrums like infant McEnroes. Such children quickly knock all confidence out of their parents and if the problems continue through school, a trail of teachers will sign off on sick and recreation leave. Though saint-like parents have less chance of producing and more chance of managing children like these, this group would be extremely difficult in anyone's hands.

A further 15 per cent of the total were described as 'slow to warm up'. They had many of the same characteristics as the last group, but these were not so severe. The difference was that, when handled with care, understanding, persistence and patience, they had a sporting chance of doing well. Parenting this group was a major challenge, where super parents managed and normal parents struggled.

With the 40 per cent angels, 10 per cent terrorists and 15 per cent semi-impossibles accounted for, 35 per cent of the total remained in an intermediate group that was neither very easy nor very difficult. Ease of handling this group depends on the parents and on the blend of temperament characteristics inherited by each child. (There is more on temperament in Chapter 4.)

The Chamberlin study

Another New York study[4] followed up 200 children from age 2 until school age. It demonstrated the main behavioural worries for parents at different ages and set out to stir up specialist paediatricians to give more help. The behaviours commonly seen at ages 2 and 4 were listed and then ranked in the order that causes greatest concern at those two ages. At age 2, many parents said 'He doesn't do a thing I tell him'. These stubborn and wilful characteristics were top of the list. Second place was shared equally between tantrums and 'getting into everything'. Continuing these behavioural Olympics, at age 4, the gold medal was still awarded for stubborn, wilful behaviour, although now verbal abuse and 'back-talk' were also included as problems. The silver medal went to whingeing and nagging and the bronze was taken easily by lack of sharing and frequent fighting.

Also in this study, a number of parents were interviewed and asked to describe their children's behaviour at three different ages (see Table 1). This makes sobering reading: 44 per cent of New York 2-year-olds are said to attack and annoy their younger or older brother or sister; 50 per cent eat too little; 70 per cent resist going to bed; 83 per cent of these normal little Americans are said to whinge and nag mercilessly; 95 per cent had stubborn and attention-seeking behaviour. These figures may be a bit of an overestimate but it makes you wonder—what is normal?

Table 1: Mothers' behavioural description of their children at ages 2, 3 and 4

Behaviour	Percentage of age group		
	Age 2 %	Age 3 %	Age 4 %
Eats too little	50	26	37
Doesn't eat the right kinds of food	64	43	54
Resists going to bed	70	46	56
Awakens during the night	52	52	56
Has nightmares	17	18	36
Resists sitting on toilet	43	2	2
Has bowel motion in pants	71	17	1
Wets self during day	75	14	7
Wets bed at night	82	49	26
Curious about sex differences	28	45	75
Rubs or plays with sex organs	56	49	51
Modest about dressing	1	7	26
Fights or quarrels	72	75	92
Jealous	54	47	42
Hurts younger sibling	44	51	64
Hits others or takes things	68	52	46
Stubborn	95	92	85
Talks back (behaves cheekily)	42	73	72
Disobedient	82	76	78
Tells fibs	2	26	37
Constantly seeks attention	94	48	42
Clings to mother	79	34	26
Whines and nags	83	65	85
Cries easily	79	53	58
Temper outbursts	83	72	70
Active, hardly ever still	100	48	40

What about paediatricians' children?

At a recent meeting of specialists in our hospital, I asked twenty-eight paediatricians about their own children. The questions covered a wide area, with behaviour featuring quite strongly. There were also some general questions which yielded some astonishing answers. For example, four of the experts did not know the date of their children's birth; three were uncertain as to whether their children were fully immunised; nineteen stated that their storage of drugs and medicines at home would be seen as negligent by our hospital's child safety centre.

In the behavioural area, about 40 per cent had endured at least
one colicky baby and although experts were at that time disputing
the benefit of drugs in helping colic, 75 per cent of them used medication, 50 per cent swearing by it. About 10 per cent of the paediatricians had a child with breath-holding attacks, about 15 per cent
had found toilet training a struggle and about 30 per cent had been
troubled by feeding difficulties. About 40 per cent of these experts
had also experienced at least one child with sleep problems and
nearly 50 per cent considered that their discipline was often far
from effective.

As a last comment, most suspected that at some time their children would have been of interest to our child psychiatry colleagues. All this goes to prove just one thing. Toddler behaviour is
a worry to most parents, whether they are psychologists,
plumbers, computer programmers or paediatricians.

Sensible expectations

It is upsetting that so few parents have any idea what constitutes
normal toddler behaviour. We spend much of our lives feeling

guilty, inadequate, self-recriminating and believing we are the only ones who cannot control our children. Life is tough enough without immobilising ourselves with such ill-founded guilt.

All toddlers...

- crave attention and hate to be ignored. Some are quite satisfied with their parents' best efforts, others would grumble unless 25 hours a day, 8 days a week were devoted solely to their care.

- separate poorly from their caretakers. In the first 3 years a toddler prefers to play near his mother and does not like to let her out of his sight for long. For most, an unfamiliar child-minder causes initial problems, while being locked in a room or becoming separated when out shopping constitutes a major trauma.

- tend to be busy little people. Some are extremely active and hardly ever still; others are just 'active'.

- have little road sense or in fact little sense of danger. They are impulsive and unpredictable which is a hazard even in the apparently sensible child. All toddlers need close parental protection.

- show little respect for other people's property. Their fingers are drawn as if by magnetism to everything they pass. Ornaments are broken and cupboards rearranged. Those ten active little digits have an amazing power to spread a sticky, jam-like substance over every surface they meet—rather like a small bee distributing pollen.

- tend to be stubborn and wilful; some are quite militant but others will bend to reason.

- tend to be blind to the mountain of mess they generate. The tidy toddler who is neat and even picks up his own toys is the exception rather than the rule.

- ask endless questions, the same one being repeated again and again, with little interest in the answer.

- change their minds every minute. One day your toddler says, 'I like Weet-bix'. When you are at the supermarket, they are on special and you buy a month's supply. 'Don't like Weet-bix, don't like Weet-bix,' squawks the mind-bender. What is happening? Are you going mad? No, this is just brainwashing, toddler style.

- constantly interrupt adults. It is not that they want to be rude, but they believe that what they have got to contribute is much more important than the irrelevant ramblings of their parents. This trick of skilfully interrupting in mid-sentence everything that mum or dad says really jars the nerves.

- make their mothers feel inferior. Little children have an incredible ability to demoralise their mothers. Many will act as complete angels when in the care of others, reserving their demonic side exclusively for their parents. There is no point telling anyone—who would believe you? Other toddlers are difficult for their mothers and behave perfectly for their fathers. This is because they have long studied mum's vulnerabilities and know how to hit a raw nerve with perfect aim, but are not so sure of dad, as he seems some sort of less known relative.
- are extremely sensitive to upset, excitement and tension in their environment. Their sound sleep pattern can be upset by illness, holidays or stress. Often quite a minor alteration to the environment can make the child who was fully toilet trained start to leak.

Many toddlers...

- will sit and concentrate briefly to draw, do puzzles or attend to pre-reading tasks. A minority will settle for a long time but most become restless in about five minutes and look for a means of escape. Quite a large proportion of active little children will not sit even for the shortest of periods.

- are cuddly, affectionate, 'giving' children. There is, however, a minority who resent handling, are distant and seem to give a poor return of love to their parents.

- are determined and independent. Some become so belligerent that they refuse to be fed or dressed, even though they are far too young to do either task unaided. Other toddlers are passive, dependent and quite happy to be pampered and directed.

- are compulsive climbers. At an early age they will organise an expedition to the summit of the settee and once this has been scaled, will set out to conquer the benchtops, tables and anything that happens to be there. Other toddlers are more sensible and have a healthy fear of the 'painful stop at the end of the drop'.

- eat well, although many do not consume the quality of food that their parents have read that they should. Some children take food extremely seriously, never lifting their eyes from the plate until the pattern is almost scraped completely off. Others find food an interesting plaything and a bit of a joke, which is a pain to the parent committed to delivering the perfectly balanced diet from the earliest day.

- go off their food around their first birthday, a proper eating pattern not returning for anything up to a year. Some will tolerate a narrow, unimaginative diet; others will eat anything in sight. Some eat main meals; others were born to be snackers.

- continue with a daytime sleep until the age of 3 years. Others discard this at about 18 months and nothing the parents do will bring it back. Most toddlers go to sleep before 8 p.m. each night, but others stay on the rampage until close to midnight. Some are lazy in the morning, finding it hard to get out of bed; others wake at an ungodly hour and disturb the whole household. With busy children who are on the rampage from dawn until after dusk it is often hard to change their pattern with any technique less powerful than a general anaesthetic.

- have fears. Dogs, loud noises, new situations and strange objects and people cause distress in over half of this age group.

- display a multitude of irritating habits. This of course is not only a problem with children.

- have behaviour which fluctuates considerably from day to day and week to week. Some parents tell me that their little children seem almost schizophrenic, with wild alterations in behaviour. Bad days are usually blamed on teething, lack of sleep or 'something they ate'. These all make good scapegoats but it never seems to occur to parents that adults can have good days and bad days and we don't blame this on teething. Even trainers allow racehorses the odd off day.

Conclusion

All caring parents worry about their children, wanting to bring them up as best they can. Many of the behaviours that cause concern would not be problems at all, if only we knew what was normal.

No matter what we do it seems that about nine out of ten toddlers will cause us some behavioural bother with about one in ten ageing us by years. When I look at the figures mentioned in the Chamberlin Study I wonder, 'Who are the children with normal behaviour? Are they the docile, compliant, non-whingeing, non-stubborn minority, or the junior Rambos who romp around our homes?'.

4

The Difficult Child: Born or Made?

History

In the nineteenth century, writers were in no doubt that the cause of all deviant behaviour was bad breeding. Some put forward the notion that 'the born criminal and lesser sinners were beyond help due to their abnormal make-up'.

As the twentieth century dawned, this notion gradually changed, and environment was thought to be the major influence on children's behaviour. By the 1950s this notion had become highly refined: all behavioural blame was laid squarely on the shoulders of inadequate mothers. It seemed irrelevant whether the marriage was stable and the parents exceptional. Mothers still collected the blame, regardless of the untold unhappiness, guilt and suffering it caused.

The cause of difficult behaviour: the view in the 1990s

Behaviour and temperament are now known to have a strong hereditary basis. This hereditary influence gives us the basic material to work with but the final product depends very much on environmental factors, which is a polite way of saying, our standard of parenting.

Though these hereditary temperamental characteristics are obviously important, no-one is exactly certain of the relative impact of genes versus environment. Personally I believe that environment is always the most important factor, which is good news because environment is something that can be worked on by improving our parenting skills, whereas we cannot send our little ones back to their manufacturer for a genetic tune-up.

Heredity or environment—a confusion

Because life is never straightforward, the whole heredity–environment debate becomes very muddy in some cases. If an extremely difficult child comes from a home filled with fighting, tension and parental abuse, it seems a black and white case of environmental upset, but this may only be part of the story.

Often adult relationships fall apart because one or both parties have always had a way of behaving that is far from easy to live with. These behaviours have a definite chance of being transmitted through to the genes of the children. The expression, 'like father, like son' is a familiar truth. The parents' behaviour also upsets the home environment and the end product is a complex coalition of heredity and handling.

A stranger in the family

It may seem a strange observation but sometimes a family gets a child that does not suit them. When a peace-loving, polite, quiet, obsessively tidy family is hit by a human tornado, their equilibrium is shattered. To survive this unexpected onslaught, major adjustments must be made. A similar upset occurs when a famous heavyweight football hero spawns a docile, passive boy who prefers picking flowers to jumping on people in the mud.

When a child seems out of place in a family, don't blame the milkman. Nature has a habit of doing this to nice parents, to bring a bit of interest to their lives. Even if our children do not suit us, we have to make the best of what we've got.

Children who are too like their parents

Parents would prefer their children to copy all their best points and by-pass their weaknesses. In reality the reverse is more likely to be true, with our children seeking out our worst qualities and displaying them to a similar or greater degree.

Many children who are difficult to live with are often like their parents. For example, totally disorganised children may have totally disorganised parents. Some children who are sent to me because they are unenthusiastic and have little drive to do anything much in life arrive in the company of equally boring parents.

Overactive, impulsive, intolerant fathers frequently produce active children who are chips off the old block, which leads to a major personality clash. Some years ago I was brought 3-year-old twins whose mother complained that they would never sit still and were forever rocking and head banging. In my office I watched them rock, foot to foot, always slightly out of time, like defective windscreen wipers on a car. When dad arrived a little later he burst into my office like a police raid. It was apparent within a minute that he was an overactive, driving athlete, who had never sat still from birth. The more he complained about his children's overactivity, the more I noticed him rocking, swaying, kicking his feet, moving his hands—exhibiting a problem far more severe than his normal children.

Is behaviour worse in the 1990s?

Forty years ago, children's behaviour problems appeared to be much less common. Many writers have blamed the current increase on the artificial colourings and other pollutants we give our children. I do not believe this is the main cause; there is, I think, a much simpler explanation. Forty years ago, if one went to a doctor seeking help for one's child, it would be in the knowledge that all blame for the problem would be laid firmly on the mother, and some long-term psychotherapy for the parents might be suggested. This, in itself, must have been a major deterrent from seeking help, preventing most troubled parents admitting to anyone but their closest family that they could not handle their offspring. Behaviour problems may seem to be more common these days because of the break-up of the extended family and the highly competitive world our children live in. I believe that it's not so much an increase in the problems themselves, as an increase in the awareness of them. Now that they realise that criticism will not be levelled at them, parents are talking more openly about them and coming for help earlier. This is a healthy change for the better.

Professionals with prehistoric views

As a doctor who has lived and suffered through the aftermath of the era of psychological abuse of mothers, I am amazed that such an attitude could ever have existed. What is worse, there are still professionals in positions of power who have not yet accepted the influence of heredity on behaviour.

I would have thought that any professional who views life with even partly open eyes, could not help but see the immense variation based on simple heredity in all aspects of human nature. Any parent with more than one child would be aware of their completely different personalities. Such variations cannot possibly be accounted for solely by the different standard of care each child receives, even if it was usual for families to give different care to different children. It is my opinion that some children are born with a difficult temperament, which generates tension and upset in their environment, which then rebounds onto them. It is not a nice thing to say, but some children make themselves harder to love and get on with than others. Happily, the converse is also true.

One place where genetic influence stands out is in the newborn nursery of any hospital. Here we have babes who have hardly been touched by their mothers, already demonstrating their different personalities. In one cot there might be a quiet, loving baby exuding affection, cuddling in tightly and feeding with ease. In the very next cot could be a child in an identical state of health, who is irritable, arches his back, cries most of the time, dislikes being handled and forever spits out his feed. You don't need to be steeped in the psychiatric tradition to know that one would be a joy for any parent, while the other would be a trial for even the most well-intentioned family.

When working at night during my training in maternity hospitals, I would often see a noisy infant banished to a corridor to avoid disturbing the rest of the serious sleepers. Some of the most difficult toddlers I care for started life in this way, their hereditary load bringing problems before they even left hospital.

I am not naive enough to believe that all parents are without fault, but I do resent out-of-date experts blaming parents for temperament and behaviour which is not of their making.

Conclusion

Some children are born to be easy and some are born just plain difficult. We can't send them back but improved handling will make a major difference.

If you are lucky enough to have been sent an angel, give thanks to God for his kindness, but please don't get swollen headed and hold up this child as the perfect reincarnation of a perfect mother. If on the other hand you have a really difficult child, I do sympathise and I hope this book is of help. If you are criticised by some parents on an ego-trip with their perfect child, let's jointly hope that next time they get a proper little terrorist. Then we will know there is some justice in this world.

Remember that behaviour results from both genes and environment. Of these, environment is most important, and what is more, it is the one we can change.

5

Understanding Toddler Behaviour

'Oh why me?' you moan, your head in your hands, as junior puts on yet another Oscar-winning performance for the supermarket crowd. 'I've given him a ton of love and endless attention and still he insists on embarrassing me with these painful performances.'

As your tired brain becomes more tired, it may be easy to believe that your little loved one is in fact the enemy, out to punish you in every way possible for your innumerable faults. But I can assure you it is not like that. In reality he is just an interesting little person called a Toddler, engaging in common or garden little person's behaviour.

When I look around at all the children I see, it appears to me that almost all behavioural concerns stem from a handful of triggers. Recognising these triggers can help you deal with the behaviour that follows.

The origin of most toddler behaviour

When we parents are having a bad day, our toddlers' repertoire of behaviour may seem extensive but in fact almost every performance comes from one of seven very predictable origins. Awareness of these brings all behaviours into perspective and allows you to achieve a firm foundation for effective discipline. Here is a rundown.

Attention seeking Toddlers crave attention. If they can't get it by fair means they lower their sights, irritate their parents and grab it by some annoying act. This is by far the most common cause of toddler problems.

Jealousy and competition Toddlers can be pretty antisocial when others step into their limelight.

Frustration Toddlers' bodies cannot keep up with their brains. They become frustrated at their own inabilities.

Fear of separation Toddlers like to be close to their parent and can be difficult when separated.

Reaction to illness, tiredness, or emotional upset Toddlers can be irrational, irritable and hard to handle when unwell or upset.

Unreal parental expectations If parents expect a toddler to have adult values, they are in for trouble.

Parental dramas Parents bring problems on themselves by taking an unimportant event and beating it into a great drama.

Attention seeking

Toddlers are not unlike pop stars, politicians and other well-known adult exhibitionists. They need to be the centre of attention all the time, a demand which many parents find hard to understand. Why do they need to behave so badly to get attention when they are getting masses of it already? Well, it may not seem very sensible to you but that's how toddlers act.

One of their main troubles is that they are little humans and, like most adult humans, they are never fully satisfied with what they have. They are forever wanting more. You only have to look at many billionaires to see that despite an already obscene amount of wealth, they cannot wait to get their hands on another billion. Toddlers simply behave like the rest of us, only they go about it with less subtlety and sense.

Interpreting behaviour

At one stage in my career, I undertook some formal training in child psychiatry, during which I was taught how to interpret behaviour in psychodynamic terms. We talked of bonding, sibling rivalry, castration anxiety, Oedipal conflict and other high-blown notions. When I say we talked, I mean this was by far our greatest skill. We were able to tell any mother how she had caused the problems in her child. Unfortunately, we were much weaker in giving the practical help, emotional support and management advice that was really needed. Fascinating though these theories are, I have since learnt to interpret toddler behaviour in a much simpler and more practical way.

When a little child performs some particularly antisocial act, stand back and ask yourself why. 'If I was doing what that little terrorist is doing, what percentage would there be in it for me?' For toddlers, the answer is nearly always the same: 'to gain attention'.

While attention seeking may well be at the root of most behavioural problems, the trouble is that we parents are often too tired and tense to realise what is happening before our very eyes. Our friends can see that we are being utter twits from where they stand, but we are seated too close to the game to see which side is scoring the points. The secret is to stand back a pace and ask, 'What is going on here? What percentage is there in this for junior?'. If their antisocial actions are grabbing attention then it is time to look critically at the quality of the attention you are giving.

Grades of attention

Attention is deceptive. It comes in many grades and guises. The aim of every parent should be to give as much high quality attention as possible. This is extremely important to the happiness and emotional well-being of the toddler. But remember, at the end of the day you will feel just as tired if you have given the best, as you would if your home has been a war zone. You might as well resist giving poor quality attention, as there's no percentage in it for you.

If we visualise attention as a spectrum, graded from A to Z, we see two colourful extremes with many shades in between. Grade A (the best) includes all those close parent–child interactions like talking, reading books, playing together and cuddling. At the other end of the scale, Grade Z (the worst) is where children are completely ignored, their presence not even acknowledged.

As we move across the spectrum from A to Z the reward for the child gets progressively less attractive. Our children will usually aim for the best level of attention they can get, and if the best is not on offer they will descend through the grades until they find one that gives them what they want.

Examples through the spectrum

- If parents have their hands full and Grade A attention is not on offer, toddlers will drop down a grade or two to B, C or D. They will probably start asking endless questions, although they are clearly not in the slightest bit interested in the answers. At least it keeps the lines of communication open and gives them some reasonable attention.

- If Grades B, C or D don't work, a bit of arguing and debating is often seen as good value. They can argue that black is white, give you a most plausible explanation of why the world is flat and debate with all the skill of an 'egg on face' politician extricating himself from a corruption case. As far as toddlers are concerned, the cause is irrelevant as long as the parents take the bait.

- Now down in mid-alphabet, toddlers find that saying 'No' to everything will get mum's undivided attention. If this, by some mischance, doesn't work, they can always climb on top of the baby, turn off the TV halfway through your favourite show, or do unspeakable things to the cat. All these activities are bound to stir up lots of attention.

- Verbal abuse is another great way of guaranteeing a rise out of mum or dad. 'I hate you mum. You love Kylie more than me.' Such statements will be delivered again and again, just as long as the target audience responds with the necessary attention.

- By now we are descending into the lower letters of the alphabet of attention. These are the ones which harbour the really big gun stirrers. Tantrums, breath-holding and even vomiting on demand lie in this nether region. Their payoff may be a long way from Grade A but when top quality attention is not on offer it is still worth the effort.

- The bottom line of attention is of the very poorest quality. Parents shout angrily at their child and may even deliver a few well-aimed smacks. Difficult as it is to understand how such pain and anger can please, bear in mind that even a smack can hurt a child less than being ignored altogether.

Jealousy and competition

Little children are not richly endowed with values of sharing and seeing the other person's point of view. They like to be the star of the show no matter what and when they are dispossessed of this role they can get mighty upset.

Behaviour varies greatly from child to child. A few are pretty laid back and humanitarian in their attitudes but most are downright possessive and resent intruders on their pitch. Jealousy and competition can bring problems for parents and arise from some quite predictable situations.

Nose out of joint with new baby

The arrival of a new baby causes confusion to the toddler. On the one hand it is fun to have this interesting, animated little doll around to play with but the sudden change in attention causes competition and jealousy. Usually toddlers and babies settle in well together but there can be problems if parents are overpossessive and unthinking.

It's quite natural for new mums to be overprotective but it can cause all sorts of difficulties. If a tense mum chucks a wobbly every time the toddler approaches the baby, soon the negative vibration associated with being near the child will damage the developing brother–sister relationship.

Another hazard is the discovery that a quick poke to baby will ensure a fireworks display of Bastille Day proportions. Now all the toddler has to do is poke, prod or pinch to have mum's undivided, if somewhat bad-tempered, attention. It can be a powerful weapon.

Tensions can also arise when friends visit the new arrival and tactlessly by-pass the sitting tenant. There is another potential for problems when tired parents feed, change nappies and give the baby comfort, forgetting that there is another little person who is in need of some attention.

With insight and sense it usually comes together well in the end, particularly if started off right. (See Chapter 16, Sibling Rivalry.)

Sibling rivalry

Parents who have only one child rarely realise just how much their life will change when they have two. Two together are usually the best of friends but they can also be fierce rivals. Most behave best when alone and are at their worst when competing.

Young ones resent not being able to do things as well as their older brother or sister. They feel others get privileges they don't. They compete for attention and object when they think they have got less, be it love or a serving of pudding. Little ones taunt older ones and older ones taunt the littlies. This is what we call sibling rivalry and it is behind many an annoying display of bad behaviour. It is quite normal in toddlerhood, and probably will continue through to the age they leave home.

Adults who get in the way

When toddlers are taken out shopping they may resent the delays that occur when you stop to chat to friends. They wriggle, run off and tell you that it's time to get the show back on the road again.

During a long session on the phone, don't be surprised if your toddler engages in some well-planned demolition work, generally

just out of eyesight, but with the right amount of noise to have you running to see what's up every two minutes.

When dad arrives home, it may be hard for the parents to chat about their day or impart important news to each other as toddlers interrupt, so complex dealings are best left until after toddler's bedtime. Even a simple cuddle between husband and wife is often out of the question, as toddler will squirrel his way in between to get his share of the action.

When good friends drop round for a deep and meaningful discussion, they may be in for a disappointment. Most toddlers will regard this as unfair competition and may react by jumping up and down between you, asking to be taken to the toilet, or clambering all over you to ensure that coherent conversation is quite impossible.

The solution is to be selective, sensible and brief when interacting with other adults if toddlers are about.

Competition caused by other children

Toddlers generally enjoy the company of other littlies but they can still be very selfish when it comes to sharing their parents or their possessions.

For example, a visiting child is held by mum and made a fuss of, whereupon the resident toddler molests the cat, an act that miraculously regains his mum's full attention. Day care mothers can also find that their own child's jealousy may sabotage the work of looking after other people's children.

Time will soon cure this behaviour. Six more months can make all the difference.

Many toddlers resent others touching their toys. This is a quite normal reaction at this age and doesn't mean that you've bred someone who is destined to grow up as a mean and selfish adult. When faced with this behaviour as parents, encourage the child to share but by no means start a Holy War over the matter. A year down the track it will all be past history.

Frustration

Tiny toddlers have ideas way above their abilities and when things don't go as they have planned they can become mighty frustrated.

The 15-month-old loads food onto his spoon but the cargo shifts on the circuitous route to the mouth; and the 2½-year-old's almost completed construction falls apart and the militantly independent

toddler gets two legs stuck down one leg of his pants. It's tough being a toddler.

As parents we should accept that a certain amount of grizzling and tantrum throwing is due to frustration and not just bad behaviour. The toddler is trying to come to terms with the limitations of his abilities and at this time it is a cuddle and encouragement he needs, not punishment.

Fear of separation

Toddlers usually want to be close to their parents and get upset when separated. This is a normal stage of development and not a sign of sickness or bad behaviour. Anxiety over separation starts at about 7 months of age, intensifies to a peak just after the first birthday, and gradually wanes over the next 3 years. This explains why some are so hard to leave with babysitters or in day care. Their protest is not naughtiness, they are just telling you that you are important and they would prefer to stay close to you. Usually this can be overcome gradually with gentleness, not scolding and punishment.

It has been said that children who wake repeatedly during the night do so due to separation anxiety. The children's point of view is that they love their parents and whether day or night, it is nice to call them in to check they are still there and get a bit of a cuddle. This has to be healthy, normal and nice for children but there comes a point when shattered parents must put their foot down. Separation anxiety is an interesting concept for academic but good rested relationships are more important in real life.

Illness and upset

When toddlers are sick, teething or have a temperature it is unreasonable to expect them to behave well. They feel uncomfortable and irritable, so why shouldn't they grizzle, dig in their heels and make a big drama out of life's trivial events.

In times of sickness, it is best to accept this all as inevitable, then freewheel for a while, establishing a firm hold again once they are better.

When the home is unsettled and routines disturbed, behaviour may also take a turn for the worse. Starting work, moving house, new babies, illness or death in the family, visitors, late nights, holiday travel and family fights can all cause upsets. With changes and turmoil, expect a little bad behaviour and work on the cause of the tension rather than combating it with the stir of punitive discipline.

Toddlers are not adults

Many non-problems are beaten up into big dramas by parents who expect 2-year-olds to act like adults. Toddlers have little sense, live for the here and now and certainly do not behave like grown-ups. Trying to make them grow up before their time is painful, pointless and a common cause of friction.

No sense

Very young children don't have much sense. By the age of 3 they have probably acquired a certain amount but before this time it is in extremely short supply, especially between 12 months and 2 years, when there is practically none at all.

The 18-month-old who clambers up onto the kitchen bench top and precariously plays the tightrope walker is not being badly behaved, he is just enjoying climbing and doesn't have the sense to understand the dangerous implications. In just the same way, if you leave poisons, pills or sharp knives about, toddlers will not have sufficient sense to avoid hurting themselves. It is up to parents to protect them, not punish them for their lack of maturity.

If they don't get what they want some (usually at around 18 months) may bang their heads hard against the floor. This may seem a pretty painful method of trying to get your own way but they lack the sense to see the futility of the exercise. If left unattended beside a road, swimming pool or unguarded fire or stove they may get injured. It is not that they set out to be naughty. Their instinct is to explore, which is natural at this age. But exploration without good sense can be, as we know, a dangerous journey and the explorers must be protected.

Not thinking of others

In general, young toddlers are not renowned for their Good Samaritan attitudes. They tend to be jealous, self-centred and not talented in sharing or seeing the other point of view.

This of course varies from child to child and improves rapidly with age. Though there may be little thought for others at 2, this is much better by $3^{1}/2$ and by adulthood they may well have turned into selfless Christians.

Sharing is a particular problem. When someone else has the toy they want, it is quite likely that toddlers will grab it, push the other child over and in general lay on an utterly antisocial scene. Our role here is to encourage a more accepting attitude in the child without having a nervous breakdown in the process. Take heart in the fact that time will always cure this problem and if the worst comes to the worst, then just sit it out the best you can.

Non-adult values

Toddlers are often confused by their parents' behaviour. 'Why is mum so angry, when last time she seemed really impressed with what I did?' The problem is that toddlers understand nothing of adult values, especially when it comes to expense, money, ownership and tact.

If you leave an open box of chocolates on the table, they will be eaten. There is no deception or dishonesty here. It is like climbing Mount Everest. They do it because it is there.

Money may be taken from a purse but this is not a criminal activity. Toddlers are nosey, have no understanding about money and have no idea of the concepts of ownership.

When grandma's special toy gets broken on the first day of use, why is she so upset? Toddlers don't know the true meaning of $30.

As they 'hype' around the house, something is bound to get broken sooner or later. If it is an old pot, there is little reaction. If it is some priceless piece of porcelain, you have a seizure. They feel your displeasure, yet they cannot grasp the different values.

Children of this age behave just the same whether we parents are having a good or a bad day. When mum is tense, exhausted or has a headache, that is her problem and toddlers don't know to keep the volume down. Little children will be excited when dad comes home at night. They want to talk and play and certainly aren't interested in allowing him to sit down quietly and watch the evening news. It is their dad they want and they are wholly unimpressed by the antics of the Super Powers or the state of the economy.

Toddlers do not understand the meaning of the word 'Wait'. They cannot see why they should have to hang on until it suits mum to get going. Queues, or hanging around and waiting turns, are not in their way of understanding. And then there are the strange rituals that their parents seem to adhere to. Toddlers want to eat, for example, when their stomach tells them they are hungry, not at some fixed ritual mealtime which fits in with other people. When they think grandma's cooking tastes terrible, they tell her so. Honesty, as far as they are concerned, is the only policy and they know nothing yet of the diplomatic mistruths we adults use to avoid giving offence.

All this shows how normal little human beings think and behave. With time, they eventually conform to our strange adult attitudes. What happens in the meantime, however, should not be construed as naughty behaviour and what they require at this stage is understanding and gentle guidance, not heavy-handed punishment.

Behavioural beat-up

I spend a lot of my life pulling parents and children away from each other's throats. The pattern is nearly always the same: child upsets mum. She retaliates and further upsets the child who, in turn, comes back even stronger, and so on and so on. Adults and children often treat those they love most with the least sensitivity and kindness. We can let so much tension develop between ourselves and our children that all it takes is a trivial trigger to plunge us into the bloodiest of battles.

Major wars have small beginnings. One bullet is fired and six are returned and in no time millions of people are involved. As parents, we are often so near the front line that we cannot see how we are creating an inevitable and unwinnable war. Both parents and toddlers can be very stubborn, but only mums and dads have the age and experience to know when it's best to back off. Try to muster all your insight and intelligence to see when you are causing harm and not helping a situation. It takes two to develop a behavioural beat-up and as 50 per cent of the combatants, we parents should aim for peace and a quick and fair solution. Life is quite tough enough without unwittingly damaging our closest relationships.

Conclusion

Most toddler behaviours start from a few predictable beginnings. Every child has an individual pattern and degree of those behaviours, but still they have much in common. The trick is for us parents to learn how to take a step back from our position at the front line to see who is making the gains and losses in the overall battle. Few toddlers do anything that is truly premeditated or aggressive. They simply behave like 2-year-olds.

When we understand what to expect and how to read the game, then we have a strong foundation, from which discipline comes easily. The techniques of discipline and how to put them into practice are covered in Chapters 8 and 9.

6

Introducing Discipline

Every one of us, whether school child, toddler or adult, needs discipline. We all feel much happier and more secure when we have a disciplined lifestyle and know exactly where we stand. If you have ever worked in an office or been in a relationship where there are uncertain or unreasonable rules and limits, and where no-one encourages, notices or seems to care, you will be able to understand how some children must feel. Children are happiest when they know that their parents are united, consistent and concerned enough to care how they behave.

Good discipline starts in the home and spreads, eventually preparing our children for a smooth passage through school. When they start their education they will be expected to sit, settle, share and behave. It will impress no-one if their academic performance is like an infant Einstein and their behaviour like an infant.

Bringing up children may be no game but it will be more peaceful if all the players know the rules and have no doubt that the referee is both fair and in control.

The theories of discipline are easy to write about but they are not so easy to put into practice. Such are the individual differences of each of our children and such are the differences of opinion from the current epidemic of experts, that most modern parents are pretty confused. For what it is worth this is how I see it.

What is discipline?

When the word discipline is used many parents become flustered because they associate it with punishment but this is not what it is all about. The word discipline has a Latin origin which means teaching or training. The similar sounding word, disciple, comes from the Latin for 'a learner'. Discipline is a far more attractive concept when viewed as a learning experience for our children rather than one of pain and punishment. I like the idea of little children as disciples. They were the ones who learned through love and example—but in the background there were always clearly defined laws.

Discipline can be imposed on us from outside or it can come from within as self-discipline. Obviously young toddlers have no idea of self-discipline and at this tender age all direction must come externally from us, the parents. By pre-school age, children are ready to start taking some responsibility for their own affairs and this process can be helped if we loosen the reins and allow a little freedom of choice. This lets them feel the repercussions of their right and wrong decisions. By school age this loosening up process can be extended, putting them more and more in control of their own decisions. The ultimate aim is to have self-discipline firmly established by the time they up and leave home.

Attitudes towards discipline

At the beginning of this century life was harsh. Almost one in five of all infants died before their fourth birthday and attitudes towards child rearing were pretty severe. Adults were seen as adults, children seen as children and there was no questioning the fact that the big ones were in charge. This approach started right from birth. Babies were fed and handled with rather frigid, rigid routines and children were brought up on a brand of discipline that focused on rules, obedience and punishment. This was a time where politeness and respect for the older generation was demanded.

By the late forties the pendulum had started to swing and by the seventies had overswung into an extreme of permissiveness. Then it was taught that babies should be fed, lifted and comforted the moment they cried. The older child received gentle guidance, not firm discipline, while home became a democracy where adults and children were almost equals. As the expectations of acceptable behaviour changed, some parents began feeling guilty and apologetic if they dared to use firm discipline.

In the nineties, this gentle, more permissive view continues to be promoted. It finds favour with the best-selling, academic authors. These experts read extensively in the university libraries but don't work daily with difficult children. For them the thought of waving a wooden spoon, smacking, or marching junior off to his bedroom is utterly abhorrent. I like the theory of guiding with gentleness and love but the practicalities of implementing this approach are too vague. As I struggle down at the coal face of child care I don't need philosophy, I need hard techniques that work.

The more time I spend with families, the more concerned I become with the current view of child care. We have overswung from strict, to democracy, to a prevailing position close to anarchy. I believe the nineties should be a time for a more balanced middle-of-the-road position: happy children who know where they stand with confident, together parents, who are firmly in charge.

Strict or permissive

There are many ways to discipline our children and each one is as correct as the others. There are, however, two approaches that are universally wrong—the extremes of strictness or permissiveness.

Parents who are excessively strict and punitive can rob their children of independent thought and in the long term, when freed from this repression, there is a chance that the children will resent and rebel. At the other extreme, we impose no limits, which gives a poor foundation for both schooling and life. With excessive freedom, children may feel that their parents do not care enough about them to care what they do. If parents are as weak as water, this does not buy love, but loses respect.

If we keep away from the punitive and permissive extremes, this leaves a middle ground from which to choose the style that suits us. Each parent and each child is an individual with distinct needs for discipline and the style of giving it. The choice is ours.

And what of the future? Take as an example two happy, stable families, both committed to giving their best to their children. One uses discipline which is strict within reason, while the other favours a more laid-back approach. If you were to follow up these youngsters at age 20, you would have to look quite hard to see any difference in their behaviour, emotional adjustment or happiness. They will however have carried into adulthood quite different attitudes to child care which will resurface when they themselves become parents. The strict will tend to be strict while the permissive will favour that approach. As each adult enters marriage with some undiscussed but quite strong attitudes to child care, this will add a bit of interest to life when children arrive on the scene.

When to start

The view in the nineties is that infants in their first year cannot be spoiled. The overall aim is to establish security and closeness which glues parent and child together with an epoxy-like bond. Some of the older generation say that babies who get all this attention are destined to be more demanding but in fact there is now the suggestion that this may make them more secure and independent. Babies in the first year certainly do not need discipline. They need love, routine and closeness.

Toddlers are completely different little people. They are at that interesting stage when they flex their muscles and challenge all around them. They most certainly need discipline, the amount of which depends on the temperament of the individual child and the tolerance of the parents.

Those who have been blessed with an infant like a living saint will need to use little discipline before 20 months and even then an occasional soft whisper will produce a disgustingly perfect child. For those who have a toddler with the temperament of an urban terrorist, it is not as easy. These parents may have already had to deal with guerilla attacks on the guests at the first birthday party and this book will be well used by then.

Starting discipline is a very individual decision but the main message is to go gently at the beginning. Before the age of 2 our children do little which is devious, aggressive or nasty. Their actions just lack thought. Gentle firm guidance is usually sufficient, leaving the wrath-of-God-descending-like-a-thunderbolt, firmly in reserve.

7

Discipline—Making Life Easier for Yourself

Our children's behaviour depends on two competing factors: their God-given temperament and the environment they inhabit. This knowledge puts a lot of responsibility on us, the parents. While we are stuck with their temperament, environment is something we can always modify as we try to handle day to day situations better.

Many parents I meet seem hell bent on making their lives as difficult as possible. They are not driven by masochism but are so close to the situation that they cannot see how they are stirring things up.

This chapter is about some extremely simple ideas which we can all use to make life easier. Although most of these will be known, it is an unfortunate truth that when we are in a tired and demoralised state, commonsense is not too common.

Aim for calm and peace—don't stir them up

I see each family as a group of delicately balanced dominoes. If one is rattled this shakes those around, the chain reaction affecting all. As parents we can't stop our little dominoes rattling but we can stop them from rattling us.

Although most parents know the situations that bring out the worst in their youngsters, they continue to stumble into them with amazing regularity. Toddlers may not have university degrees in psychology but they still seem able to read us like a book. They plant little detonators which bring about major parental explosions. If we are one step ahead, sensible and calm, these detonations will be nothing more than a series of damp squibs.

Australian and New Zealand parents in the 1990s have many worries: jobs, relationships, and the major problems of money, mortgages and housing. I have no miracle cure for these troubles but we can work on minimising the damaging effects they generate. All I ask is that we become aware of just how infectious tension can be, then do our best to prevent it stirring up our children. There are many ways in which we can help the situation.

Don't nitpick

Some adults never seem to get off their children's back. In my office these parents nitpick non-stop. 'Look at Dr Green when you talk to him!' 'Say please.' 'Use a tissue.' 'Don't touch that toy.' 'Sit up straight.' There can be no peace in an atmosphere like this where every little gesture is used to generate tension.

This kind of over-disciplining is counter-productive. Notice what matters, concentrate on that, and selectively screen out the rest.

Avoid escalation

Many parents seem to seek out some trivial occurrence and then go over it again and again until it has escalated into a monumental hassle.

There they are sitting at home and their child drops a crumb on the carpet. 'Pick it up!' 'Pick it up now! This instant!' 'I am warning you, you will be in for big trouble!'

How can a crumb ever justify such a behavioural beat-up? If you had ignored it, the dog would probably have eaten it.

Once finished—forget it

Children may forget quickly but some parents just cannot let a matter rest. A child who commits a major crime early in the day should be punished then and the episode followed immediately by forgiveness and peace. Parents who are slow to forgive their children, write off days of their lives with a form of ongoing psychological warfare. This ensures that tensions remain high, bad behaviour is encouraged and maximum home unhappiness is guaranteed.

Holding grudges only produces parents with hypertension and ulcers—not stable, loving children.

They do it—you discipline—you forgive.

Turn down the volume

Loud music is known to make spotty teenagers want to dance and a mere fanfare of trumpets can move great armies to march off and fight. Likewise, toddlers will become greatly stirred up in a noisy situation. It is hard to discipline the young in a home where the adults are arguing, children are fighting and the television set is going full blast over the top of it all. Calm and peace are highly infectious qualities. Toddlers think and behave best when volumes are low and there is little distraction around.

Wind down overactivity

Activity is contagious and winds up all those around. When three children in a group are 'hyping' about, it won't be long before the fourth is compelled to join them. Toddlers love rough play and get very excited when springing around with a parent. If you spend time stirring them up, you must also allow for time to let them unwind.

A child who comes straight from frantic horseplay to the dinner table will not display the manners taught at finishing school. Any child who is overexcited and overexercised just before bedtime is unlikely to sleep.

Children's parties are dynamite to the active youngster. Parents assure me that this is due to the Coke, chocolate and sugar in the birthday diet. The behaviour would be just as high even if all they got was preservative-free bread and pure spring water. You don't need to be a genius to know that their bounce comes from being so close to activity, not food. If you are looking for peace and calm, don't 'hype up' little children.

Accept the inevitable

Tension may be minimised if you try to view life with a degree of philosophical acceptance. Some things happen to us and our children that are just inevitable. They are going to occur whether you burn yourself out with worry and tension, or lie back and adopt the philosophical approach of an Indian guru.

When our little ones are sick, they will wake just as many times at night whether we accept it as inevitable, or fight it. The wise approach is to salvage what sleep you can with thanks; the foolish approach is to so resent the situation that when at last your head hits the pillow you find you are too keyed up to sleep anyway.

In child rearing it is fairly difficult to view life from a calm plane of philosophy but on the other hand, beating your head against a brick wall is a futile exercise. The calm approach is not gained by sitting cross-legged, chanting mantras and chewing vegetarian delicacies. As parents, all we need to do is to open our eyes, stop blowing our tops and start using our brains.

Consistent discipline: 'There's only one set of rules in this house'

Children cannot live happily in a home where messages are inconsistent and conflicting. If one day they are let get away with murder and the next crucified for half the offence, they become confused and brainwashed. If one parent says 'Do this' and the other immediately countermands the request, then you have just witnessed the end of effective discipline.

It would be an unusual family where both parents agree completely about child-rearing but despite this, we need to become a coalition and present our children with a united front. In each home there can be one and one only set of rules.

If today the police let you drive on the right hand side of the road, tomorrow the middle and the next day you are summonsed for not driving on the left, you would become confused, insecure, angry and feel extremely vulnerable. The same goes for toddlers living in an environment of inconsistent, rapidly changing laws. They become angry, unhappy and unmanageable.

In some marriages, one parent is so pig-headed and has so little respect for the other party that each occasion of discipline becomes a dispute. The child is quick to spot the disagreement and will play off one parent against the other until the situation becomes intolerable. Where there is such major disagreement between parents, behavioural help is unlikely to work until the warring parties can reach a truce.

Angry, unthinking parents who use a child as a weapon with which to beat their partner are practising a form of legalised child abuse which can cause an immense amount of harm. In my experience, parents who openly disagree on discipline and use their little children as a means of hurting each other, have a relationship which is on such a downhill slide that separation is generally both inevitable and beneficial.

Don't use grandma as a scapegoat

Parents with uncontrollable children like to blame someone else for their problems. So often I hear parents say 'How can I discipline him when the next day he goes to his grandmother and she spoils him stupid?'. This is a complete red herring. You cannot go through life blaming child minders, teachers and others for your child's imperfections. The buck, as the saying goes, stops here, with you. Anyway, toddlers show an amazing ability to cope with the different disciplines in different loving situations. Of course they realise that there are different limits when at pre-school or grandma's, but they should also know there is one clear set of rules in their parents' home which will be enforced.

Parents are the majority shareholder and as such have the majority influence and responsibility for the standard of behaviour.

It takes two to fight

Fighting with little children is unproductive and on the whole it's best avoided. With toddlers, even the fight you win you lose. After 10 minutes the child has forgotten all about the fight, yet as much as an hour later steam is still gushing from the victorious parent's ears.

Every day parents tell me: 'He keeps fighting with me,' to which I invariably reply: 'Surely you mean you keep fighting with him?'.

Obtuse as some of us are, no-one can fight by themselves, like a tango it takes two.

You know that when you've got your dander up and are spoiling for a fight the result will depend on how the object of your fury reacts when you meet. If they also explode and get out of control then you've got the makings of an intergalactic conflict. If, on the other hand, they refuse to be drawn into battle and remain cool, calm and collected, there can be no fight.

You alone have the power to enter or avoid fights with your children. You only have to go to the complaints counter of a major department store to find out what truly calm, collected people are like. As the customer's voice ascends in octaves of rage the only reaction coming from the other side of the desk is invariably 'Oh, I am sorry the blade flew off your new food processor and cut off your finger. That certainly has never happened before with this model. I'll draw it to the manager's attention for you.' Parents too, believe it or not, have this power to encourage or prevent fights, depending on their reaction. Fighting with toddlers is as futile as playing tennis with a coconut, so exercise your veto in order to stabilise your blood pressure, maintain your sanity, and generate some domestic peace.

Structure and routine

Little children tend to be much more secure and happy when they live in an organised, structured environment. As well as knowing when they are going to be fed, when it is bedtime, and when it is time to go to pre-school, they also need to know the behavioural limits that their parents will tolerate. Most children thrive on routine and will immediately be thrown out of kilter by late nights, late meals, unexpected visitors or mum or dad going away on business. Wherever possible, parents should try to organise things well in advance so they can warn their children of what lies ahead for them. Disorganised parents can produce disorganised children, and the combined effect is a sure recipe for chaos.

Beware of the triggers

By triggers, I mean those situations that always seem to lead to trouble, like dragging their feet until they are almost late for school, refusing to bath, brush their teeth, eat their vegetables or being unable to pass an ice-cream shop. Minor triggers can create big repercussions and it is always better to avoid the trigger than to have to mop up after the 'Big Bang'.

If you stand back and try dispassionately to analyse your child's repertoire of tricks, you will find that it is in fact pretty small. You are probably being stirred up by the same trigger day in and day out but you are too close to see it.

Take a step back, open your eyes wide and see what exactly is setting off your child's bad behaviour. Then you can use a bit of cunning to steer around these triggers.

Positive is powerful

My toddler taming techniques are most successful when carried out by positive parents. First you must believe in what you are doing, then communicate clearly to your children. I refer to this brand of positive parenting as the evangelical approach —'This is the way it is going to be, brothers!'. This will be mentioned again and again throughout this book and if at any time your discipline seems to be slipping, stand back and check that it has been delivered correctly. Remember, positive parents are powerful people!

Beware the negative rut

Now it is all very easy for me to philosophise about being a 100 per cent positive parent but this is never quite so simple to put into practice. From time to time everyone hits a bad patch and with this, 'No!' can become a much over-used word. When things get really bad, each day of life becomes a negative battle of 'No', 'Don't', 'Stop it'—then Slap! After existing through such a day parents feel demoralised and numb behind the eyeballs. As they crawl into bed they think, 'What good thing have I said all day? Is this what the joy of parenting is all about? I wish I had taken contraceptives three years ago'. But it is all too late.

Sinking into such a negative rut alters our attitude to everything. Next morning you greet the dawn with a negative sigh and the thought 'What awful thing will he do first today?'.

A helpful technique is one used quite frequently with the families of the handicapped children in our care. We actively seek out good points in what at first appears an arid desert of bad news and general negativity. We look carefully for talents, skills and attributes and once they have been recognised, we build on them in the hope of lifting some of the despair and gloom that surrounds the family.

With toddlers, if all appears negative and full of unending bad behaviour, lift your sights and seek out some good. I have to admit that the behaviour of some of the children I see is so appalling that it takes a vivid imagination to spot anything that remotely resembles good. With the most difficult, start by rewarding the 'nearly good', using the thin end of the wedge to build up a more positive attitude and, with this, better behaviour.

Trying to be more positive is an admirable but often impractical goal. If you fail, just try to be less negative. In the long run this must have the same effect.

Sensible expectations

I believe that most of the major problems we experience would never surface if we had more sensible expectations of our children. The truth is that no 2-year-old is going to think or behave like an adult.

'Normal' toddler behaviour has been discussed in Chapter 3, so you should be under no misapprehensions about it. Try to readjust your sights and approach your toddler's upbringing with more sensible expectations. Some of the more common areas of conflict are mentioned below.

Mess and breakage

Toddlers by nature are noisy, dirty and messy. If allowed to pour their own drinks, a good proportion of it will inevitably land on the floor. In wet weather, mud and dirt walk into the house with your toddler, and toddlers are rotten judges of the dirt-resisting properties of your best quality Berber carpet. They have absolutely no sense of the adult monetary system and our strange values, failing to realise the difference between breaking a milk bottle and a priceless Waterford crystal vase. Animals they fondly cuddle yelp for release and ornaments they handle in genuine interest seemingly disintegrate in their fingers.

Toddlers aren't malicious, they are merely impulsive, non-thinking and often accident-prone. If you leave anything of value in their reach you have only yourself to blame if it is broken.

Broken toys

If you give a toddler an expensive toy there is a sporting chance that it will be broken before the sun has set. Toys do get damaged, and it is stupid to blame the toddler; it is probably you who should be reprimanded for spending too much money in the first place or buying poorly made articles. Little children do not need expensive, easily broken toys. They have such an imagination that an old cardboard box or the tube from the middle of a toilet roll can give hours more creative fun than any expensive plastic creation.

Father's return

By evening, the toddler is bored with his mother and as he hears father's key turn in the lock he happily comes to life with renewed energy. Dad is viewed as an exciting new entertainment-giver, and the toddler has little respect for dad's tiredness after a long working day and his wish to sit down, put his feet up and talk to his wife or read the evening paper. It's far from easy, but fathers must try to see life from their child's point of view and allocate a period of attention at the time of their return each night. The child will expect it and is unlikely to accept rejection without a fight.

Social honesty

Children of this age have not yet developed the quality of 'social dishonesty', which is expected of any of us who wish to succeed in the grown-up world. Toddlers are not backward in pointing out different skin colours and people's handicaps, as well as informing people of their disastrous hairstyles or ugly features. When out visiting, if the cooking tastes rotten, the child will not beat about the bush, using the vague dishonesties of an adult; he will say it in plain English for all to hear.

Whether we should change the toddler's honesty or the adult's dishonesty is an interesting philosophical point that we will not argue here. Suffice to say that, in the long run, it is hard to live in the crazy world of adults without behaving like one.

Toddler proofing your home

Life can be made so much easier if you live in a suitably fortified home. Child proofing becomes a necessity just after the first birthday when the toddler is becoming extremely inquisitive and much more mobile, with sense at a standstill. I have seen some parents take child proofing so seriously that they crawled around the house on their hands and knees doing a trouble shooting survey from toddler level. This is a bit over the top but however you do it, toddler proofing is important.

Fiddly fingers and the collapse of the dream home

When newly weds move into their first home they love to display their prize possessions, usually at toddler height. It comes as a rude shock when a little terrorist bursts on the scene and starts fingering the ornaments and taking the house apart. Now a major rethink is called for.

Some stubborn parents adopt the attitude that 'We were here first and he will have to live here on our terms'. Sure you can leave those tempting trinkets lying around and if you say no, divert and smack enough, he will eventually learn not to touch them, but it is rarely worth the hassle. Sensible parents keep temptation out of toddlers' way, gradually reintroducing things several years down the track. Without toddler proofing, parents need eyes in the back of their heads. Once home is secure we can relax, a little.

Latches, locks and prohibited areas

If you have a fast-moving, inquisitive toddler, child proofing is not just advisable, it is a necessity. You cannot be expected to fortify the whole place like a suburban Fort Knox but a few modifications are well worth the effort. Keep breakables in a child proof cupboard or up high on a shelf. If you have good furniture in a good room with a snow white carpet, it is often best to declare this out of bounds. If your teaspoons are flushed down the toilet—put a latch on the cutlery door. Some cupboards will need to be latched and out of bounds, while others are open to play in and explore. Cupboards with saucepans, vegetables and thick-skin fruit are always popular and safer, whilst those with plates, glassware, sharp knives, detergents and drain cleaners are an absolute no-no.

One way to prevent inquisitive little fingers getting into cupboards and drawers is to buy one of those rolls of wide super sticky tradesman's tape. A short length stuck across a drawer, cupboard, or fridge, dissuades all but the most determined toddler, yet it can be easily peeled back for adult access. As the stickiness wears out new lengths are introduced. The aim is that by the end of the roll sense will have arrived.

Immobilise the refrigerator (if necessary)

Some parents come to me with what they believe to be a really profound question. 'Dr Green, how do you stop him taking the lemonade from the fridge?' The simple answer is not to keep it there, or ask the manufacturers to design child proof lids. It is not so easy when it is milk they are taking and spilling.

Little people can be kept out of the refrigerator with a remarkably simple technique. Take a short piece of elastic cord, the type used to hook articles onto the roof rack of a car. Clip the hooks around the back of the fridge and you have a spring-loaded door. This opens only a short distance and will slam closed before the toddler can extract the goods. This method usually allows parents easy access, while providing the child with exercise equipment not unlike a chest expander. Some rope, a length of sticky tape or a wooden wedge between the door handles may be equally effective.

Make-up, creams and indelible markers

Many toddlers have wonderful artistic talents, particularly when it comes to finger painting on bench tops, the floor or mirrors.

Make-up creams and indelible markers should be kept well out of reach. Any pen with ink that is not easily and instantly washable must be kept under the tightest security.

Dangers, dogs and sharp toys

Houses with glass doors or windows that come down to floor level pose a danger to the child. If he falls through the glass he will suffer severe cuts and even greater injury if he rides his tricycle through an unprotected first floor window to the ground below. Block such dangers with furniture, fit temporary bars across the window and use safety glass where possible.

Safety plugs should be fitted over power points as young children have the sort of fascination with electricity that a fly has with a zapper. It is not a bad idea to have a commercial circuit-breaker fitted to your junction box outside, and then at least you can rest safe in the knowledge that even if he does poke a hairpin into the electric toaster he will survive to poke another day.

Toys with sharp edges that are likely to cut or damage either him or something else are best removed altogether. It is imperative that all medicines are stored safely in a securely locked cupboard high up out of harm's way. It is a common mistake for people who are very conscientious about storing medicines to leave even more dangerous products within easy reach in the kitchen or laundry. Bleach, rat poison, weed killer, drain cleaner and dish-washing detergent are the sort of offenders that must be locked well away.

Pets and toddlers generally mix well but there is no place in the same house for a savage dog who bites when teased, however important his role as a guard dog may seem. Such animals should be sent back to the jungle where they belong.

Fortify the compound

Coping with an active toddler is always easier if you have access to a secure garden. They need the space but you can never relax unless there are fences and gates to prevent escape onto the road. Where there is particular danger, some parents find chicken wire is a cheap form of fencing and though it does not create a compound as escape proof as Colditz, it is an affordable start.

Where fencing is inadequate and roads are busy, all doors leading from the house must be immobilised. The best methods are a high-level latch, security chain or deadlock. If you have one of those quiet, angelic, predictable children or are surrounded by acres of gently rolling parkland sweeping majestically to the horizon, this will all seem a bit unnecessary.

The playpen

The playpen seems a marvellous invention for keeping active children out of mischief. Although sound in theory, it rarely works in practice, because extremely active children need space and protest if put in a playpen.

Some parents tell me that the playpen is for their own use. Inside it they place a comfortable chair, then sit back and read a book, while the child runs around the house.

Absconders and reins

Toddlers need to be supervised closely as they have no road sense. Fortunately most do not like to be separated from their parents when out of the home and tend to stay close by. Others have no such worries and bolt at the first sign of open space. Some of these children enjoy being chased after, others have no fear of separation from their parents and get lost with monotonous regularity. Here we go again in the supermarket as they announce 'Will the mother of the grubby 2-year-old with a faded yellow T-shirt collect him immediately'.

This period of attempting to abscond is generally quite short lived, and though I dislike the use of reins, there are some instances when they are literally life savers.

Parents can use a short length of rope with a boy scout knot around the waist or one of those lightweight ties, like a telephone cord. If your child pulls like a Melbourne Cup mount at the starting gate a full heavy duty harness will be necessary. Reins may raise some eyebrows with your friends whose perfect children stay clamped beside them every outside moment. They are welcome to their opinion but for me, reins are preferable to exhausted parents worrying themselves and the local constabulary into nervous breakdowns every time they venture out.

Apathetic, helpless parents

Never a week goes by without a brilliant mother telling me of a new child proofing technique she has invented. Other parents seem to have no imagination, initiative or motivation to improve anything. They are apathetic and helpless, as they sit there and tell me 'It is impossible to lock the door' or 'It is impossible to immobilise the gate' or 'It is impossible to stop a 2-year-old drawing on the walls'. This is ridiculous. In the 1990s astronauts are blasted from the earth to fly for weeks through space before landing back where they started and it seems unbelievable that in this super-scientific world, an intelligent 25-year-old cannot devise some method to prevent a 2-year-old child from opening a door. We do not need the high technology of computers, space suits and rocket fuel; a latch, a piece of elastic, or a length of string can all produce dramatic results.

Fighting with children is such a waste of time and emotional energy, it is important to toddler proof your home, for your child's safety, the security of your belongings and your own peace of mind.

Avoid no-win situations

Beating your head against a brick wall is a painful and unproductive part of life. If you seek a peaceful existence, it is wise to reserve time and energy for the worthwhile causes and avoid at all costs those that cannot be won. The clever parent is quick to spot when they are on a losing wicket and extract themselves gracefully.

The main no-win areas involve feeding, toileting and sleep. Other problems arise when time is limited, the venue is very public or there are too many interfering adults around.

We parents have to be sensible. Sometimes our children chuck a boulder before us as we go down the highway of life and when this happens it is easier to steer around it than hit it head on and cause a major confrontation.

Feeding

It is easy to sit a child at the table and place food in front of him. What is difficult is to get it down the 'big tube' if he has decided it is not going to happen. Medical science is advanced but I am sure there is a Nobel Prize awaiting the person who discovers the switch that makes the reluctant toddler eat.

Fighting over food is a complete waste of time, which entertains children and ages their parents. Remember that no toddler has ever starved to death through stubbornness and forcing food down a child's throat is a cause of feeding difficulties, not a cure.

Toileting

You can take your child to the toilet, you can encourage him to sit there, but no amount of parental jumping up and down will make something drop out if junior has decided it is not going to happen. This is yet another case when you must accept that he may be small but he has the ultimate veto.

Sleep

In exactly the same way as you can lead the proverbial horse to water but cannot make him drink, parents can put a child to bed but there is no way that an unwilling child can be made to go to sleep. If the parent demands sleep immediately, the little rascal will generate unbelievable powers of wakefulness, just to show who is boss.

Parents can put them in their beds, keep them in their bedrooms, but have to accept that they cannot make them go unconscious. That is of course unless you fire tranquillising darts through the keyhole or pump anaesthetic gas under the door.

Limited time

It's a hot summer day and the 2^1/2-year-old is romping around naked under a hose in the back yard. In exactly ten minutes you need to have him dressed, in the car and up at the school to collect big sister.

The toddler knows this and is darn sure that there is no way you will get him dressed and there on time. You could be bloody-minded, but it's all a bit hot and humid for that. Why not avoid the boulder, forget the clothes and put one naked toddler in his car seat and hope you don't have a breakdown?

There are times when confronting the toddler is just not worth the trouble.

When the going gets tough—get out!

Despite all the best behavioural advice in the world, there comes a point when some children's behaviour becomes unbearable. This usually happens on those wet, windy days when the single bedroom apartment seems oppressively small. When the whingeing starts, it seems to reverberate around the walls and ceilings, going right through your head and jangling your nerves. At this point, discipline becomes difficult and I believe it's best to cut one's losses and run. Take the children and head for the wide open spaces. Noisy children never seem quite so loud when their efforts are muffled by the great outdoors, and the movement of the baby buggy is usually very soothing to the active toddler. It's worth getting wet just for the peace of mind.

One mother of a particularly difficult child recently told me: 'When I am losing control, I get outdoors straight away. There, things never seem quite so bad, and even if I was driven too far, we are both much safer, I could never harm him in public'. Now there is a piece of wise, honest advice.

Out of control and birth control

I am often asked whether I believe the first, second or third child is most difficult. My answer has no research backing but it is my belief that the last child is usually the most difficult. It seems to me that if you have a really difficult child you make sure that this is going to be the last. A difficult child is the ultimate contraceptive.

When I see parents who cannot cope with their children, I always ask what are their plans for further additions to the family. Some whose children are completely out of control tell me that they may or may not have more, as 'It's all in God's hands'. Far be it from me to interfere in other people's affairs, but if we as parents cannot cope with our present brood, it is absolutely certain that an extra child is only going to make matters worse. Perhaps these parents should seriously consider some reliable form of avoidance rather than leaving all the responsibility in God's hands.

8

The Techniques of Discipline

The parents I see today are confused about discipline. They fear they will lose their children's love if they are firm, when they are more likely to lose their children's love and respect if they are weak and ineffectual. They have heard that there is a short critical period of emotional development in these early years and if you start wrong, all that follows is doomed. This is an interesting idea but it is just not true.

Parents blush as they admit to me that they have waved the wooden spoon at their young John. In fact, such occasional appearances of the spoon usually act like a magic wand, producing an instant Lourdes-like cure. Most are embarrassed when they admit they smack. They are all too aware of the promoted view that an occasional smack can produce emotional damage, encourage violence in children and may later lead to wife and child abuse. This is a complete misreading of the facts but that does not stop its popularity.

Other misconceptions are that putting an out-of-control child in his bedroom causes sleep problems and that diverting the attention of an about-to-tantrum child is degrading. Some psychologists quibble that rewards for good behaviour damage a child's self-esteem. Parents are apologetic as they tell me they are inconsistent, lose their temper and don't always set a good example. These are normal parents like you and me who should be congratulated for having the insight to see what they are doing. I write for and work with real people and have little time for impractical dreamers. None of us is perfect and certainly our standard of discipline will reflect this fact. The bottom line is that we can all do it better and this is what this book is all about.

Discipline—what really matters

Today's parents have been bombarded with so much academic small print they cease to see what really matters. With discipline, if we filter out all those trendy ideas that are interesting but impractical, we are left with a list like this.

Love Successful discipline can only come when there is a strong framework of love, being wanted, respected, cared for and feeling important. If children don't have this prerequisite it is both difficult and unwise to firmly mould behaviour.

Consistency Children need to know the limits and exactly what is expected of them. They should sense that their parents are in agreement and in charge. Discipline must be applied consistently and not depend on the fluctuating moods of a tired mum or dad.

Staying calm and in control Don't argue, don't debate, don't stir, don't chuck an adult 'wobbly', don't shoot from the hip.

Communicating convincingly Use the positive line: 'This is the way it is going to be!'. Discard the wishy-washy approach: 'Maybe we will do it this way but if you complain and whinge enough we will go for a recount!'.

Avoiding trouble Toddler proof your home, don't fight over trivialities, recognise when you are on a losing pitch.

Boosting the best Reward the behaviour you want with encouragement, interest, warmth, fun and attention. More tangible rewards may be given, even bribes.

Underplaying the undesired Try to dampen down the unwanted behaviours. Don't rise to the bait. Become skilled in the art of selective blindness and deafness. Don't get it back to front so that you spend so much time fussing, fighting and encouraging the bad that the good moments pass unnoticed. Sometimes parents stand too close to see who is scoring the points.

Commonsense and cunning Recognise and avoid triggers to bad behaviour. Divert attention. Keep little bodies busy. We parents cannot give full attention all the time, so learn to use side stream attention.

Sensible expectations Little children are not adults and will not behave as adults. Listen to what they are telling us, as their behaviour may not need disciplining but comfort, reassurance and a cuddle.

Safety valves When your tired parental brain is close to self-destruct, use Time Out to separate the warring parties. Use a bedroom, go outside, find space and engage in an activity.

Remember Tension at home, parental point-scoring, depression, conflicting opinions, confidence in your boots, all make effective discipline difficult. Each one of these can be helped but we parents need to be committed to lift our game.

Sense of humour The toddler antics I see before me each day could only be classed as amazing. Keep smiling, this circus doesn't go on for ever.

Behaviour modification therapy

When I mention behaviour modification therapy, parents cringe as it suggests some sinister brainwashing technique. They have a vision of secret police moulding an unwilling dissident to another way of thinking. Even worse, others have heard that behaviour modification has been used to train dogs, pigeons and all sorts of circus animals. But don't panic, this is not some dog doctor's piece of animal psychology. It is old, it is effective and I am sure that even though your parents had never heard the name, it was the way they brought you up.

Encouraging the good—discouraging the bad

The theory of behaviour modification therapy is remarkably simple. It states that any behaviour that is reinforced by rewards will tend to be repeated. This is what happens at the end of the concert when the audience applauds enthusiastically. Such is the reinforcement that the group gives an encore—you get a repeat performance.

Behaviour modification also has a reverse side which states that any behaviour that is not noticed, encouraged and reinforced will probably disappear. This time the concert finishes but the audience is bored senseless and the applause silent—tonight there will be no encores.

Imagine the scene: your 2½-year-old stands up, smiles, then in front of the visiting church committee, with perfect articulation, says 'Bum!' Mother blushes and there follows a fireworks display. With such reward and reinforcement, before long all you will hear is 'Bum!' 'Bum!' 'Bum!'.

This could have been handled differently. When the child said 'Bum', mum could have remained distinctly unimpressed, yawning quietly and continuing to chat. Now junior stomps off muttering 'What a bummer—no audience—no show'.

In young children behaviour modification will work best if the good behaviour is rewarded quickly. Even a minute after the event the reward will have lost some of its power at this age. The technique must be used consistently if it is going to be effective. If a behaviour is going to be ignored and underplayed this must happen five out of every five times it occurs. If the ignoring is restricted to four out of five occurrences it will always be worth trying you out. It is like feeding a poker machine; if you play long enough, odds are that eventually you will score a jackpot.

What sort of rewards?

Rewarding children for performing is not degrading, it is part of our Australian way of life. I get rewarded with money for working, and I get no pay if I don't. If I give a successful lecture people thank and flatter me and before I know it I have agreed to give another. If rewarding adults is thought appropriate, then children deserve the same.

In behaviour work there are two styles of rewards. There are the soft or social rewards and then there are those which are hard and tangible.

Soft rewards

These refer to giving attention, praise, smiles and touch. Of these, attention is the main reinforcer and, as will be seen later, when used wisely it can be very powerful. When misused, however, it can promote some mighty unwelcome behaviours. Both children and adults are very sensitive to soft, subtle boosting of behaviour techniques such as being noticed, or by the warmth of your voice, or that twinkle in your eye.

Hard rewards

These are the more tangible items like a smiley stamp, a gold star on a chart, a 'Thomas the Tank Engine' sticker, or a host of little toys. Then there are all those sweet rewards that tend to turn both your child's teeth and the dentist's bank balance black.

Rewards and bribery

There is a very subtle difference between reward and bribery. Most behavioural experts get quite upset at the thought of bribing children and encourage rewards. A bribe is seen as a form of blackmail, where the child is told that he can only have something after he has performed a certain task. The behaviour modification reward is given when there is no talk of what will happen until after the good behaviour has appeared and then the reward comes as an immediate and unannounced bonus. Very often the difference between bribes and rewards is far from clear and though I would prefer rewards, if a bit of good old-fashioned bribery achieves the desired effect, then go for it.

Soft or hard rewards?

When deciding whether to use soft or hard rewards, the child's age is an important factor. Most toddlers are very happy with soft rewards, particularly attention, whilst older children are more aware of the value of objects and may do better with hard rewards, especially those that jingle in the pocket.

Getting it back to front

These behaviour techniques allow us to steer a stubborn toddler around trouble without becoming drawn into any futile fights. Behaviour modification, however, does have one great weakness. It is far too easy to get back to front. The technique has no safety lock which makes it boost only the good, while selectively filtering out all that we do not wish to see.

Though we use behaviour modification every day, many times we unknowingly get it so reversed that it becomes an enemy, not an ally. Most of the behavioural difficulties which confront us are actually created by us. We fuss over trivial little problems thereby producing big ones.

Some years ago I was examining a little boy as he lay on his mother's knee. When I felt his tummy he quite involuntarily straightened one leg and kicked me. As a bit of a joke I jumped back, holding my knee and made a great fuss. A few seconds later my foolishness was rewarded by a sharp kick on my other knee and this time it really did hurt. Again I jumped and by the end of the interview the little terror was tramping on my toes, kicking my shins and having a ball. A week later I was working quietly at my desk, my office door burst open and before I knew it he dashed in and gave me a kick.

Now admittedly this seems a particularly silly way for a paediatrician to behave, but it illustrates clearly what happens when we make a fuss over some trivial event. If the first unintentional kick had been ignored, that would have been the end of it. But I made a big deal out of it and created a rod with which I was beaten. I should have done it differently, or purchased shin guards.

A common example of getting behaviour modification back to front would be with feeding. You put food in front of the toddler, he takes one look at it, and says 'Yuk!'. Immediately the adults start to act like toddlers. Mum makes aeroplane noises, dad juggles oranges and the dog probably performs circus tricks. With so much reward for not eating, the mouth remains shut, tight as a Scotsman's purse. Now you have created a feeding problem.

Start again. He looks at the food: 'Yuk!' You ignore this. He either eats or ends up with hunger pains, but you maintain your sanity and have no future fights over food.

Changes come gradually

Some parents leave my office with a behaviour plan, convinced that if it does not work within an hour, my techniques are a rip-off. Behaviour modification gradually moulds the way a child behaves. It is time, cunning and consistency that brings results. There is no point expecting that a child will touch the hem of Dr Green's garment and be instantly cured. After all, they have been practising their particular performance for months and it seems reasonable to allow a few weeks to bring about change.

Things can get worse before better

For some time your child has studied his parents well, knowing your every raw nerve and point of vulnerability. If you suddenly smarten up your act, close the chinks in your armour and cease to respond, he will feel he is losing his touch and will have to turn up the pressure. Militant toddlers may initially try more of the same but with even greater persistence. When your defences remain strong, they go back to base to re-plan the campaign and attack on a different front.

If after a short while you show clearly that there is a new you who is in charge and really means business, then peace will soon return. In life we often have to put up with a bit of extra pain on the route to a long term cure. Before embarking on any major behavioural change, be sure you have the strength to handle that dark which comes before the dawn.

Behaviour modification is not some dubious new technique but a well-tried method of moulding behaviour. When this technique is used properly much can be achieved without recourse to raised voices, tantrums, force, threats or parental insanity. Consistency is important and so is care, not to get it back to front.

Smacking—let's be sensible

So much has been written and said about smacking that the parents I talk to feel embarrassed if they deliver even the gentlest tap. My views on this topic may be out of step with most modern child care authors, but I suspect them to be very much in tune with how parents feel. I object to all the philosophical hype that surrounds the push for legislation to make corporal punishment of one's own child a criminal offence. I worry that those who push this particular political barrow have not grasped the difference between an occasional smack in a together home environment and severe, frequent beatings in a disturbed family.

When lecturing to parents I often ask how many in the audience smack their children. At this point the hall goes quiet and out of a hundred people, a few hands tentatively poke up as heads turn uneasily, wondering if they are the only child beaters in the auditorium. Those that dare admit to this look apprehensive as though the whole proceedings were being recorded by camera and transmitted direct to the office of the welfare department. In response to my next question: 'How many of you never smack your children?', rarely more than two hands appear out of the hundred—a changed picture.

Whether it is a good or bad way to treat children, it is a fact of life that most parents will smack their children at some time or other.

Smacking—don't get the wrong end of the stick

First let me state unequivocally that I am not a smacking enthusiast. I feel that as used by most of us, this form of discipline is generally unhelpful and frequently makes things worse. I could never support any family who uses smacking as the main form of discipline—this is very wrong. In no way can I condone beating, excessive punishment, violence or child abuse. These are degrading, damaging and, I believe, often signs of a deep family sickness.

Having said all this, I do take great exception to the deliberate misleading and misreading of the facts by some anti-corporal punishment lobbyists. They use their position and misinformation to cause unnecessary concern in the majority of good parents who are not averse to the occasional smack.

The research quoted by the anti-corporal punishment groups, if taken on face value, certainly shows that smacked children have more chance of becoming child and wife abusers at a later age. If the statistics are looked at more carefully, it soon becomes apparent that the academics have got the wrong end of this stick.

We know that all children are very sensitive to the emotional happiness of their home. Those who are reared in a disturbed setting, often have difficulties in having close and loving relationships with their parents. This sets a poor example and gives an unstable foundation to all relationships which follow. It also puts them at greater risk of making unsuitable marriage partnerships which all too easily can bring the same problem straight to the next generation.

What has all this to do with smacking?, I hear you say. It is well-known that children of emotionally unhappy homes are much more frequently exposed to excessive corporal punishment, child abuse and domestic violence. If this was present in the first generation and if the lack of love disturbs relationships in the next generation, the violence that often accompanies this is liable to reappear.

Certainly there is a link between excessive beating of children in one generation and pathological relationships, with abuse, in the next. I believe that beating is not the cause but rather the symptom of the pathological relationship, which can go from generation to generation in a disturbing vicious cycle.

If lobby groups genuinely want to improve the emotional wellbeing of children, it might be more useful to first address some of our present forms of legal child abuse. Maybe they should be lobbying for a law to give more protection to the children of heroin addicts or the families of the chronically intoxicated. Maybe they should suggest that the parents who upset their children by continually fighting and abusing each other in front of them should face criminal action. Possibly parents and lawyers should be charged when they use innocent children as point-scoring pawns in messy divorce cases. When these and a hundred other common abuses of children's rights are addressed, then you will find me right at the front of the anti-smacking brigade.

Smacking misused

Though smacking small children is not the evil some say it is, the way most parents apply it, it still remains a pretty ineffective form of discipline. It usually falls flat because it has been doled out in a time of temper, following which our little ones capitalise on all our guilt and weaknesses and use them to their own advantage.

Smacking not followed through

Most smacks seem to descend when we parents are angry. At the time this may make us feel better but it is often ill-aimed, badly timed and inappropriate. The problem for most of us comes about two minutes later, when after a flood of tears, our anger turns to guilt and then the game is lost.
Imagine the scene. You have had it but they go on until—smack! They start to cry—you feel bad. They know you feel bad, so cry louder—you feel even worse. They know how you feel and cry even louder, knowing victory is within their grasp. You give up and they get a cuddle.
   A quick smack may diffuse a situation and regain control but unless we follow it through properly it is all too easy to blow it.

The last straw smack

Most of the smacks we parents dole out are at times when we have had a gutful and can take no more. Often the smack arrives after a long series of annoyances and is precipitated by some trivial, unimportant event which becomes the last straw that finally breaks a parent's back. This sure relieves a lot of tension for the parents but it confuses the children. Be careful with these last straw smacks. We adults are supposed to be more intelligent and in control than the average toddler, but at times I am not so sure.

Smacking back

Another occasion when smacking gets you nowhere is when the smacked child immediately smacks the parent back. The blow is returned and the toddler reciprocates. Soon you have been drawn into a minor war that was much easier to get into than out of.

As the battle heats up the parents get more and more angry and although the toddler is receiving a few minor flesh wounds it becomes the best game for weeks. Toddlers are negative, stubborn and have little sense. If their parents are even better endowed with these qualities, the fight can go on 'almost to the death'. Unless you are obsessive, almost to the point of autism, you don't have to cast the last blow.

I never felt it!

Some toddlers have the most amazing theatrical talent. When smacked they stand stoically like Rambo under interrogation, look you in the eye and with the dumbest of dumb insolence say, 'That didn't hurt'. Of course it hurt but they know that this reaction will infuriate and punish the smacker for laying a finger on one so important.

It is hard to believe but I have had a child referred to our clinic accompanied by a note from the family doctor, 'Please investigate the nerves in his legs. He appears to feel no pain'.

Smacking used correctly

Smacking must be one of the oldest and best tried techniques known to man. If you think logically, it cannot be all that damaging to children. If it was, then our ancestors, right up to our parent's generation, must have ended up a pretty disturbed lot.

Best in the younger child

Smacking has its main usefulness in the younger child. At this age words are less effective than some decisive action. You can debate all day with a defiant 2½-year-old. You can explain about the finer points of love, example and character building and even your evangelical views against corporal punishment, but the chances are that words may miss the mark, while a gentle gesture of a smack may land centre bullseye, right on the target.

Quick results

Smacking has one major advantage over most other forms of discipline in its ability to bring a rapidly deteriorating situation to a quick resolution. A firm, positive rebuke and Time Out (see later this chapter) are also quick and effective but the rebuke is often ignored and Time Out is only of use when there is a suitable room available, which limits it to use at home.

Registers limits clearly

A well-considered smack registers a firm message which states that these are the limits, you are in charge, and will be extremely firm if there is any further challenge.

Aborts escalation

Most behaviour wars start with some minor trigger. Some relatively unimportant decision sets in motion a train of events which seem to run rapidly out of control no matter which tack you take. In the end there is such a blow-up that the whole house is tense and unhappy for hours. A smack delivered at the right moment can curb this frightening escalation.

Resolves a stalemate situation

Smacking is also useful when toddlers and parents find them-selves locked in a hopeless stalemate situation over some issue that must be seen through to the end. When all else has failed and our authority is on the line, either a short period of Time Out or a well directed smack will usually bring resolution and peace within minutes.

Deterrent to danger

I believe that smacking can be a worthwhile deterrent to ensure that a dangerous life-threatening act is never repeated. I see noth-ing wrong with giving an immediate hard smack which will strongly reinforce the message that whatever has just taken place must never happen again. Cats may have nine lives, but as those of us who work in big hospitals know, this does not extend to chil-dren. Children only escape once or twice when dismantling electri-cal appliances, playing with fire or running across busy roads. Even if a painful smack did produce minor emotional trauma, this must be a small price to pay if it prevents the major pain of injury and keeps our children alive and healthy.

Imagine your toddler climbing onto the edge of a high balcony. You can debate democratically saying 'Dear Cedric, that is rather dangerous. It is fifty metres onto the road below and you might sustain a nasty injury'. On the other hand, a hard smack might do more to engrave the message that this must never happen again.

Conclusion

In the 1990s we are looking for a peaceful life with powerful, pos-itive parents who are in charge. Smacking used selectively will, for some, be part of this process. After a smack has diffused the situ-ation, forgive, be warm and don't hold grudges. Whether smacking is good or evil, it continues to be used by many good, loving parents.

I have never blindly accepted a view because it is politically correct. Though smacking is a poor form of discipline, it is used by real parents in real life. It certainly has some effect on the easy temperament child, but for this group there are far better forms of discipline.

Parents with an oppositional challenging child need all the means of discipline they can muster. Now, when smacking is most needed, it is both ineffective and dangerous. Desperate parents resort to a smack, and when it fails they smack harder, escalate, and the relationship nosedives. Soon you have anger, resentment, hate and potential abuse.

The firm cuddle method for treating tantrums

Some writers view tantrums differently to you and me. They do not see them as symptoms of militant little people trying to challenge the umpire's carefully considered decision. They believe the tantrum is the sign of children trying to find their inner selves. Instead of ignoring all the wriggling and crying, they recommend that children should be held close against their parent's body until their inner rage subsides. I believe there is too much academic hot air in this textbook technique for the real world people I work with. Of course it has a place when the little one is frightened or frustrated, but in the deliberate limit-testing tantrum, it is not only useless but also dangerous.

When mums are devastated, tired, run down and past thinking about scientific child care, few are capable of being asked to stay locked closely to a wriggling angry child. If methods like this are promoted for the average parent, one might see the incidence of child abuse escalate.

Parents need to remain calm, sane and emotionally in control. With major tantrums, it is best to separate the warring parties so that each has a chance to calm down.

Diversion

Diversion is one of those good old-fashioned remedies that has stood the test of time and still comes out with flying colours. Think back some years to when you were at grannie's, just about to de-leaf her pot plants like a dose of Agent Orange. She says quietly, 'I just remembered I have those lollies in the big jar in the kitchen'. With this your hands disengaged from the plant and you were off to the kitchen with the speed of Phar Lap from the gate. With all this never a voice was raised, peace was restored and the plant continued to do its bit to combat the greenhouse effect.

Today's parents can use the same technique with equal success. It is particularly useful with younger children. When it seems you are about to run headlong into a bit of bother, it is often easier to quickly divert the child's attention before the obnoxious behaviour has time to take hold. There is an exact psychological moment that the clever parent can sense and if grasped, the situation is saved before control has been lost.

Some parents take exception to the use of diversion as they believe it deceives children, is dishonest and downright degrading. My answer is simple, it has been used and proved effective for centuries. It works. It prevents fights and helps people live in peace. Anyway, if it is so degrading, why do our politicians use the same technique on us intelligent adults.

Imagine the scene. The talented tantrum-thrower is just about to stage yet another amazing Oscar-winning performance. 'Sesame Street is just about to start,' you say. With this the faint hearted performer diverts. The militant tantrum-thrower is another matter, dealt with in Chapter 9.

Selective deafness—selective blindness

Peace loving parents must be careful not to notice and punish every trivial offence. When we overdo discipline, home becomes a place of, no! stop! don't! no! With this we become tense and get into such a negative rut that we wonder what happened to the pleasure of parenting. To keep sane and happy it is best to install a sort of filter in front of your eyes and ears, one that lets you see what matters and shuts out all the rest. This extension of behaviour modification is called selective blindness and selective deafness.

I first discovered this as I watched how husbands react when their wives talk to them. It seems that a line like 'Did you put the garbage out?' often fails to register whilst 'Would you like a can of beer?' seems to squeeze itself along the hearing nerve and be clearly registered by the brain.

I have to admit that I was once troubled by this problem but my medical wife soon sorted it out in her own quiet way. She just booked me into the Hospital Hearing Clinic to get my ears tested and at that point I heard what she was trying to tell me. Selective deafness is of particular use when our little ones abuse us verbally or try out some of those words that were heard, but not taught, at pre-school.

Imagine a 3-year-old militant who is not getting everything his own way. He turns to his mother: 'I hate you'. Now the upset mum gets flustered, feels that the hate is genuine and responds with such effusive assurances of love that it is like a soap opera.

It would have been much better to hear nothing, or if a reply was needed, it was kept short, e.g. 'Well, I love you' and then leave it at that. You don't need to be a psychoanalyst to know that he really does love you. There is no doubt who he wants close by him when he is sick or frightened.

The basis of behaviour modification is to boost the best behaviour so that it will be encouraged, whilst the rest is ignored and underplayed in the hope that it will gradually fade out. Ignoring is one of those things that experts find easy to write about, but we parents find hard to do. I am sure it would be different if I were writing for Wonder Woman or Superman but in the real world we get tired, cease to see clearly and then shoot with both barrels blasting at any behaviour that moves. Parents do best when they aim carefully and shoot only at clear targets. Of course it is impossible to ignore all irritating behaviour but we must try. This is helped along by a bit of selective blindness.

Imagine a 2½-year-old boy who wants to overdose on chocolate biscuits. After three, his mother says, 'That's enough!'. He knows she is a softie and puts on an interesting bit of theatre—he stands running on the spot, in one of those 'vertical type tantrums'. Now, despite all this huff, puff and stamping of feet you must stand firm and put on an even better act. Play this one completely serene, calm and in control like the Mother Superior in the Sound of Music. 'That's interesting,' you say as you take a pile of washing, walk out and hang it on the line. Now there are few actors who like seeing the audience walk out in mid-performance and even the most thick-skinned toddler will tend to get the message.

Time Out

Time Out is an excellent technique which quickly brings an escalating situation to an end. Like smacking, it brings rapid results but is much more useful and calming.

Getting the warring parties to separate

The aim of Time Out is to remove the child from a deteriorating or stalemate situation and place him, for a short time, in another room. This takes the child from his position on centre stage to a less prominent place, where his antics pass unnoticed. He has time to cool off and this also permits the parents to calm down. With difficult toddlers it takes two to fight and if either party can regain their cool, the exercise has been worthwhile.

Time Out is probably one of the more useful techniques I give to parents who are having great difficulty. It is a safety valve that lets them know what to do when their back is hard-pressed against the wall.

Time Out is probably most effective in the 2 to 10-year-olds but it still can be helpful in those who are very much younger. When all your best discipline has been tried and is getting you nowhere, when you are rapidly losing control and your little one knows it—don't snap, don't smack, use Time Out. Once you shout, argue, become irrational and behave like a toddler, the game is lost.

As with all well-proven techniques, this one also has its critics. Some parents with 'God-given' angels and heads full of theories find it offensive. They also make all sorts of excuses as to why it doesn't work.

That is their business but in my experience Time Out has been a life saver for thousands of families who are close to snapping. Don't forget, real parents with difficult children do have their breaking point and it is never smart to see how close you can get to this very dangerous situation.

Which room?

The ideal Time Out room would be a dull, quiet place, of easy access but far from all excitement. This is nice in theory but in practice the nearest we can provide is our child's bedroom.

The experts are quick to tell us that use of the bedroom is a mistake. They believe that the child will associate this room with punishment which develops fears and results in sleep problems. This response, though sound in theory, in my experience has not been proved correct.

If putting a toddler in his bedroom will put him off sleeping, then presumably putting him in the bathroom will put him off washing, the dining room, off eating, the lounge room, off sitting, the kitchen, off dishwashing and so on. I choose the bedroom because it is sufficiently soundproof and far enough away from the rest of the living area to give both parties the space they need to calm down.

The technique

The main purpose of Time Out is not to punish the child but to separate the warring parties and give enough time for both to cool off. As said many times in this book, big bangs start with little triggers and it is much easier to use a method like this to defuse the situation in its infancy than wait so long that you have to mop up after an incident of international proportions.

The technique is simple. When the child reaches a pitch of crying, aggravation or limit-testing that can no longer be ignored, this is the moment to decide whether to plunge into full scale battle or use Time Out. There shouldn't be a moment's hesitation: Time Out it should be.

Calmly take him by the hand or carry him, then decisively put him in his room. Be gentle, and in no doubt that you are going to see this through. Once inside, state clearly in your 'This is the way it is going to be' voice that you are not going to argue but he will stay there until he has calmed down. Then shut the door and move quickly from the scene.

Don't lock the door

Time Out in the bedroom must never be mistaken for that unfortunate carry-over from the last century of locking children in their room. This is more likely to terrify than help. It is part of the outdated view that little children should be punished, seen, and not heard, and has no place for day-to-day discipline in the nineties.

The naughty corner

Making a child stand in a corner may have worked well in our own school situation but in my experience few parents find it effective in present-day homes. No sooner than your back is turned, the child sneaks out, gaining great pleasure as he winds up his parents. On the other hand he may stay in the corner and gain even more attention with a flow of rude noises, or obscene 'taxi driver' type gestures. For most parents this is a useless form of discipline, which provides the child with little more than an enjoyable game. Time Out in the bedroom is real Time Out.

When Time Out does not work

Sometimes when I have suggested Time Out, parents return saying that it did not work. When I hear this, I know that it has failed for one of a few reasons.

Immediate reappearance

The main complaint is that of rapid escape. The child is put securely in his room and before you have taken five paces he is out the door like a bullet from a gun. I find this can usually be overcome if the parents harden their hearts and are 100 per cent firm at the time of banishment. Little children are very quick to sense when disobedience or a course of whingeing will get them what they want and they are equally aware when their parents are serious and not about to give an inch.

Other parents complain bitterly that the child won't stay in the room. When I ask them where they are at the time of the child's reappearance, I usually discover that it is directly outside the door. Children are not stupid. If they know there is a welcoming party ready to greet them, of course they will come out—anything for a bit of fun and attention.

Other pathetic parents complain that the child is out of the room before they have even turned their back. It seems unbelievable to me that a 2-year-old can run across a bedroom, manipulate a door handle and escape faster than a fit adult can sprint from the scene. If this is the case it might be better to stop complaining and enrol immediately in a fitness class.

In my experience, if the parent puts the child in the room with commitment, closes the door firmly then clears off quickly, reappearance is extremely rare.

Occasionally an escape artist does need some heavier guidance. At the first escape he is put back with complete firmness. The next time he gets a gentle, limit-registering smack and if the challenge continues, the door may then need to be immobilised for a short period. It sounds tough but remember Time Out is the bottom line safety valve. This is where you go when everything else has failed.

Screaming and kicking

'Oh, I put him in his bedroom and he screamed and screamed until I had to let him out' is something I often hear. When I ask where the parent was standing at this time, again the answer is 'Outside the door'. Your toddler may be only $2^{1}/_{2}$ but he is exhibiting considerably more intelligence than the parent who hangs around in such a position. Obviously if there is a captive audience listening to every whimper there will be a Royal Command Performance inside. Put him in the room—close the door—go away quickly.

Now and then I hear that Time Out is unsuccessful because the toddler forces the door handle. 'What were you doing at the time?', I say. 'Oh, holding the other handle!' Toddlers love this; it's like being a big game fisherman and hooking a whopper.

Sometimes parents complain that their very young children lie against the door and kick. Generally they only do this if you are within earshot and anyway if a bit of paint is displaced, this is always easier to repair than a parent's shattered nerves.

Wrecking the room

Many parents tell me that they cannot put their child in his room because he is liable to wreck it. In fact most are speculating that this will happen and it is extremely unlikely that they have put it to the test. Over the years I have seen very few children do this when their parents act as though they are in charge.

It is important not to have dangerous or destructive items left lying about. Paints, Textas and anything that makes a mess should be put away.

When a child shares a bedroom with a brother or sister, parents may find it hard to relax, fearing that the angry, attention-seeking toddler will reorganise the other's property. When this is a problem it may be necessary to use another 'neutral room'. When space is really limited, on occasion we have had to resort to a bathroom.

When the captive child does wreak havoc in his own bedroom you are left with three options. You can pretend (with great difficulty) to be completely unimpressed with what has happened and later, when the air is calm, tidy up together. You can pass a firm comment that you are far from happy, and then insist that he should tidy up. Finally, the wrath of God can descend on junior and a message is firmly engraved which states that this is not acceptable behaviour. I would favour the first option but it is best to go with the one that suits you and works.

Example. At about the age of 4 I find some children are bored with being toddlers and make life extremely hard for their mums. One wilful young girl had studied the art of tantrums and was now practising it with savvy. When put in her room she would cool off but then do a bomb job.

When I heard that the very necessary Time Out was being so effectively sabotaged, I started by getting the parents to clear the room of all breakable objects, pens, paint and any other messy substances. The next time she was placed in her room, she did not bother to cry as she knew that a little rearranging of her belongings would have much more impact on her mother. Ten minutes later she came out of the room in perfect control looking extremely pleased. Her mother steadied herself as she glanced in the door to see the bed wrecked and clothes out of every drawer on the floor. But mum had got the message and as she walked past merely remarked 'Oh dear, that looks a bit of a mess'.

The little madam was taken aback as she was sure this would have scored a direct hit on mum's rawest of raw nerves. As she sensed a 'change in the balance of power', she was extremely careful to avoid any tantrums for the rest of the day. Now when bedtime arrived she was sent in to get her pyjamas but returned complaining that she could not find them. 'I think they may be under that pile of clothes,' said mum helpfully. She then asked how she was going to be able to sleep in her unmade bed. 'No problem,' said mum, plonking one blanket from over there and another from that corner over her. The same procedure was followed the next morning when the girl looked for her clean clothes. Again the untidy pile of clothes was pointed out and a message came across in the clearest of terms: wrecking one's room got no major reaction from mother but was a complete pain to the wrecker.

I talked to the mother by phone first thing the next morning and we decided that mother and daughter should set about tidying the room together in an enthusiastic and positive way. All the clothes were gone through and those that were too small were set aside to be sent to the 'needy children'. The toys were tidied and mother and daughter made out a list of possible presents for Christmas, which was fast approaching.

I was impressed with the control and strength of this mother and delighted that the habit which in the past had prevented the effective use of Time Out was quickly extinguished. In the wake of such a showdown, mother and daughter were able to salvage the situation, build a much closer relationship and turn a disaster zone into a fun place to live. The room was never damaged again and surprisingly the tantrums were greatly reduced with less need for Time Out.

While occurrences like this are exceptionally rare, Time Out is an excellent safety valve for all of us parents and if carried out correctly is seldom sabotaged.

Unrealistic expectations

Time Out is often said to have failed when, in fact, it is the parents who have failed to realise what they are trying to achieve. Five minutes in a bedroom does not guarantee angelic behaviour for the rest of the day. No method I know, other than possibly a straight-jacket, could ever give such a guarantee.

Many parents expect the child to walk out, head bowed, to stand before them and say, 'Dear mother, I have done wrong and will behave perfectly for the rest of the week'. Others refuse to let the matter rest and constantly remind the child of how naughty he has been. This maintains a high level of tension which is guaranteed to destroy everyone's ongoing happiness. The purpose of Time Out is to allow both parties to cool off and thus prevent major fights.

The child does not have to apologise. The only expectation is that he should re-enter in a more reasonable frame of mind.

Other parents claim that Time Out does not work because the child repeats the original behaviour. If he walks straight out and immediately and defiantly does the same, then he must be put straight back in the room. When parents complain that their child repeats the same behaviour they generally mean that it recurred, an hour later.

Time Out is a technique that defuses a rapidly escalating situation at one particular time. Once this has passed and peace is regained, the method has shown itself to be effective.

Some parents feel they have been cheated when the child goes into his room in mid-tantrum and remains there to play happily with his toys. I must repeat that Time Out is not a punishment; it is a technique aimed at separating two people who are hell-bent on a 'barney'. Whether the child plays with his toys, stands on his head or sings Waltzing Matilda in his room is utterly irrelevant, just as long as he cools off and parents are allowed a little time to relax.

Conclusion

Time Out is a very effective technique when used properly. I use it with toddlers, the handicapped, and even some quite difficult older children. It is a powerful method of maintaining peace in the home and if used in the way mentioned, it reduces a lot of emotional tension without frightening or upsetting the child. As the tension settles and the child understands clearly the limits placed on him, this leads to a closer and happier life for all. Remember that in the 1990s children are to know exactly where they stand and parents are to be back firmly in charge.

Team effort

If you want an adult to do something in the workplace, you use diplomacy. If I ranted and raved at my staff, I would be ignored and then quietly told to 'Take a tablet', if not worse. The diplomatic way is to give a goal, set an example, and lend a hand.

The same applies to the toddler who, after all, is a little adult but twice as stubborn. Often a straight demand will be greeted with a paralytic lack of movement, whereas if you say 'How about us picking up these toys together?' you are in with a sporting chance.

When working with very young toddlers it becomes obvious that they love things to become a game. At this age they may be blind to stains on the carpet, finger marks on the wall and rooms in a mess but they love to help mummy scrubbing, wiping and tidying, as it is fun to be in the centre of activity and attention. It is best for them to be helpers and play friends, an approach which makes for fun, not fights.

With the older toddler and early school child, you can often smooth things along by following a request for action with a consequence they wish for. 'You tidy up your toys and I will get that milkshake ready for you.' 'You help mummy with the dishes and I will fix the puncture on your bike.' Whether dealing with toddlers or adults, diplomacy, team effort and carrying them along with you, brings about quiet achievement.

Debating, arguing—is there a place for democracy?

With the modern move towards democracy for children, many of today's parents believe that every little detail of what is going on in life must be explained to their toddler. This is a commendable and charitable action but it often leads to trouble when a highly intelligent but functionally blind parent is unaware that he is being manipulated by an infant, barely the height of his kneecap.

An amazing amount of parental energy is consumed each day here in Australia, arguing, debating and being democratic with little children. It has certainly hit almost epidemic proportions in my practice and seems about as useful as discussing differential calculus with a Masai warrior.

Toddlers love attention and one of the main ploys to guarantee a constant flow of this commodity is to ask endless questions. When you examine what is asked, you will find that their range is remarkably small, little interest is shown in the answers and the same question is repeated again and again, as long as we parents rise to the bait.

Now, to ask lots of questions is a rather quaint characteristic of the young child and should be encouraged up to a point but when debating, questioning and arguing goes on and on, bearing no relationship to the quest for knowledge, that is a different matter. When this verbal ping pong starts, parents must ask themselves 'Is this getting us anywhere or is the real reason for the exercise to stir us up?'.

Take for example the case of an acrobatic toddler who bounces up and down on your new coffee table. You communicate clearly and convincingly that he must get off but he immediately asks 'Why?'. If you are more into democracy than preservation of property, it is all too easy to embark on a long dissertation concerning the lack of strength of modern chip-board furniture, or possibly mention Mrs Smith who lives in the unit downstairs, outlining the characteristics of her nervous disorder that account for her intolerance for loud overhead noise and her sensitivity to large sections of plaster landing from the ceiling onto her loungeroom carpet. All this will avail you nought, when the sole object of the question was to hijack your attention. I believe the question 'Why' can be answered once and after this it is better to divert, become selectively deaf or pull rank and say 'Don't—because I say so!'.

Many of our toddlers are at this moment playing games with

their unaware parents. With so many words and so little action, all this verbal incontinence does nothing but stir the home. Educate and listen to little people but when the sole object of the exercise is to wind you up—drop democracy.

Shouting

We all know that we shouldn't shout at our children, but we do. You don't need to have a university degree in communication to know that a bit of volume helps grab a toddler's attention. The trouble is that shouting stirs and often makes behaviour worse.

Young children are extremely easily wound up by noise, activity and tension in their environment. Pre-school directors often tell me that their class becomes almost airborne with the noise and movement of a windy day. At home the more tense we become and the more we shout, the worse our children behave.

Toddlers don't think before they open their mouths, but parents should. Calm is infectious and spreads to those around, so for peace in life, let us aim to keep the decibels down. Communicate important messages clearly and firmly but don't get into a shouting match.

I have to admit that there is an opposite extreme of controlled communication that makes me cringe. Some parents talk to their children with every word carefully articulated, considered and brainlessly boring. It is almost as though they were afraid to relax and act naturally for fear of dislodging a suppository they were trying to contain.

Toddlers are so charged with enthusiasm for life, they need enthusiastic, fun-loving people around them, even if we do occasionally go over the top and shout.

Threats

Thinking back to student days in my home town of Belfast, I clearly remember bus travel to and from the hospital and two things stick in my mind. I will never forget the winter rush hour with its overcrowded buses, their interiors smoky and thick with brown globules of condensation dripping from the roof. The occupants only took their pipes or cigarettes from their mouths to embark on a spasm of coughing that would have done credit to a tuberculosis ward.

Equally vivid is the memory of mothers on buses with their un-controllable offspring. The trip from the city centre was punctuated with 'Stop that,' 'Do that again and I will smack you,' 'I am warn-ing you,' 'I'll get the conductor to put you off'. Threats, empty threats, are a common and usually futile form of discipline.

Children should know the limits of acceptable behaviour and the consequences if they overstep the mark, but this should not be constantly told to them as a form of threat. It is also important that when you say something is going to happen, then it should be carried out as promised.

On those Irish buses, the children knew their exhausted mothers were all talk and no action. They had heard the threats often before, it was all water off a duck's back, a daily ritual that stirred up the mother and did nothing for the child.

Waving the wooden spoon

Parents who use a belt to threaten their children are a big worry. Though they would have fitted in more comfortably in the last cen-tury, I still see a disturbing number and this form of discipline is too close to child abuse for my liking.

Waving the wooden spoon is a more benign pastime and still sur-prisingly common. From my academic background I don't like the idea but from my pragmatic perspective, if you wave it occasionally and it works well, then I am not going to have a tantrum.

It seems that in Australia, the fly swatter is almost as popular as the spoon. Parents tell me it makes a most impressive swish as they wave it about but it does little other harm, unless you are a fly.

Don't forget that waving spoons and swatters are both forms of threat and there must be so many better ways of helping behav-iour before you have to descend to this level.

Negotiated settlement

The technique of negotiated settlement is common in sorting out industrial disputes when the union members may agree to build an extra car a day in exchange for say, longer smoko breaks, and ten weeks' holiday a year. Bargaining with toddlers is usually a com-plete waste of time but the early school-age child is often interested in coming to such a settlement.

With children over the age of 4, I sometimes get the parents to draw up a list of behaviours they would dearly like to see changed and then balance this with a list from the child. Though we rarely revolutionise the child's behaviour with this method, there is always some improvement.

The youngest age I would use this negotiated settlement is just below the 4-year mark. Most recently I saw a girl of 3 years and 11 months, whose parents were greatly upset that she still liked a dummy with her by day. Now they should have just taken it from her which would have been most appropriate at this age, but they didn't. Instead they went for a gentle negotiated settlement. She was a bright little girl and clearly aware that we lived in a consumer society, so we negotiated this contract in her presence. On her fourth birthday she was to be taken to a large toy warehouse where she would be allowed to choose a special doll. What happened after this had been fully negotiated and went exactly to plan. Both girl and doll would come to the checkout where the shop assistant wrapped the doll but did not hand it over until the dummy had been carefully posted in the nearest rubbish bin. In this case a negotiated settlement passed off without a hitch.

I have to admit it does not always go quite to plan. Trying the same technique on a 3-year-old girl recently wasn't quite as successful. The dummy had been given to the local chemist in exchange for some much wanted item. The next day the little lady woke up and felt that the new item was no compensation for the dummy. While out shopping she whinged and whinged and at the chemist shop demanded to go through the rubbish bins and abused the chemist when she discovered it had gone for good.

Delayed punishment and the removal of privileges

Young children do not have a very far-reaching view of life. For toddlers, an hour ahead, tomorrow or next week is all quite beyond their understanding. Discipline and rewards for the toddler must, therefore, be immediate. Withholding some treat tomorrow or waiting until dad comes home is both unfair and ineffective. If the toddler has to wait until the evening he has long forgotten his misdeed and the delayed punishment will come as a thunderbolt from the blue. This will do more to frighten and confuse the child than it will improve his behaviour or act as a long-term deterrent. With young children, punish immediately and make that the end of the episode. Young children do not think much about the future or future events, so removal of privileges is a pointless exercise. By the age of 5 or 6 the situation changes with a clear statement made as to the standard of behaviour expected and what will happen if it does not occur. Now the child who won't do his homework, stays out late, or commits some major transgression can have his television viewing restricted, the front wheel taken off his bicycle, or the productivity bonus removed from his pocket money. In toddlers this is pointless and should not be attempted.

The reign of terror

The reign of terror is an old-fashioned philosophy based on the belief that any child can be battered into shape if the parents are firm enough. This method was popular in Victorian times and many a drawing room echoed to such sayings as 'Little children should be seen and not heard'.

Some parents still believe that a house run on strict, authoritarian lines can create the perfectly behaved child. On the surface this may appear to be the case but underneath such forced compliance lies resentment and potential for rebellion.

Model children produced through intimidation continue to behave well just as long as the threat is present. Once it is lifted they rebel: going wild, getting boozed up or having super orgies when their parents go away for the weekend. They usually leave home at the first possible opportunity, making a rude departing gesture as if to say 'Thanks for nothing'. Like government by intimidation, discipline of children by the same method is only good as long as the repression continues. It never creates respect, long-term stability, independence or happiness.

When on top: keep on top

In my work I watch many parents with young children move from a position of power to one of definite defeat, often within the space of five short minutes. What is worse, these parents usually bring this deterioration on themselves.

At the end of a lengthy interview with a family, all their tired toddler wants is to be shot of my office and get out quickly. At this point there is peace, the parents have been given some practical ideas and their attitude is positive—but then they blow it. 'Shake hands with Dr Green.' 'Say thank you to the nice doctor.' 'Pick up all the toys.' 'Park the tricycle over there—No! move it even further over.' After this the parents drag their feet, fiddle about looking for their car keys and chat to the secretary about the weather before they leave.

By this time the child is protesting, the parents are rising to the bait, the air is full of tension and those who were in charge have carelessly thrown away their previous position of advantage.

When I finish a family session with a twitchy toddler, my door opens and they are out and away immediately. When you are handling material that can sometimes be unpredictable or highly explosive, you don't hang around looking for trouble. Don't release your grip; keep little ones interested and on the move.

When on top—keep on top.

9

Dealing with Tantrums and Other Tricks

Now, after three chapters cram-packed with theory and techniques, it is time to see how all this works in practice. How do we stay calm as the toddler performs theatrically on the lounge room floor? How can you get through to a child who turns deaf the moment you ask him to help? What about those spectacular tantrums in the supermarket?

In this chapter we'll look at putting practical discipline into action.

Tantrums

Tantrums are the trademark of the toddler. They start around the first birthday, but generally by the age of 4, most children have learnt that there are better ways to get what they want. As we look around at our adult friends, it seems that a few never grew out of tantrums, lapsing into the most childish behaviour when they do not get their own way.

All children are born different: some are quiet and controlled, with a great frustration tolerance; others come with a remarkably short fuse. To discipline them is like juggling with sticks of unstable gelignite. You are never quite sure when things will go well and when they will blow up in your face.

In the hands of the skilful toddler a tantrum is an art form which can be brought about by a number of different stimuli. Not all tantrums are caused simply by a parent thwarting a wilful child in mid-activity. Some come from the inner frustrations of the toddler himself, who is being stirred up, or is impatient with his lack of ability.

The treatment of the tantrum depends on the age of the child, the reason for the behaviour and where the performance is being staged. In the first year of toddlerhood, before the second birthday, behaviour often just happens, without much thought or reason. Where possible at this age it is best to guide, and be gentle. It is different when you have a 3-year-old who uses a tantrum to openly defy his parents' authority. This is absolutely not on. When authority is challenged, the parents must be consistent and stand firm.

Some toddlers play their parents like poker machines. If their efforts still score jackpots, then they will continue to play. If the parents review their discipline and rig the odds so the toddlers never win, they may crank away but all to no avail. At this point even a 2-year-old should see that it is just not worth the effort.

If a young one becomes frustrated and throws tantrums because he has plans and designs which are way ahead of his technical ability, then it is not punishment he needs but a helping hand and comfort. Any child who is sick or in a home which is upset needs the gentle approach.

Tantrums—the major league

The highest quality toddler tantrums come with all the skill of a Broadway stage production: every detail is designed to elicit the very best audience reaction. Once the tantrum starts, its length and intensity depends on the sort of feedback the actor receives from the theatre.

On centre stage is a wilful toddler who is being prevented from doing something or other that seems immensely important to him. He quickly sizes up the situation and makes instant preparation for a spectacular tantrum. First he takes a quick look over his shoulder, to check that the proposed area for a crash landing is clear of hard and potentially hurtful objects. Next he takes a look at the audience, checking that they are well positioned and watching and that the lighting is adjusted to the best effect. Then quick as a flash, he is off. Crash! He hits the floor and the performance has commenced.

Tackling tantrums is easy in theory but never quite as simple in practice.

- The 2^1/2-year-old music lover decides he wants to fiddle with big sister's Walkman. This is not wise; you take it gently from him and place it safely on a high shelf.

- Explain calmly, clearly and in three words or less why he can't have it. He is not satisfied with the situation.

- He ignites his engines and they start to rev up in preparation for take-off.

- This is a good time to divert his attention. 'Here is dad home early,' you say as you look out the window. 'Oh no, it was another white Commodore.'

- This hasn't worked, he is now revved up almost to full thrust. Now a tantrum is inevitable—CRASH!—he hits the deck, arms and legs going with all the grunts, groans, hype and genuine hurt of a professional wrestler.

- Now even the most serene and best adjusted parents are severely stressed. Hands tremble, palms are sweaty, blood pressure has surged, you are close to having a stroke.

- This is the time you should ignore, but this is not easy. Luckily it is sufficient to pretend to ignore.

- Stay calm, don't fuss, don't notice, don't argue, go about your business.

- Move away to a different room. Wash the dishes, peel the vegies, hang out the laundry, get outside for a breath of air.

  Note: *Now think for a moment what is going on in the mind of a tantrum-throwing toddler. Here he is having put on his best Oscar-winning performance and in mid-act the audience has upped and walked out. With most actors if this happened, they would stop there and then, but of course they are not toddlers.*

- Now that the audience has moved away and is ignoring him, the faint-hearted toddler gives up, waves the white flag and with a sniff and sob, goes for comfort. If this happens forgive, forget,

don't lecture, be gentle. Don't be over-effusive; after all the victory was the parent's and the tantrum must not gain a great reward.

- Meanwhile, back on the loungeroom carpet, the militant is still in full flight. 'This is a bit off,' he thinks, stomping out after mum and putting on twice the tantrum at mum's feet.

- The volume is now rising, your heels are being kicked and you are rapidly losing your grip. Don't forget that we parents are the big people who should stay in control and in charge. While still on top use Time Out. Lift the little one gently, without anger or hate, and put him firmly and decisively in his room.

- Do this with complete conviction, leaving him in no doubt that you are 100 per cent serious.

- As you leave, say very firmly, in few words, that he must stay until in complete control, then extract yourself rapidly to a distant part of the house.

- Whether he comes out in one minute or in fifteen, the time is irrelevant, as long as the tension has eased and the unwinnable confrontation has passed.

- Forgive, don't point score, don't hold a grudge and get him moving along to some new and interesting activity. Loosen up and leave the tantrum and tension in the past.

The supermarket special

Tantrums are not usually difficult to manage when at home but are a different matter when thrown in some prominent public place. When outside you are much more vulnerable and there are always crowds of interfering people, watching to see how you will extract yourself from some unpleasant situation. What is worse, whatever you do, half the people who watch will think it is wrong. Tantrums whilst out shopping are a real pain. Probably one in six of the parents I see find shopping stressful. Many are ashamed when they are out in public, convinced they are failures who can't control their children.

Don't be fooled, what you see out there is modified by a form of natural selection. Yours may appear the worst in the shop, the Mall or even the entire city but there are always many more difficult little ones, whose mothers have learnt from experience not to take shopping. While you are being embarrassed in public, crowds of similar children are left with a neighbour, casual care, or maybe even in a heavily fortified dungeon at grandma's place.

Designers of modern supermarkets have much to answer for as they have created an exciting environment, designed to bring out the worst in a difficult toddler. It starts on the walk from carpark to complex where one finds all those coin-operated rides. For a small sum they will bounce and shake your child but never to the point of complete satisfaction, they must always have another ride. It is best to avoid ever putting a coin in one of these mechanical highway robbers, as once it has been primed, it becomes almost impossible to walk past without fuss. It's like puffing your first cigarette; after a few goes, the habit may be hard to break.

Once inside the shops, the noise and bustle stirs up most children. It is an exciting place and a great learning experience, if they behave. Each child has an individual time limit for shopping and once it has expired every effort must be made to gather up your business and get out as soon as possible. Getting out of supermarkets is never easy, at the best of times, because the checkouts tend to be slow and crowded. To make things worse, the management takes great care to leave rows of sweet stuff beside the queue, strategically placed at knee height.

As you wait, it is not surprising that junior grabs a Mars Bar.

He may not know that it is new, improved and 15 per cent bigger but he is quite convinced that he wants it, 'Now'.

You say 'No!—put it back'. He glances at you, now at your most vulnerable with arms full, purse open and surrounded by an audience holding their breath just waiting to see what will happen.

The little one grizzles a bit and you repeat 'No!'. CRASH—now you have a full blown tantrum and if the other shoppers held scorecards this would rate at least 7.6 for style.

Now you have three options.

1. Give in to this blackmail and buy the bar.

2. Try hard to ignore the antics.

3. Deliver a sharp, well-aimed smack.

The trouble is that whatever you do will have its problems.

- If you weaken and buy the bar, each visit that follows will cost you.

- If you pretend that you are deaf and walk on quite unmoved, you can hear half the audience mumble 'Disgraceful. A woman like that shouldn't be allowed to have children'.

- If you smack, the other half says 'Shame, that's a child basher if ever I saw one'.

Your hands seem tied but there are some things you can do. In my experience, most children who throw a tantrum when outside do the same at home. It is sensible to focus first on the tantrums at home and once these have been tidied up, this control usually spreads to outside. If this fails and you still have the supermarket terrorist on your hands, then only four options remain.

1. Suffer stoically, buy a rinse to hide the grey hairs and wait for age and maturity to bring about some better behaviour.

2. Use grandma, a neighbour or occasional care, to allow tantrum-free shopping.

3. Use late night shopping or bring your partner on a Saturday as an extra pair of arms, a minder and entertainer.

4. When all else fails, opt for smash and grab shopping. The S and G shopper knows exactly what she wants to buy before leaving home. She enters the supermarket, toddler in tow, with sparks flying from the trolley wheels. She speeds round, scooping products off the shelves, with direction, determination and not a shred of hesitation, then through the checkout, pay and away. If you are lucky, this leaves the stunned little spectator still revving up for his usual supermarket performance, but it is all too late.

He won't do a thing I say

One of the most common complaints I hear from parents is, 'When I ask him to do something he doesn't seem to hear. Could he be deaf Dr Green?'. Well if he is deaf he seems to be able to become 'undeaf' again with ease. Though he does not hear what he is asked, there is no difficulty picking up the hiss of an opening Coke bottle at one hundred paces.

This is not the case for a hearing aid but some simple behavioural encouragement.

- If you don't get a response, don't make a fuss of the event unless you are sure that it is a message which must be registered. (Don't fight over trivia.)

- Communicate clearly—gain their attention and eye contact, then transmit a short, positive statement. Don't nag, otherwise nagging will always be needed to get action.

- Don't slow the pace of life to allow excess time for arguments and debates. Jolly them along, help them, keep the show moving.

- When obedience is really important, repeat with conviction.

Then when all gentle techniques have failed, Time Out or a soft smack will clarify who is running the home.

Tidying up toys

Some children seem to be born tidy, while others are quite oblivious to the disaster area they inhabit. The former are easily trained to be neat, the latter will pose a problem, but things can always be improved and made easier.

- Have sensible expectations. Cleanliness and tidiness are possible but not usual in the under 3-year-old.

- Restrict the number of toys on offer. Little children don't need an entire warehouse full of playthings. Put some away, then rotate and reintroduce bringing new interest in forgotten toys.

- Avoid any product which comes apart into twenty tiny pieces. If you don't you will write off weeks of your life, looking for the lost bits.

- Have a big cardboard box for toys and try to establish a habit which encourages it to be filled at the end of play.

- Give a positive statement that it is time to tidy. Softly reward their efforts to help with appreciation. Then move on to some rewarding activity.

I have to admit that teaching tidiness was never successful with my own children. At one point I got so frustrated that I went out and bought a plastic garden rake. This allowed a room to be cleared in seconds, then with a quick burst of the vacuum it looked like new. This was finally sabotaged when an interest developed in glass marbles. These seemed to slip through the rake and then hit the innards of the Hoover like a landmine.

Behaviour—discipline questions

As I have talked to parents over the years, the same questions seem to come up time after time. Many are about sleep, toileting and feeding (see Chapters 10 to 13), whilst the vast majority concern behaviours which are really non-problems which would not arise if we had more enlightened expectations of our little ones. Here follows a list of quick questions, most of which are best answered with understanding, not discipline.

'I tell him no. He stops momentarily, then when I have turned my back he does it again.' This is an example of a toddler who is determined to find out how far he can stretch the limits without getting hurt. If the toddler is clever and his parents lack insight and are blind, it is fun and rewarding to watch us grab the bait.

- Ask yourself if this behaviour is worth noticing. Probably it would be better left ignored.

- If you do respond, be clear, concise and convincing.

- Divert, move them or yourself from the situation, keep little bodies busy.

- If really important, warn again, then use Time Out or a carefully considered smack as the bottom line.

'Every time I raise my voice to discipline, he disintegrates into floods of tears.' This is a common situation where correct and appropriate discipline backfires leaving the parents punished, confused and feeling guilty. Of course there are a few children who are truly sensitive and must be treated with gentle discipline. Others are little Mata Hari's who use their seductive talents for reasons of subversion. They know they have a losing hand but use tears to trump their parents.

- With a genuinely sensitive child—stay close, be gentle.

- Tread carefully in times of separation or family stress.

- If these antics become a major form of manipulation, stand your ground.

- Be sensible, selective and single-minded about discipline. Divert, talk, comfort and calm, move away, don't lift or cuddle.

'If I say no, he whinges until I give in.' Little children are extremely clever at getting what they want from their parents. Some have developed whingeing into an art form, which so grates on their parents' nerves, that the most convincing No! can be turned to a yes with only two minutes of torture.

- Was the issue worth fighting over? Next time don't rise to trivial triggers.

- Be firm, consistent and convincing. Don't ever give in to the whinge. Divert. Move away.

'Our 2¹/₂-year-old grizzles, kicks and complains when putting on her shoes to go out.' This is yet another piece of limit testing, attention-seeking manipulation. They know you have to

be up at the school in ten minutes and every delaying tactic is certain to get a good response. It may not be as much fun as being cuddled or read to, but at moments like this they still have 100 per cent of your attention.

- Be organised, be ready, then move gently but with single minded determination. Transmit clearly who is in charge.
- Be decisive, produce the shoes, put them on.
- Don't allow diversion with complaints about the colour, the style or the socks.
- Don't hang about. Get the show on the road.

'My 2-year-old screams and pushes if any visiting child dares touch his toys.' Young toddlers are not heavily endowed when it comes to socialisation and sharing. They believe they are important people, they know that the toy is theirs, so they expect all intruders to keep their hands well clear.

Don't panic, the fact that your children do not socialise or share at the age of 3 years does not indicate that they will still be mean and antisocial by their twentieth birthday. At this young age they need gentle guidance, after which time and maturity will bring about some major miracles.

- Briefly mention the expectation to share. Don't force the issue, don't make a scene.
- Compensate the empty-handed visitor with the majority share of attention.
- Introduce another area of entertainment. Time Out and smacking are not appropriate here, unless there is a repeated heavy assault on the visitor.

'No matter what I say he disputes my decision and argues.' Toddlers will always argue black is white if it gains good attention from their parents. Fighting with little children is pointless and one of those things one learns to avoid. It takes two to fight and if either party stays calm, there is usually peace.

- Communicate positively, clearly and mean it.
- Become deaf to dispute and debate.
- Stay calm. Do not show upset or emotion.
- If the situation escalates, try Time Out.
- Arguing and debating will not depart overnight, it will take consistency and time.

'You tell us to ignore undesirable behaviour but you cannot ignore him when he is fiddling with the television or video.' Toddlers see adults adjust their electronics and as apprentices to the big people, they copy what they see. To prevent breakages, this must be discouraged and where possible keep vulnerable valuables secure and out of reach. When this is not possible there are several options.

- Persuade gently that touching will not be accepted.
- If the gentle approach fails you may need to be tough. Where touching is being done not through natural curiosity but as a deliberate attempt to defy, gain attention and wind up, be 100 per cent firm.
- Use Time Out and possibly a smack as the absolute bottom line.
- For the very young use a playpen. Put the video, not the toddler, inside. This acts as a palisade to protect your property.

'When out shopping my 2-year-old often attacks other children.' We know by now that many 2-year-olds are lightly loaded with social skills. When out in public some push, nip or throw insults at some innocent infant they pass. This does not come with premeditated malice, it just happens. It may appear a great worry at the age of 2 but don't despair, it will not last long. Socialisation will usually have set in within 6 months or a year at most.

- When concerned keep the toddler tightly in tow.
- If this is minor and occasional it may be ignored or given gentle correction.
- If major hurt is inflicted and repeated, intervene early, warn clearly and be tough.
- Quickly extricate, don't philosophise, smack if it works..

'When I say no, he goes to his father, hoping to be told yes.' If mother and father are united, no child will bother to play this game. If a toddler ever gets wind of a split in the leadership he will hone in on this and prise it wide apart. Like political parties close to election time, there is room for different opinions in private but the public profile must always be one of complete unity.

- Remember, united we stand, divided we fall.

Non-problems need no discipline

'*He uses the pen by the telephone to scribble on the wall.*' Put the pen out of reach.

'*My 3-year-old is not as tidy as his twin brother.*' Don't compare children. If they were all the same, life would certainly be pretty boring.

'*When visitors come I cannot get my child to go to bed.*' This seems very sensible. When there is so much excitement around, they want to be part of it. Give them time, have a later bedtime or get a baby-sitter.

'*My toddler won't say please or goodbye and cringes when kissed by grandma.*' That all sounds pretty normal, they are a bit young to understand these empty adult utterances and kissing probably spreads germs.

'*I tried your behaviour techniques but they made things worse, not better.*' When children find their old antics don't get results, they have to switch up the volume, which is generally the sign that you are starting to get through. Stick at it for success.

'*When dad comes home tired my 2-year-old won't let him watch the evening news.*' Why should he? After being apart all day toddlers want to talk and play with dad. Toddlers see the affairs of the family as more important than the affairs of the world. What's more they are right.

'*What do you do with a toddler throwing a tantrum in the car in rush hour on the Sydney Harbour Bridge?*' This is the sort of impossible question that exhibitionist parents ask in a crowded meeting, knowing quite well there is no answer. Tantrums in the car are often associated with tantrums in the home and these should be treated before focusing on the untreatable.

'*My toddler keeps taking chocolate from the fridge.*' Don't keep chocolate in the fridge.

'*How do I take comforters and cuddly toys from my toddler?*' Why should you take comfort from a toddler? There is a move afoot to prise thumbs, pacifiers, cuddly toys and comforters away from children at the youngest age to promote independence. We all need our comforters; why rush children and rob them of their childhood.

'*At the end of each meal my toddler throws food on the floor.*' He is telling you it is time to wipe his hands, clear the dishes and put him down. Food is for eating and not entertainment. Don't let these aerial food drops be used as attention-seeking antics.

'When his father is away from home he comes to my bed at night.' This sounds sensible. When one parent is away the child often wants to stick close to the other, just in case. Try to return him to his own bed, but go gently. Be really firm when dad returns.

'When I put him to bed he immediately asks for a drink, a wee wee, a brighter light, etc.' Many children procrastinate at bedtime in an attempt to keep those they love close as long as possible. Give lots of attention before you put them down, then be decisive, firm and go.

'On a wet, miserable day their behaviour is awful.' Active little children cooped up with tense parents in bad weather are hard to manage. Try to entertain more, divert and when it gets too difficult, rug up and get out.

'My 2-year-old seems to want snacks all the time and does not eat big amounts at mealtimes.' Toddlers eat when they are hungry and are not governed by our artificial adult mealtimes. Healthy snacks can provide excellent nutrition. If they are thriving, healthy and energetic, with a reasonable diet—relax.

Effective discipline

- Have sensible expectations. A 2-year-old will not behave as an adult.
- Keep temptation away from inquisitive infants. Child proof your home.
- Don't over-discipline. Don't fight over trivia. This makes home negative and causes tension.
- Encourage and reward the good. Ignore and underplay the undesired.
- Don't get this back to front. Take a pace back and check that you are not boosting the bad and missing the good.
- Steer around trouble. Divert. Keep fiddly fingers and busy bodies entertained and active.
- When you mean it, say it with conviction and see it through.
- When losing control use Time Out.
- An occasional smack will let a child know exactly where the limits lie or abort an escalating, unwinnable situation.

- Avoid no-win situations. Be quick to retreat and regroup when on a losing wicket.
- Remember, tension at home, conflicting opinions and parental point scoring sabotage effective discipline.
- If you love and enjoy your children, then use a form of discipline that feels right and works for you. You can't do better.
- If home is happy and secure, never be afraid to be firm. The adults of the twenty-first century will be happier and healthier if the parents of the 1990s are firmly in charge.

Toilet Training

Despite anxious parents, grandparents, the interfering neighbour and a host of other people who think they know better, children become toilet trained when they, and only they, are ready. No child can be trained until the appropriate nerve pathways have sufficiently matured, a process that is completely outside the influence of even the most brilliant parent or doctor. Once sufficiently mature, the process is controlled by the child's will to comply or his determination to defy, which, in turn, is dependent on the child's temperament, as well as the skill and cunning of the trainer.

It seems that at the beginning of this century children were trained much earlier than today, with the process starting at about 3 months, and there are many reports of children being completely trained by their first birthday. There was a lot to be said for early training in those days of cold water, poor detergents and washing by hand. It was also a time when people had a great obsession with bodily functions and the clockwork regularity of bowel movements. It was vigorously drummed into new mothers that if the baby was started off on the right path in his earliest months, he would be saved in later life from the scourge of constipation. Most of what was labelled as toilet training was in fact an unrecognised, involuntary bodily reflex—Toilet Timing. Although we are now ninety years on, the myth of early toilet training still confuses and worries parents.

Most toilet training difficulties today are really non-problems caused by unrealistic expectations and misleading advice. Parents often start training too early, motivated by ideas more akin to the 1890s than to the 1990s. Turn a deaf ear to all those well-meaning but interfering friends and family. Do not start too early: this invariably leads to unnecessary problems. Remember that the child alone has the ultimate power to go where and when he wishes. Don't hurry, don't fight, just relax.

Toilet timing, toilet training

Babies, from their earliest days, tend to empty their bowels or bladders when their stomachs are full after a feed. This is a completely reflex action, being no more clever or voluntary than a knee-jerk reaction. If a child is put on the potty after a meal there is a sporting chance that something will 'pop out'. This is most interesting but it is nothing to get excited about. This is toilet timing.

Toilet training is something completely different. Here an older toddler uses his brain to decide whether he wishes to go to the toilet and then makes a deliberate attempt to oblige. This is a voluntary action and the child is in full control.

Most of the crazy ideas concerning early training are put about by those interfering know-alls who mistake toilet timing for toilet training. No child is toilet trained at the age of 1 year, and children who give this appearance are just demonstrating a particularly strong toilet timing reflex. The effect may reduce the load on an overworked washing machine but this is a temporary lull, often relapsing as soon as the child starts to exert voluntary control.

Toileting: normal development

During the first 1½ years of life there is no proper bowel or bladder control, just the toilet timing reflex. As the child approaches 18 months this reflex appears to weaken and voluntary control begins to take over.

It is pointless to consider serious toilet training until the child knows at least when he is wet or dirty. The realisation rarely dawns much before 18 months of age. In the months that follow this discovery, the child becomes aware of his toileting needs before the event rather than after. This great breakthrough occurs somewhere between 18 months and 2 years of age, but with urine training there is one unfortunate flaw. Although warning is given, the child's alarm system is only adjusted to tell of the impending puddle 5 seconds before it arrives. By the age of 2, the amount of warning has increased and you can start to notch up a few successes. At about this time bowel control will also become established, in some children before urine control and in others after it. By the age of 2$^{1}/_{2}$ years, over two-thirds of children will be dry most of the time; the majority can take themselves to the toilet and handle their pants without too many mistakes. At this age night-time wetting also starts to come under control, the child initially needing to be lifted onto the toilet in the middle of the night, and later holding on unaided. Although most children are dry and bowel trained by the age of 2$^{1}/_{2}$, the whole procedure is still surrounded by a great sense of urgency—the child needing to go 'now' rather than when it suits the parents.

In toilet training development, there is a great variation from child to child. There is a strong relationship with family history, and parents with late bladder training, especially at night, frequently find that their children are endowed with similar characteristics. Girls tend to become trained slightly earlier than boys, possibly because of their slightly more advanced development, different anatomy or, perhaps they have a more compliant personality at this age. Early training is no more a sign of intelligence than early development of teeth. As far as I am aware intelligence comes from the brain, an organ somewhat distant from the bladder.

Our teaching today is clear.

- Eighteen months is the earliest age to consider toilet training.

- Two years is probably a more realistic time and if you wait till 2$^{1}/_{2}$, it won't worry me.

- The average young Australian will be night trained at 33 months.

- The normal young Australian will become night trained somewhere between 18 months and 8 years.

- One in ten of all normal 5-year-olds still wet at night. That is three in every kindergarten class at school.

- If one parent was not night trained before the age of 6 years, 40 per cent of their children may follow suit.

- If both parents were not night trained before the age of 6 years, 70 per cent of their children may follow suit. (Children—please choose your parents carefully!!!)

- Forcing little children causes tension and tension causes little humans to clamp closed all bodily openings. Don't force—relax. Relaxed little children find toileting easiest.

The fundamental rules

1. A child must first learn to sit on the toilet before he can learn to open his bowels on that toilet.
2. A child must know the difference between the feeling of wet and dry before he can be urine trained.
3. A child must be able to produce some dry nappies at night before you can expect a dry bed.

These are my basic rules for toilet training children. It seems pretty obvious that you have to sit before you can perform on a toilet. Seagulls may be able to do it as they fly over Sydney Harbour, but little humans need to be firmly in place if they are going to hit the target. It is equally obvious that you are wasting your breath trying to convince a youngster that he should have done his wee wee in the toilet when he is quite oblivious to the fact that he has just done it in his pants. If the nappies have been consistently wet every night, it stands to reason that if you remove them the bed will become wet every night.

Bladder training

Some time after 15 months of age little children start to realise when they are wet and they don't like the feeling.

The majority just set to and bladder train themselves. They see mum doing it every day, they love to copy their mum. They sit, then one day they surprise themselves.

There is, however, a certain sub-group who seem quite oblivious to the feeling of wet, much to their parents' despair. We do have a simple cure—trainer pants. Now if you get rid of the well-insulated nappy and trade it for a pair of these thin towelling pants, you are in with a chance. They may do little to protect your best Berber from seepage but when wet they evaporate and cool. As the wind whistles off the high hills, the chill factor increases in the lower regions and brings icy feelings to sensitive spots! Now they know they are wet and you are in business.

Trainer pants have the added advantage of being quick-release. This is of great benefit given the precarious state of toddler urgency. Now they know they are damp, it is time to encourage them to sit regularly each day, if they are not already doing it. Put them on the pot at times of coming in and out of the house, as well as all major meals and minor snacks.

Some children will be enthusiastic and keen to oblige while others with a negative streak will use it as an excuse to exert some of their excess power. Forcing is a complete waste of time.

If they sit you encourage, if they rebel you ignore. If something happens you praise, if they do nothing you keep going with patient optimism. When handled in this gentle way, bladder training will rarely cause problems.

The plan

- Are they old enough to start training?
- Do they know the difference between wet and dry?
- If your carpets can cope, use trainer pants.
- Sit regularly before mealtimes and as a double act when toileting yourself.
- Don't force, don't stir, drop subtle hints of encouragement.
- When it eventually happens, notice and reward.

Bowel training

There are many different ways of bowel training a toddler. Most are effective as long as they are not started too early and not pushed too hard. There are three methods that you might consider:

- the 'grunt and catch' method;
- the 'broody hen' method; or
- the 'sit and wait' method.

The 'grunt and catch' method

This method is self-explanatory. The parents do nothing until they hear a grunt, and see that strange look which appears at times like these on the toddler's face. This is accompanied by an ominous silence, an odd posture and finally a characteristic smell. At the first sign, the child should be rushed to the pot in anticipation of the big event. This may be easy in theory but it often fails in practice. Firstly, the parent needs all the speed of an Olympic sprinter to reach the toilet on time and the dexterity of Houdini to untangle the obstructing nappy. Then, if all goes smoothly and the child reaches the pot on time, there is a sporting chance that he will then announce he has changed his mind. It is not a bad method to try, but I suggest it be used only as a back-up to the more reliable sit and wait method.

The 'broody hen' method

This is my term to describe one of the common but perhaps slightly bizarre training methods. When the child dirties his pants, he is immediately taken to the potty instead of being changed. Here, his offering is placed in the sacred chamber, and the child is made to sit above it like a hen incubating a newly laid egg. This is a form of conditioning, getting the child to associate bowel motions with the toilet. I know many parents who swear by this method but I find it a bit kinky.

The 'sit and wait' method

This is the best way to train all toddlers, whether they are malleable or militant. The method is not very scientific but is just a large chunk of good, old-fashioned, commonsense. Start with Green's first rule of toilet training—a child must first learn to sit on the toilet, before he can learn to open his bowels on that toilet.

Initially you use gentleness and guile to achieve a regular sitting habit. Once this is established you give a discreet emotional nudge of encouragement which plants the seeds of success. If you establish these good routines, encourage and don't force, eventually it will happen and then you set off the fireworks.

Don't commence training until both child and parent are ready. Eighteen months is the absolute earliest, 2 years is more sensible and a $2^{1}/_{2}$ year start would not worry me, though it might wear out your washing machine.

Like so much in this book, this is not going to work unless the parents are fully committed and prepared to persevere with the technique. If you don't feel strong enough to see it through at present, then wait a while. If home is in turmoil with visitors, a new baby, holidays, illness or family tension, there will be more success if you postpone until the dust settles.

The method starts by getting the toddler to sit happily and regularly on the potty. Aim for three sits a day, preferably after meals. The secret of success is to make this fun. 'How about sitting on the potty? I'll read you that story we had last night. Once upon a time there was a girl called Goldilocks who went into the wood one morning ...' Maybe at such a young age they don't understand the finer points of Goldilocks but they sure understand the meaning of being the focus of all attention at centre stage.

This is another application of behaviour modification, the technique that is behind most of the methods in this book. The idea is to encourage the desired behaviour—sitting, and not make a fuss of the undesired—refusal to sit.

The trouble is that it can be all too easy to get this back to front. Fighting over toileting often backfires on us parents. Imagine the scene, you have dragged him to the toilet, and say sternly 'You will use the toilet at once!'. With this the eyes twinkle with devilment and a little smile comes onto his face, as he says to himself, 'That's what she thinks!' You force him to sit for five minutes before realising you are beaten. It is unfortunate that this is often not the end of the saga. Ten minutes later junior reappears, a coy smile on his face, nappy at half mast and an interesting manurial odour in the air. Now you have got your just reward. Getting worked up over toileting leaves the child with a trump card that can be used mercilessly to batter the parents when the spirit or bowel decides to move.

As for the length of sitting, that will depend on the child. Some active toddlers find it almost impossible to sit for two minutes, while others are content to remain in an almost catatonic state for most of the day. The law of diminishing returns operates here, however, and if there has been no sign of action after five minutes, then there is little point in prolonging the process.

Once the sitting habit is firmly established, it is time to engage in a little amateur psychology. Gentle hints are dropped to get them thinking positive thoughts about a bit of action. 'Gosh, you are almost 2 and big 2-year-old girls do poohs in the potty.' 'We could give all the nappies away and get new pants.' 'Grandma is going to be pleased.'

What you say is nothing more than a gentle emotional nudge. It must never suggest anxiety, frustration or impatience on your part. Remember, you can only make them sit, they have the ultimate control over what happens and they know this. Even if two minutes after leaving the pot empty they dirty their pants, this must be dealt with calmly, saying nothing more than 'Next time you may do a pooh on the potty—Daddy would be proud'.

If the child sits regularly, is relaxed, encouraged and not forced, eventually something has to drop out in the pot. At this age soft rewards of fuss, attention and praise are best. Grandma is contacted and dad dragged to the phone at work to hear the piece of earth-shattering news. This may seem a bit over the top but it works.

Once training is established there remains an air of urgency for some time before it becomes more stable. Relapses are very rare except in times of diarrhoea, constipation or sickness.

The plan

- Start after 18 months of age at a time when both parents and child are ready.
- Sit the child three times a day after meals. Make it fun. Never force. Don't make a fuss over defiance.
- Once sitting is established give a gentle emotional nudge and then wait patiently.
- When the big day arrives—set off the fireworks!

The untrained 3-year-old

As a child care columnist in a leading Australian magazine, I get hundreds of requests for help each year. One of the most common is from the parents of the 2½ to 3½-year-old child who refuses to use the toilet. These parents often feel that they are the only ones in Australia who cannot toilet train their toddlers. 'What have I done wrong?', they write. The truth is they have done nothing wrong and thousands of other mums are in exactly the same boat.

It is very difficult to deal with children who scream and protest if you as much as take them near a toilet, then wriggle off in seconds, or sit stubbornly but don't deliver. After a year which started out gently and degenerated into forcing, pushing and punishing, the tension level is now running extremely high. At this point both toddler and parent have dug in for a siege and while in that position, neither they nor their bowels are likely to move.

The best course to steer now is to back right off, cool down and put all the fights and failures of the past year behind you. Defuse the tension by suspending all attempts to train, as a first step. Once calm is established, all attention must focus on sitting. Gently and cunningly build up a good sitting habit, then sow the seeds of success, stay cool, wait and reward when the big day comes. This approach will work with both the child who has never been trained and the one who has regressed. With this latter group a medical opinion is wise, to ensure they are not overloaded and constipated.

When refusal to sit has become an insurmountable barrier to training, it is easy and possibly correct to interpret the show of hysterics as a sign of tension or fear of a painful toileting experience in the past. Whether this is true, or whether they just got off on the wrong foot, an alteration of attitude usually secures success.

The majority of these apparently impossible toiletters start to sit when there is calm and their parents approach them in a confident and convincing way. Occasionally one needs to resort to a little desensitisation. This starts with the potty in front of the television, the child seated with trainer pants in place. From here there is a gradual move to no pants, no television and no nonsense.

Toddler bed wetting

Most doctors say that bed wetting (nocturnal enuresis) is so common in the toddler that it is a 'non-problem'. This may be scientifically quite sound but it offers little comfort to parents who know that their child is still wetting the bed, whereas their friends' children were all dry by the time they were 3.

The average age of attaining night-time dryness is about 33 months, but 10 per cent of 5-year-olds still wet their bed regularly. After this age, about 15 per cent of them are cured of the habit each year, until it becomes relatively rare in the teenager. The parents of the 5-year-old who wets his bed must be reassured that, although other parents are not openly declaring the fact, two other children in their child's class will also be regular bed wetters.

Delay in bladder training at night seems to have an extremely strong genetic relationship. Some studies show almost 70 per cent of wetters have a parent or sibling with a similar problem. Bed wetting is also more common in boys; while I find that day-time wetting in the older child is almost completely confined to girls.

Some doctors get very worked up when they hear of a dry child who regresses to becoming a wetter again. They believe that this secondary enuresis is caused by infections or emotional trauma. Certainly infections can cause a relapse but other unmistakable symptoms such as urgency or pain are usually very much in evidence. As for emotional trauma, it may well be a triggering factor but in most of the children I see, I doubt whether even Sherlock Holmes could find the real trigger.

Treatment for bed wetting

The best time to start night training is when a few nappies have made it unannointed through the hours of darkness. Attempts can be made before this but it tends to be a long uphill battle.

When you move from having a couple of dry nappies each week to using no nappies at all, this change often acts as a catalyst to speed up the night training process. Though getting rid of the nappies at this time usually brings training together, some toddlers seem to stick with watery beds with no relief in sight. Now you have to make a decision whether to reintroduce the nappy, relax and rely on your washing machine, or try some other tricks.

Some parents believe that restricting the fluids you offer in the early evening will do much to reduce the wetting. Unfortunately most experts claim this does not work, but experts are not necessarily right. From my simple way of thinking, it seems that what goes in must eventually come out and if it doesn't go in it is less likely to leak out. I am told that this is faulty logic, but for your child you must be the judge.

Many parents find that if they get the toddler up and put him on the toilet late at night, just before they go to bed, this greatly increases the chances of a dry night. This is a sound idea, just as long as the child doesn't become too distressed and as long as it works.

When the toddler has a dry bed, that is the time for encouragement and praise. When the bed is wet, notice is made of it but there is no fuss, punishment or implied blame. I remember asking a rather silly mother if she punished her child when he wet the bed. Her answer was: 'No, I don't punish him, I just rub his nose in it'.

We know that when you start to get a number of dry nappies you stop using them altogether, but what do you do if you never see a dry nappy? Whether dry or wet there comes an age when nappies have to go. This is some time about 4 years of age, but it depends on how the child handles the wet nappies and how you handle wet beds.

When 4 years old, out of nappies and still untrained, there is little more to do but wait. Some suggest star reward charts to encourage them to 'think dry', but in my experience soundly sleeping children have little interest in my stars. It used to be popular for paediatricians to prescribe a medicine for the older wetter, which had some effect. This is out of fashion at present and even though it often works, the effect only lasts as long as the prescription.

At the age of 6 years, a bright light appears at the end of the tunnel. This is in the form of the electronic bedwetting alarm. This gadget has two electrodes in the bed, kept apart by a thin dry sheet. When the bed gets wet the sheet shorts out and bells start to ring. With this, parents descend like a swarm of chamber maids, sheets are stripped, bed remade, new pyjamas supplied, alarm set and off again. No-one seems sure why this works but in children 6 years and over, more than two-thirds will be dry within a month. If you have a wetter of this age, don't psychoanalyse the situation, book in for an alarm and get results.

When a child is ready to train he has no respect for the seasons, but when possible try not to begin in a cold wet snap. For a start the sheets will be hard to dry but also it is less likely to be successful. When a warm child lies in a warm bed, he sweats and loses fluid. When a cold child lies in a cold bed, there is little reason to sweat and the fluid may choose another route for escape. This leads to a full bladder, probably a wet bed and cold parents who have to change the clothes.

Summary

- The time to night train varies greatly from child to child. The average is 33 months but the range of accepted normal is anything from 18 months to 8 years.

- When you find a number of night nappies make it through to morning still dry, it is time to take them off. For most this accelerates the training.

- If bladder control remains unreliable, lift and take the child to the toilet before you go to bed. This suits some and helps them stay dry.

- If you have no success by the age of 4 years, night nappies must soon be withdrawn, leaving the load on the washer.

- Medication is known to help some but the effect is temporary and its use unfashionable at present.

- Star charts are more use for astrologers than night wetters.

- When 6 years and still wet, get a bedwetting alarm. The results are excellent.

Potty or toilet?

One of the decisions that parents have to make is whether to use the toilet or a potty. There is no right answer to this; the method of using them is more important than the equipment itself.

Most parents start their child sitting on the potty, and most toddlers prefer this to the toilet. It has the great advantage of being portable, so it can be taken from room to room and even out in the car. There are, however, a number of independent little toddlers who are bored with being children and who wish to use the toilet like grown-ups. If this is the case, I offer the following suggestions.

Sitting perched high on the toilet with legs waving in mid air is not the physiologically ideal posture for moving one's bowels. If the child is using a toilet, I recommend bricks or a step under his feet. This makes it easier for the child to climb up, and gives support for his legs when pushing down. A small child's toilet seat should be put inside the adult one which gives more stability and dispels any fears of falling into the bowl. Whatever you do, don't flush when they are still sitting, or they will think they are about to blast off and join the astronauts.

Chain flush toilets are pretty obsolete now but I remember in one old hospital where I used to work there were vintage toilets in the children's wards, which gave one adventurous toddler a most terrifying experience. After using the toilet, he climbed on to the seat, just managing to grasp the dangling chain before losing his balance. The toilet started to flush, and still holding on tight, he hung like Indiana Jones over the raging whirlpool below. Eventually, as his strength ebbed, he fell, becoming wet to the knees and having his toilet training delayed by at least six months.

The right thing in the wrong place

Some children have good control of their bowels but they insist on displaying the fact in various places around the house and garden. This can cause anxiety and anger in parents, many of whom believe that it is an early sign of deviant behaviour. All that needs to be done is to quietly mention to the child that this is not welcome, and give great rewards when the right thing is done in the right place.

Boys: should they sit or stand?

Some experts philosophise painfully over the pros and cons of whether little boys should learn to wee standing or sitting. It honestly doesn't matter one little bit. If you opt for standing, urine training may come fractionally faster due to the rewards of hearing so much tinkling water and also being in charge of one's own equipment.

There are, however, several drawbacks. Toddlers at this age are prone to what I call the 'Fireman Syndrome'—they are hellishly inaccurate and spray water all over the place. In addition, some get so carried away with this new skill that it's almost impossible to ever get them to sit. So you've promoted urine training but delayed the bowel habit.

In the first edition of *Toddler Taming* my only cure for inaccuracy was to remove all carpets from the bathroom, after which you had to call in the plumber to insert a big drain and then all you had to do was hose the scene down with great regularity. I have now discovered a better, and dare I say, more scientific, way. Tear up some bits of paper and roll them into little balls. Drop these into the pan and there before your very eyes floats the entire Australian navy just waiting to be bombed into oblivion by the better aiming toddler. Alternatively you may drop a ping pong ball in the bowl and encourage your little bomb-aimer to sink the *Bismarck*.

If your child gets locked into standing and resists sitting, don't worry, this is only a temporary problem and easily rectified by using one or other of the methods outlined in the next section.

The reluctant sitter

I have seen children from 2 to 12 years old who refuse to sit on the toilet. This bad habit may be due to pure stubbornness, to being too busy to spare the time, to fear of toilets, or to the pain of trying to move constipated bowels.

No child of any age should be forced, but rather encouraged. With the very young, I get the parent to read to the child as he sits on the potty, initially with his nappy on. Once the sitting has become an established pattern, then the nappy can be removed. If he leaves his seat prematurely, there should be no fights, but the reading and the attention simply stop. Most young children respond very well to this simple technique.

For those who are frightened of being left in the toilet, it is best if the mother initially stays near by, gradually moving away until eventually the child learns to 'fly solo'.

Other children will establish a good sitting pattern if rewarded with praise and attention when they comply. In the older child (over 4 years), I use a star reward system which is very effective, or I negotiate a simple, no-fuss agreement such as, 'You go and sit and I will have a milkshake waiting for you when you come out'. Strong-arm tactics do not work on toddlers. There are much easier ways of getting things done. If the child has been constipated and possibly also has a small tear in the anal area, there may be great fear of using the toilet. Laxatives and faecal softening agents are useful, as well as a little lubricant cream for the tail end.

Toddler urgency

When you are out shopping with a toddler, you learn very quickly that when he says 'Wee wee, now,' he means now—and not in five minutes. At this age, parents are forced to throw modesty to the wind, aiming the child towards the gutter or helping him water the flower arrangement outside the Town Hall. Car travel is also difficult, with frequent stops often being required, usually in places where it is impossible to pull over.

Urgency is normal in toddlers. Small patches of dampness appear, particularly when the child is excited or engrossed in play. Major accidents also happen for at least a year.

Rituals

Some children will engage in quite extraordinary parent-manipulating toilet rituals. A stubborn little 3-year-old girl I saw recently had it down to a fine art. She had been bladder trained long before but when it came to bowel motions the fun really started. When such a motion seemed imminent she summoned her mum. A warm, freshly laundered nappy had to be brought and carefully pinned in place. The little dictator then gestured the family to assemble at the dining table. She sat in her chosen chair, her favourite doll seated on her right-hand and mum on her left. Then her favourite book was opened at a special page and placed in front of her. Then, when all was exactly to her liking, she gave a great heave and peace was restored for another day.

The cure for all this followed a rather bumpy course. As a first shot I got all her nappies donated to a newborn baby down the road. Our little lady's response was swift. She entered a stage of concrete constipation. A large dose of laxative was administered which worked like a dream, the trouble was that the resultant movement was in her pants. At this point mum and I wondered if dirty pants were really any sort of improvement on the ritual. But we were pursuing greater goals and persevered, and with a great deal of guile and gentleness a good sitting habit was started and in three weeks we had achieved a complete cure.

The obsession with regularity

Parents' concern over what goes in the feeding end of their child is rivalled only by their obsession as to what comes out at the other. It is best to interfere as little as possible with toddlers' bowel patterns; there is a wide range of normal, which nature usually takes care of quite adequately. An eminent doctor once claimed that the normal toddler's bowel habit was between five times a day and once every five days. This may be a rather extreme view, but it is probably more sensible than many parents' over-concern.

The two common conditions that upset parents most are constipation and diarrhoea. Some children are born with a 'sluggish' bowel and always tend to be constipated. Others become constipated as a result of bad toilet habits, and others have problems that started following a feverish illness. Whatever the cause, parents need reassurance that, though it is best for bowels to open every day, this does not always have to happen. A bowel pattern as irregular as, say, once every three days, does not cause headaches, bad breath or lack of energy. Constipation does, however, lead to a vicious circle in which the more constipated the child becomes, the more difficult it is to pass a motion, and the more reluctant the child is. If this is associated with a small tear in the anal margin, the resultant pain may cause a major problem of withholding.

Diarrhoea can occur as a result of the slightest variation of diet or even minor illness. There is a strong relationship between the extremely active child and an extremely active bowel. There is also a condition known as 'toddler diarrhoea'. The child passes many motions a day, which are often very watery and usually contain undigested peas, carrots and other bits of fibre. When the parents view this vegetation, they fear the child has some major malabsorption syndrome. This is far from the truth. Toddler diarrhoea is benign and temporary. Treatment for it is covered in Chapter 12.

Conclusion

You can't go far wrong, just as long as you don't start too early, don't force the child, and just take your time. As the poet said: 'They also serve who only stand and wait.'

Sleep Problems—the Answers

Toddlers who don't sleep well can be the cause of great unhappiness to their parents. Sleep deprivation, as any well-practised torturer will avow, is a sure method of breaking your spirit, determination and ability to think clearly. The mother who says, 'He's not getting enough sleep.' is in fact talking in code. What she really means is, 'Forget the kid, I'm a walking zombie'.

The night-time antics are really only half the story. It is the after-shock the next day that causes the real harm. Then a tired, irritable mum with a befuddled brain has to struggle valiantly to manage a tired, irritable and unreasonable toddler. The result is often complete disaster.

As far as my work is concerned, sleep problems are probably the speciality of the house. My interest started in 1974 when I became disturbed at how many parents were suffering because of their little insomniacs and how hopeless most of us professionals were at helping.

At that time there were four popular ideas on treatment. Some childless doctors suggested that you let the hysterical child cry all night, whilst others recommended a strong sedative. Philosophers believed it was a mother's duty to be up all night, every night, with her crying child, no matter how it disturbed her. Then there was the psychodynamic view that all sleep problems were caused by separation anxiety and if we improved the relationship with our children by day, the sleep problems would disappear.

Of these the only idea that worked consistently was to let them cry for long periods. Unfortunately this also unnerved the parents and as the children became hysterical it did no good for them either. In the end it was this method which I modified, taking its strengths and discarding its upsetting elements, to become the foundation of my controlled crying technique.

If you are an exhausted reader, with a sleepless toddler, relief is now in sight. The methods that follow offer a 90 per cent chance of cure within a week.

The science of sleep

Let us start by getting the science of this straight. Sleep is not one consistent state of unconsciousness, it is a cycle of deep, light and dream sleep punctuated with regular brief periods of waking. Brainwave studies (EEGs) back this up. These show a different electrical pattern for each stage. First we drift off to sleep, then hit the deepest plane of unconsciousness, we dream for a while, then lift to a lighter state before coming briefly to consciousness, to stretch, turn over then drift off again for a re-run of the cycle.

These electrical tracings indicate that the average newborn has a sleep cycle of just under 1 hour, a toddler about $1^1/4$, hours, whilst we adults go about $1^1/2$ hours between awakenings. Other studies confirm this. One of particular interest recorded children with a video camera as they slept in their own homes[5]. Parents of the children studied believed that their little ones were sleeping soundly right through the night, but the recordings showed otherwise. It appeared that even apparently good sleepers may wake a number of times to sit up, look around, play with their toys, kick off their covers, then perhaps have a quiet grizzle before slipping back to sleep. We have to accept that all humans will wake regularly each night, but we do not have to accept that human children should disturb their parents when they do wake. As adults we surface regularly to hear a window rattle, notice it is still dark or that the clock says one minute past three. We register this then turn over and zzzzzzz, we don't kick our partner and say 'Hey, it's one minute past three. How about getting me a drink?'. The same must apply to children. They can kick, wake, grumble and make some noise but they cannot expect you to share in their nocturnal activities. Waking should be discouraged, not encouraged, but we often get this back to front.

Think for a moment from the toddler's point of view. You are 16 months of age, you dream, then lighten a bit, and as you come near the surface you stretch and grizzle. A minute later as you open your eyes there out of the darkness a breast approaches. That's great, you think then, zzzzzzz, down once more to the deep. An hour later you come to the surface, grizzle, the eyes open and there it is again! You have learnt that a good grizzle or a grumble makes a breast appear, and now you believe in the Genie of the Lamp. If mum can do this and still feel rested, that's fine. If not, she now has a problem.

It is normal for children to wake briefly throughout the night but toddlers should be encouraged to act like adults and learn to settle themselves back to sleep.

The statistics of sleep

No two studies have ever shown exactly the same incidence of sleep problems in a population but a few figures are shown in Table 2 that give some insight into how other people's children behave at night.

Table 2: A profile of some sleeping habits[6]

| | Percentage of age group | | | | |
Problems	1 year	2 years	3 years	4 years	5 years
Wakes once or more every night	29	28	33	29	19
Wakes at least one night each week	57	57	66	65	61
Requires more than 30 minutes to fall asleep	26	43	61	69	66
One or more 'curtain calls' before settling	14	26	42	49	50
Requests comforting object to take to bed	18	46	50	42	20
Goes to sleep with lights on	7	13	20	30	23
Nightmares at least once every two weeks	5	9	28	39	38

The Chamberlin study in New York found that 70 per cent of 2-year-olds, 46 per cent of 3-year-olds and 56 per cent of 4-year-olds regularly resist going to bed; 52 per cent of 2-year-olds and 3-year-olds and 56 per cent of 4-year-olds regularly wake up during the night; 17 per cent of 2-year-olds, 18 per cent of 3-year-olds and 36 per cent of 4-year-olds regularly have nightmares.[7]

By comparison, studies in the United Kingdom gave lower figures for waking at night with only 27 per cent of 1 to 2-year-olds[8] and 14 per cent of 3-year-olds doing so.[9] Another survey in the United Kingdom found that 37 per cent of 2-year-olds living with their parents were waking up at nights. These were compared with children of the same age who lived in a residential nursery and found that only 3.3 per cent awoke at nights.[10]

This lends weight to my own belief that the more readily available the comfort at night, the worse the sleep pattern of the child. Certainly when the child enters a period of semi-wakefulness, he is more likely to roll over and go back to sleep if he realises, from past experience, that crying does not bring rapid Grade A attention.

When is waking at night a sleep problem?

What appears to one family to be a massive sleep problem may not concern the next. A problem is, therefore, only really a problem if parental well-being and happiness are compromised. A child who wakes up four or more times a night may not necessarily have the worst sleep problems. He may merely wake, cry briefly and go straight back to sleep after a reassuring pat on the back, and the parents may return to sleep within seconds with no real problem occurring. Another child may only wake once or twice in the night, but each awakening may be followed by considerable difficulties before sleep returns. By the time the parents have paced the floor and bounced the child up and down, the child may be fast asleep again but the parents are wide awake, wound up and incapable of further sleep.

It's not the number of times a child wakes up at night that constitutes a problem but the effect this disturbance has on the parents.

I am constantly criticised by influential experts who found their own children no hassle at night and from such a fortunate position judge my methods as unnecessary and extreme. They are welcome to their views but if your experience is different and sleep deprivation is removing much of the happiness of life, ignore such opinions, read on and the chances are you will soon have a complete cure.

Just who suffers

I used to think that it was only parents who feel the effect of sleep-less nights, but that is wrong. The shock waves are felt by all around. They influence the mother, father, other children, the neighbours and most of all, the child himself. Each year hundreds of parents write to me, with a simple message: 'Since sleep returned, home life is ever so much happier. Once again I am enjoying my children'.

Parents

Mothers who have not had enough sleep tend to be tired, irritable and less patient. As a result, their ability to look after their children both by day and by night may be affected. Many get so tired that life with a toddler is viewed as a form of penance to be endured, with child care giving little joy. I have seen wonderful mothers in tears because they are genuinely scared they will hurt their children unless they get some sleep. Others have slipped past coping and sunk into a pathological depression. It seems crazy that the toddler is often the instrument of his own destruction. He has the power to greatly damage his mother or father, who, uninten-tionally and unavoidably, then transfer the wound.

The marriage

A tired mother makes a tired wife, who needs the help and support of an understanding husband. Where this is not forthcoming a great strain is placed on the marriage. I see many husbands who deliberately spend as little time as possible in the disturbed atmos-phere of home, while others have to put up with being ousted from the marital bed to make way for a sleepless, kicking child. Husbands and wives need to have some time alone together if they are to communicate effectively and remain a strong team. If a child stays up half the night, destroying all meaningful conversation, this is almost impossible.

Brothers and sisters

Most brothers and sisters of sleepless toddlers develop an amazing ability to sleep through most of the night-time antics. A few are, however, sufficiently sensitive to noise to become sleep-deprived, just like their parents. They cop it twice, which is most unfair: once from having their sleep disturbed, and again next day when they inevitably suffer unjustly from the wrath of tired parents.

Neighbours

If you live in a double-brick, detached residence set in the middle of nowhere, you can afford to ignore the neighbours. Unfortunately most of us don't live in these ideal circumstances, and complaints from irate neighbours always add to parental harassment. Even worse I have known excellent parents who have been reported to the police and local child welfare agencies by their intolerant neighbours. It seems grossly unfair that these parents are accused of child abuse, when in fact it is the sleepless child who is abusing his parents.

The child

I used to reassure parents that when the toddler would not sleep, they were the only ones who suffered, as the child always got all the rest he needed. Recently, I have altered my opinion. I now believe that the child who sleeps all night becomes more settled, happier and easier to control by day than the child who has sleep problems. An even stranger phenomenon has come to light with some of the younger children I see.

Once the night-time sleep pattern improves, there seems to be a lengthening (or reintroduction) of the daytime nap. This is a paradox but it appears that more night-time sleep encourages more daytime sleep as well. It must be due to the combined effect of both child and parent being more relaxed and calmer, thus producing a sleep-inducing environment.

Sleep problems—the main offenders

When it comes to sleep, there are three strategies children use to pain their parents. By far the most damaging is that *middle-of-the-night wakening*, where the child cries once or many times night after night and month after month. This can turn happy smiling people into the 'living dead'. Then there are those who *won't settle when put down at night*. This does not exhaust parents or deprive them of sleep but it robs them of valuable time alone together.

Lastly, there is the child who goes down alright but then in the wee small hours *wriggles his way silently into his parents' bed*. By itself this is a fairly innocent habit but as many night visitors also kick and push parents out the side, this is not much fun.

Children wake on other occasions when they are sick, teething, frightened or when home life is disrupted and of course these are not sleep problems. At times like this children need comfort, not discipline.

Repeated middle-of-the-night wakening

The night wakers I see are of two sorts. Most have had a reasonable sleep pattern at some time in their lives and have now slipped from the straight and narrow, while a few have been appalling sleepers right from birth. Generally those who were good and then slipped lost this sleep skill at a time of teething, illness or home disruption. What happens is that ill children wake, are comforted and enjoy the attention. When they get better they think 'That was a bit of alright, let's keep calling for comfort,' and they continue to wake every night thereafter.

As a rule of thumb I can cure almost all of those who at some stage had a reasonable sleep pattern, whilst the born insomniac poses a greater but not impossible challenge.

When children wake at night their cries are often interpreted as a sign of sickness or fear. Now I can never be completely certain but if the disturbed sleep has gone on for some time, it is likely to be a bad habit, not an illness. With just a few days of waking you should always give the child the benefit of the doubt but if it goes on, and on, blaming teething or sickness would stretch the limits of credibility.

Over the years a procession of parents has come, complaining of sleep problems which really don't need treatment. If a child wakes once at night, gets a gentle pat or even a drink, and everybody can get straight back to sleep, then no harm is done. It is a different matter when middle-of-the-night wakening starts to damage the happiness of both parents and children and that is the time to come on extremely strong.

There are some parents who come to me seeking a cure but they are only interested if it involves no effort on their part. They speak as if they are motivated, then make innumerable excuses to ensure that anything I suggest fails. I must stress here that as a prerequisite to any attempt at treating sleep problems, parents must be absolutely certain that they want a cure. They must be determined to see it through, and have the strength to put up with a short period of greater difficulty that usually precedes the complete cure. If you have that sort of commitment, let's look at the method which will do this: the Green Controlled Crying Technique.[11]

The controlled crying technique

We have seen that all humans have a sleep cycle that brings us close to waking almost every ninety minutes. All adults and most children learn to wake, roll over and put themselves back to sleep without disturbing the household. When toddlers are comforted, fed and fussed over every time they come near the surface, the chances are that they will wake regularly to capitalise on so much good attention. When comfort is not readily available to toddlers, they generally decide it is easier to settle themselves and go back to sleep.

We also know that leaving wakeful children to cry unattended dissuades them from waking in the future. Having said this, we don't let children cry for long periods in the 1990s. This is an old-fashioned idea which causes children to become confused and hysterical, while few parents are insensitive enough to put up with so much upset and crying from those they love.

Controlled crying refers to my method of letting children cry for a short period, then coming in to give some, but not full comfort, letting them cry a little longer each time, giving more incomplete comfort, gradually increasing the crying time between comforting until eventually they say: 'I know she loves me, I know she will always come but it is just not worth all the effort'.

In 1974 I would only use this method on children 18 months of age and older. By 1980, I found that 10-month-old babies could be treated and in 1990 we know it is useful right down to the age of 6 months.

We recently ran a research project with this technique in which 140 children were treated over a period of 12 months. The results showed that over the age of 2 years, 100 per cent of our group responded, usually within 3 days; between 1 year and 2, 93 per cent were cured, usually within a week. With those children 6 months of age to 1 year, 80 per cent got better, though it often took as much as 3 weeks and often needed some modification to the method.

The technique

- Toddler wakes at 3 a.m. Initially there is gentle crying, which soon turns to a noisy protest.

- Leave them crying for 5 minutes if you are average, 10 minutes if you are tough, 2 minutes if you are delicate and 1 minute if you are very fragile. The length of crying depends on the tolerance of parents and how genuinely upset the child becomes. Don't give in easily to grumbling or noisy crying with dry tears, but genuine upset with fear and hysteria needs quick comfort.

- Go into the toddler's room; lift, cuddle, comfort. Occasionally you can get away with patting them as they lie in the cot, which is all the better.

- When loud, upset crying turns to sobs and sniffs, this is the God-given signal to put them down and walk out decisively.

- They are taken aback that you dared to walk out. Immediately they start crying again in protest.

- Now leave them to cry 2 minutes longer than the previous period (10 + 2 minutes, 5 + 2 minutes, 2 + 2 minutes, 1 + 2 minutes).

- Go in, lift, cuddle, talk, comfort. At the moment the crying comes towards control, put them down and exit immediately.

- Once again increase the period of crying by 2 minutes. Then comfort, increase period of the crying again, comfort, increase, etc.

- Be extremely firm, continue for as long as it takes. It is pointless starting this technique unless you are prepared to see it through.

- Once they fall asleep, get yourself back to bed and try to get some rest. If they wake again, once more be completely firm. Do the same tomorrow night, the night after and for as long as it is needed.

- If no success is in sight and you are approaching the limit of your endurance, don't give up, combine the technique with a small dose of sedation for several nights.

- After half an hour of unsuccessful controlled crying technique, give sedation. This will take a further half hour to act and in this period, keep the technique going with firm resolve. With sedation you are guaranteed to get your sleep after an hour and the child still hears a very firm and consistent message before finally dropping off. Sedation is strictly short term.

• It can be helpful to get a friend to act as a 'sponsor'. As you struggle away at 2 a.m. trying to be tough, it is a whole lot easier to be firm if you have to report your efforts to someone outside the combat area in the morning.

Common questions

Each year I talk to thousands of parents and questions about my sleep technique always top the list. Here is a selection of the most common.

I have tried your controlled crying technique and it does not work. I hear this every time I talk and when I get exact details of what has been done, the questioner has usually missed the point of my method. If you are going to use this technique it must be carried out correctly. You must be committed to a cure and be totally firm, especially in the middle of the night. When you appear to be getting nowhere, short term sedation in association with the technique is necessary. This allows parents to remain rested and resolute even through a quite prolonged campaign.

When performed properly, it is extremely rare that a cure, or at least a significant improvement, cannot be achieved.

My child wakes to grizzle, grumble and fuss but doesn't really cry. Remember that each of us and each of our children will come to the surface repeatedly throughout the night. If they wish to grizzle and grumble at that time, that is their business and we should not interfere. Children who call out or want you to come and play at 2 a.m. are also best ignored. Children who behave like this in the night can be left unattended, as they are neither frightened nor truly upset. The controlled crying technique is only for use with those children who cry consistently to grab their parents' attention.

My 18-month-old wakes and demands a feed. Is this necessary? Toddlers may enjoy little snacks delivered during the night but these are not necessary for their nourishment. We adults might like our partner to get up and make us a hot drink on several occasions during the night but we have more sense than to ask them. Drinking, nibbling and sucking may be nice for children, but they are more interested in the comfort than the calories. If you are going to use the controlled crying technique, no bottles, breasts or high class comfort can be offered between dusk and dawn.

What do I do? His father works very hard by day, he needs his sleep and I cannot let the toddler cry. I hear variations of this feeble excuse almost every week. I feel it is an insult to mothers, implying that they can be up all night because what they do during the day really cannot be classified as work. Husbands were very generous as they shared at the time of conception and it seems only fair to me that this sharing and caring attitude should continue. The controlled crying technique usually brings success within four nights and any husband genuinely interested in his family's psychological well-being should be helping, not hindering.

We live with my in-laws and they refuse to let the toddler cry. There is no answer to this statement; you are powerless while in that position. If they obstruct yet are genuinely interested in their grandchild's welfare, maybe they should offer to do the night shift.

He shares a room with his sister and if we try your crying technique they both will be awake all night. It is surprising how many siblings are able to sleep through all this crying. When the disturbance is genuine and not being raised by the parents as a red herring, I suggest that the other child is moved to a different bedroom and if this is not available, to the furthest corner of the house. Having isolated the offending party, you are now able to perform my technique properly and within a week, two sleep-loving children will be together again.

He cries at night and if I go in immediately and insert a dummy there is instant peace. Should I use your technique? If we were being completely sensible about discipline, the dummy would be removed, the controlled crying technique used and the problem would be finished within a few days. Having said this, it is often easier for most of us to insert the dummy, knowing that minor disturbances like this are remarkably short lived. We don't need to bring our children up exactly by the book. If we are reasonably rested, happy and peaceful then that is good enough, without worrying about minor infringements.

I have used your technique effectively in the middle of the night, but what do I do when he wakes at 5.30 a.m.? This is a common question which is hard to answer. If you are tough at this hour and use the controlled crying technique, by the time he falls asleep you are ready to get up for the day and it all seems a bit pointless. Sedation so late also leaves hangovers during the day. (More on this later in the chapter.)

What sedative do you suggest? This should be prescribed by your own doctor and it is his decision. In my practice I usually favour brands such as Vallergan.

I have used sedatives and they don't work. Most parents who tell me this have unrealistic expectations of these drugs. Firstly they need to know exactly what they are trying to achieve and then if the right dose is given at the right time there will be few failures.

If parents are at the end of their tether and it is imperative that they get one good night of sleep, there are two ways of achieving this. You can use a suitable dose, given at bedtime, which will take the toddler through the night in most cases. Unfortunately a few toddlers will sleep soundly until 3.30 a.m. and then disturb you until dawn. This is overcome by the second method which is to withhold all sedation until the first time they wake. When given at this later time (e.g., 11 p.m.), there are usually no further disturbances before the dawn.

Most of the sedation I now prescribe is in conjunction with the controlled crying technique. Here we can use a low dose as the aim is not to propel them into twelve hours of unbroken sleep but to break a stalemate situation. In this instance it is now the middle of the night, the child is tired and all the crying has made him even tireder. Often it takes little more than the smell of the uncorked medicine bottle to send them to sleep.

Many experts say you should never use sedatives. Sedation as suggested is used for the purpose of making a highly effective behaviour technique work and in this instance is rarely needed for more than three or four nights. Sedation which is prescribed independent of a sleep technique is generally unwarranted, except when parents are close to collapse, when it gives them several nights of rest and allows them to recharge their batteries. My main concern with sedatives is that some people prescribe them for long periods with no attempt to introduce a sleep programme. This application does not provide a long-term cure. The main side-effect is that sedatives may produce a hangover in some children which leaves them slightly below par the next day. When used correctly, sedatives are safe and effective.

Is this technique effective on the 3- and 4-year-old? Yes, it is often so effective it seems like a latter day miracle. Children over the age of 3 are a joy to work with. Over half of those I see are cured as they leave my office without ever 'a shot being fired'. Once I have told the parents exactly what to do, I then explain it again, this time in the child's hearing. Children at this age are compulsive sticky beaks and though they appear somewhat bored as they play or look out the window, they are taking it all in. As they leave they know the score and their parents are committed to seeing it through. When the parents ring me in the morning, most of them are amazed at what happened. 'Dr Green, you won't believe it, he never woke last night!' We all know that something simple yet powerful has happened. The children know exactly where they stand and can sense that the big people are in charge, and going to see this through. It is not worth a challenge.

Are you sure your technique does not cause some psychological damage to sensitive children? There are many things we have to do in paediatrics which cause considerable upset to the children in our care. We frighten them with X-rays, examinations, immunisations and hospital investigations. Then there is the pain and trauma of life-saving surgery. Whatever we do must always be a balance of the benefits against any emotional upset. I cannot be certain that my controlled crying technique does not cause upset to children but even if it does, it would seem that the amount is minimal. Balanced against this there is no doubt that sleep deprivation can do immense harm to parents, who in turn bring stress and emotional harm to their children. I am convinced that the benefits of my technique when used correctly greatly outweigh the theoretical objections.

When they won't go to bed at night

Over half of all toddlers will play up when it is time for bed if they know they can get away with it. They seem to be designed with a sleep clock whose bedtime is considerably later than the setting their parents would wish. Some are tired but still obstinately refuse to go to bed, while others infuriate their parents by popping in and out of their rooms like a Jack-in-the-Box. Other, more subtle toddlers, create a smokescreen of requests for drinks, the toilet and various comforters, which succeed in keeping parents on the hop and gain them great attention. Most bedtime problems are simply bad habits which can be avoided with routine and rules administered by gentle but determined parents.

Refusal to retire is a much less damaging problem to parents than the antics of the middle-of-the-night wakener. All this in-and-out drama is a pest and though the parents may be irritated, at least they are not losing any sleep. Parents deserve the chance to have some time alone together, so their children should be expected to go to bed at a reasonable hour—a nice notion, although sometimes sabotaged by our little children.

One group of reluctant settlers are those who require less sleep than the text books tell us. These children will probably grow up to be prime ministers, leaders of industry or other irritating insomniacs. For them, no matter what we do, bedtime will be later than we want. Then there is another group who like an afternoon nap, but this so recharges their batteries that they continue to run on full power half the night.

Of these the first need a later bedtime and when put down they must be made to stay in their room, even if not unconscious. The others may need to lose their afternoon nap or at least make it shorter.

Some fortunate parents have the luxury of a child-free period each afternoon, followed by the same each evening. However, many of us can't have it both ways.

Medical science is not sufficiently advanced to make non-sleepers take more sleep but we are in no doubt about how to put children to bed and how to keep them there. Here are some suggestions.

The gentle approach

Good routine Try to follow a regular routine in the lead-up to bed, then put them down at a constant bedtime. Where settling poses a problem, a later bedtime may be introduced on a temporary basis. Once this is well established it is quite easy to bring it forward a few minutes each night, until an acceptable level is achieved.

Calm them down Don't fight, stir, run, chase or play wild games near bedtime. Olympic athletes do not finish the race and then go straight to sleep and we ourselves need to unwind before bed. Bath, talk, tuck up, cuddle and read a soothing story.

Leave decisively When it is time to go, say goodnight and leave as though you mean it. Do not rise to requests whose only purpose is procrastination.

If they come out If they reappear you must be firm. Don't feel guilty at being tough, after all you have given them your absolute best attention before bedtime. Never encourage Jack-in-the-Box behaviour. Over the years some parents have told me in all seriousness: I put my child back twenty-four times last night. This is not discipline. You are playing a fun game with your child and only one party is appreciating it. You put them back once, no questions are accepted, you know you are in charge, they know where they stand and that is it.

The even gentler approach

Good routine, calm down As above.

Sit until they sleep The gentlest approach is to stay until they slip off to sleep. You finish the story, cuddle, kiss, tuck up then sit beside the bed until they start to snooze. This is a very loving way to do things but many parents find it backfires as their child prolongs the process with a lot of questions and manipulations.

You sit quietly in the room either reading to yourself or just relaxing. All you are offering is your presence, not an evening of entertainment. If they lie quietly you stay but the moment they question or climb out, this gentle approach has failed and you must leave decisively.

The tough option

Good routine, calm down, leave decisively As above.

If they come out once Put them back immediately. Leave them in no doubt that you are not going to tolerate this and will be extremely heavy if they reappear.

If they come out again At this point there must be no misunderstandings. You dearly love them but you have given them a more than generous amount of your time and attention and if as much as a nose pokes out again, you will descend like lightning from Mount Olympus.

If they come out yet again At this point a serious challenge is being staged and you can either stand up and be decisive or decide to abdicate your position as a credible leader. If you believe in giving a warning smack, this is the time to do it. If not, some means must be used to block routes of escape.

With a smack, most children realise that the game is up and remain firmly in their room. Unfortunately many change the rules of the game and start to cry vigorously in another attempt to break the resolve of their parents. This of course will not work as the parents have already been instructed in the controlled crying technique and if this is used the battle is all but won for them. On first reading this may seem a hard way to treat children but bearing in mind that a complete cure can usually be guaranteed in under a week, it is a small price to pay for peace.

Green's patent rope trick For those who cannot bring themselves to smack their children but realise that they are rapidly getting nowhere, I strongly recommend the rope trick. This is one of my better inventions, which came from the drawing board when I was trying to curb the escape-artist antics of my own children. All that is required is a short length of strong rope.

Before you get worried, I am not going to suggest that you tie your child to the bed, tempting though this might on occasion be. What you do is loop one end of the rope around the inner handle of the bedroom door and attach the other end to the handle of a nearby door. Carefully adjust the rope so that when the bedroom door is forced open, the aperture is just a little less than the diameter of the offending child's head. As all of you who have had babies know, if the head is not going to get out, nothing is. It is not that they are locked in, they just cannot get out.

With your child safely in his room, he may resort to crying to break your resolve but once again this ploy will fail as you use the controlled crying technique. A light should be left on in the passageway outside the bedroom, so that the child can see and hear what is going on around the house. This means that the child will not become frightened, yet at the same time he is made very aware that bed is the place he is meant to be.

Before you all rush out to the nearest hardware shop, ordering up miles of rope, let me relate one cautionary and somewhat embarrassing tale. One late evening it had become quite apparent that there was no way our active superboys were going to stay in their room, so a loop of rope was attached in the approved manner. Following this, there was a bit of gentle crying which then dramatically increased in decibels. My wife and I knew we had to wait five minutes before we came and comforted (it had to be true because I had read it in my book) but when we eventually arrived we got a nasty shock. The boys were still in their room but unfortunately I had made the rope a fraction too long and the older boy had skilfully pushed his younger brother's head into the crack in the door, where it was firmly jammed. Extraction almost needed an obstetrician with forceps. Life is not without its troubles, even for child care experts. Don't let this put you off, though, as the patent rope trick works well.

The results

Whichever of these approaches you take, if you are determined to achieve a cure this can be guaranteed in under a week for at least nine out of ten cases. Whatever you do, have sensible expectations. This is not a way of making children go to sleep, it is only a means of ensuring that when you put them to bed they stay there.

The child who comes to his parents' bed each night

Many philosophers extol the joys of a family sleeping together in one giant, bed-bound commune and in fact I receive many rude letters if I dare suggest eviction. This may be a terrifically enjoyable state of affairs for those who are deep sleepers or are lucky enough to have children who do not wriggle or kick. If you enjoy having children in bed with you all night, every night, that's your decision. If you are all happy, let them stay there until they are ready for high school as far as I am concerned.

In my experience, about 75 per cent of mothers and 95 per cent of fathers wish their bed to be a private, peaceful place. They greatly resent intruders making a regular appearance in the small hours of the morning.

Nocturnal wanderers tend to be the more active members of the child population, seemingly incapable of lying quietly in the parental bed. It is almost as though they had different magnetism, while mother and father lie North/South they are almost drawn to the East/West position in which they can simultaneously kick one parent and poke the other. Many mothers can tolerate this intrusion but fathers, I find, are less long-suffering. The prospect of a busy day after a disturbed night's sleep will force them to flee to the peace and comfort of the loungeroom or take up position in the child's vacated bed, probably with their legs hanging out the bottom.

Many lonely mothers, whether alone because their husband is away on business, or because of a marriage break-up, subtly encourage their children to come into bed with them each night as company. This is probably quite good for both parties but it may cause problems when life returns to normal.

A child who is sick or genuinely frightened, will always have a rightful place in his parent's bed, though it is important to evict him once his health has returned. All children are entitled to that enjoyable early morning romp in their parents' bed, just as long as the sun is up and the cock has crowed. Sleep is very important to the sanity of us parents and I believe that children should be excluded from our beds if at all possible. Peace and privacy are important to people and that includes parents. Of course it is up to you but if you want a good method of evicting the most determined toddler from your place of rest, read on.

The technique

1. The moment the child appears he must be put back immediately.

On a cold night, a tired parent must be very strong to resist slipping the little intruder into bed, but such an action only reinforces antisocial night-time behaviour and must be discouraged. Some unwelcome little nocturnal prowlers can slip into their parents' bed with all the stealth of a cat burglar and lie there unnoticed for quite some time. If you are determined to stop this habit, I suggest putting a wedge under your bedroom door, which allows it to be opened a short distance but causes an obstruction that alerts you to the child's approach.

2. If the child returns, give a stern warning and, if possible, have the other parent return him to bed.

More democratic parents give the child a stern warning, leaving him in no doubt as to what lies ahead if he is seen again, and then put him back to bed (preferably the other parent than the one who dealt with him the first time). I must admit, however, that most parents feel that this degree of civility is quite unwarranted at that time of the night, and they move straight to the next stage.

3. If he returns a third time, give a light smack or immobilise doors.

In this case, either a light, symbolic smack should be used before returning him to his bed, or various doors should be immobilised with the patent rope trick or a therapeutic little wedge. Following this, the controlled crying technique is used.

4. The results: ten out of ten cured if that is what you really want.

Coming to the parents' bed in the middle of the night constitutes the least damaging of the three major sleep problems of toddler-hood. It is up to the individual parent to decide whether to tolerate their behaviour or have a showdown. The methods outlined may seem rather harsh but the middle of the night is no time for playing games, and it is worth being firm, because the chances of a quick and permanent cure are excellent.

Other sleep-related problems

Most young children, once asleep, are dead to the world and would not wake even if set down in the middle of the 1812 Overture, cannons and all. Some, however, are uncommonly sensitive to sound, which leaves the parents tip-toeing round the house at night, frightened to run a tap or flush a toilet.

The light sleeper

Problems with light sleepers are easily overcome by placing an ordinary household transistor radio beside the child's bed. On the first night, turn the radio on with such a low volume that the sound is barely audible to all but a passing bat. As the nights pass, gradually increase the volume over a period of two weeks. Most children are well and truly desensitised by this time. From there on, most children should sleep through garbage collections, car horns, the football final on television and the odd cannon.

What station should your child listen to, I hear you ask. Assess his interest. Budding merchant bankers should be tuned to the station that gives the best stock market reports, punk rockers in the making will be happy with a rock station, and a possible candidate for the clergy is probably happiest listening to hymns. Of course, I am joking. It really doesn't matter which programme the radio is tuned to. In fact some tune to FM and then go slightly off station, thus leaving the radio with a crackle not unlike Niagara Falls which gives background noise constantly without the quiet spots at the end of records or talking.

The afternoon sleep

Children in the first two years of life enjoy their daytime nap—and not only the child, I may say. Mother looks forward to this time with equal glee. Unfortunately, this peaceful event disappears somewhere between the ages of 2 and 4, and every parent mourns its passing. But in the final days before the changeover, parents are in a dilemma. If the child does not get an after[...] unbearably irritable in the late afternoon but he g[...] and sleeps soundly. If he does sleep in the aftern[...] enjoyed but it is paid for when the revitalised ch[...] the house until all hours of the night.

There is, I'm sorry to say, no answer to this problem. Parents simply have to make a choice. I favour the sacrifice of the already waning afternoon nap, believing the good night-sleeping pattern to be more important.

The right bedtime

There is no universal 'right' bedtime for all children. In my experience, 7.30 p.m. appears to be the accepted time that most toddlers should assume the horizontal. This may be the case for the sleeping majority but a significant minority won't settle to sleep at this time in a month of Sundays. The offenders are usually those difficult children who have been poor sleepers from birth. They are mostly active boys, which is surprising because one would expect them to need more sleep considering the massive amounts of energy they use up during the day.

All we can do is accept that children, like adults, have different sleeping needs and be thankful that most toddlers are snoring by 7.30 p.m. As for the late settlers, they need a later bedtime, and although they cannot be forced to sleep there are at least ways of keeping them in their rooms, which must surely increase the chances of them inadvertently falling asleep.

The procrastinator

Little children who do not wish to be parted for the night from their loving parents have an immense repertoire of procrastinating techniques. 'I want a drink,' 'I feel hungry,' 'I want you to lie beside me,' 'I want a different pillow,' 'I don't want a pillow at all,' 'I want two pillows,' and so on. This is a genuine wish to hang on to the parents' attention for as long as possible and put off having to go to sleep. This is all part of the charm of these tender years but it must not be allowed to get out of hand. A little procrastination is fun but if handled badly it can turn into a major case for manipulation. Know your child and know when to say enough is enough.

The early riser

Some children love to sleep late while others are up and on the go from the first chirp of the dawn chorus. Once again, this tends to be the prerogative of those over-active members of the toddler population. I have to admit that I have never been of much help to parents with this problem. In theory, if we suggest a later bedtime, this should cure the habit, but I find that its only effect is usually to turn a happy, early riser into a tired, irritable early riser. Cutting out the daytime sleep leaves them hard to live with in the late afternoon but they still seem to wake equally early.

One approach which sounds sensible but rarely works is to ensure that the room and cot are filled with quiet toys which will let them entertain themselves and play in the early morning. In theory this should enable the rest of the household to remain asleep, but few toddlers are interested in this. They want to get up, move, be fed, and share the full beauty of the sunrise with their parents.

When the early morning habit becomes a major hassle, the controlled crying technique can be extremely effective, but it often leaves you in the ridiculous situation of soothing a child off to sleep just in time to wake the rest of the family up for the day's activities. Sometimes it is easier for the adults to change their sleeping pattern, going to bed earlier and waking in harmony with their youngster. I fear that with early risers sometimes the most I can offer is sympathy, not a cure.

The night prowler

Some children wake up in the middle of the night wanting something to eat, or to play or explore the house. Recently I was brought a 3-year-old who had discovered that getting up at 2 a.m. and turning on the vacuum cleaner had quite an effect on his befuddled parents. Another 3-year-old of my acquaintance loved to play with his toy cars in the middle of the night. As he could not reach the light switches, he had to find an alternative form of illumination, which he achieved by setting up his automobile collection in front of the refrigerator, then pulling open the door and playing by its cold, bright light. This would have been a quite innocent pastime, except that he was often overcome by sleep in mid-activity and would be found in the morning in company with piles of defrosted vegetables.

If children are determined to play in the middle of the night, that is fine, just as long as they are quiet and do not damage themselves or other people's property. It is usually safest to deal with night prowlers by resorting to the patent rope trick, as well as making sure there are deadlocks on all the exterior doors and wedges on others to limit the child's access to danger.

The shared bedroom

Often, with the midnight screamer, parents are defeated before they ever start. They are quick to point out that my techniques will never work as they are too disturbing for the other children. I can assure you, however, that if you are really keen on finding a cure, then a shared room, although inconvenient, is not an impossible hurdle.

All I ask for is one week of absolute firmness, during which most families should be capable of rearranging themselves for a short while. Older children who share the crying toddler's bedroom usually have a much higher tolerance for nocturnal noise than their parents anyway. The controlled crying technique can usually be used without causing any great disturbance to the other room occupants. If this is not possible, a temporary sleeping arrangement must be organised and the other children moved from the bedroom to the comparative quiet of the lounge room or off to granny's for the weekend. This will leave the toddler pretty well soundproofed for the duration of the treatment, and once a good sleep pattern has been established, the children can be reunited.

It's only when the entire family live in one bedroom that my technique falls sadly apart. In these difficult situations parents simply have to give in to the child in the interests of the family's peace.

The cot in the parents' bedroom

Many newborn babies sleep in a cot close to their parents' bed, taking some of the effort out of the night-time feed. Some parents with older children prefer, for a variety of reasons, to keep them close to their bed at night. This may be fine if the parents are sound sleepers and the child remains quiet at night. But it may not be such a good idea for light-sleeping parents who are stirred to consciousness every time the child coughs, turns over or passes wind. Even children with epilepsy or other medical problems should be encouraged to sleep in a separate room, as unbroken sleep has great curative powers for the entire family.

The lost dummy

Some young toddlers can only survive those wakeful periods at night with their mouth firmly plugged by a dummy. If it becomes disconnected, help is summoned by loud wailing and gnashing of teeth, and the cries will only subside once the missing piece of junk is replaced. Many parents get sick and tired of this constant midnight drama, but they don't know how to rid themselves of this offending object. Some disposal suggestions are mentioned later in this book, but one way of keeping track of the thing is to tie a short tape onto the dummy and pin it to the child's night clothes. Children of an advanced age, who shouldn't have a dummy in the first place, are thus able to locate the lost object. Unfortunately young children seem to be unable to make contact with the tape and, even if they can, find it well nigh impossible to reel in and plug their mouths.

The only reliable cure for repeated wakening as the result of a lost dummy is to get rid of the object completely. Certainly this may lead to several difficult nights but in the long term, it is well worth the momentary inconvenience.

Night feeds

There is a major relationship between night wakening and night feeding. If night-time breast feeding continues after the first birthday, there is a strong likelihood that this will be accompanied by multiple nocturnal wakenings. So great is the comfort from breast feeding, that the child will demand the breast as an adjunct to sleep—comfort rather than sustenance is the object of the exercise.

When breast feeding and sleep are both wanted, toddler breast feeds should be given by day, on going to bed and on wakening in the morning. A strict curfew must be imposed during the hours of darkness. Bottles and beakers give less comfort. When compared to a warm breast, there is minimal joy to be gained from sucking a cold rubber teat that has been steeped in some nasty, antiseptic solution. But these should also be suspended during the hours of sleep if night wakening is to be cured. When given, they establish a bad pattern, which once again encourages the half-asleep child to cry out for sustenance rather than turn over and go back to sleep.

A basic law also decrees that 'what goes in must come out'. The more fluid the child drinks, the greater the number of wet nappies, wet beds, discomfort and excursions to the toilet.

Don't be fooled by advertisers' attempts to encourage you to combat 'night starvation'. Toddlers don't starve at night. For the sake of peace and quiet and an undisturbed sleep, all midnight snacks, be they from breast or bottle, should be discouraged.

Of course if night-time feeding is no major hassle, please continue. That's always a gentle, comforting and charitable way to go.

The cot escaper

Long before they reach their first birthday, some children have developed strong mountaineering skills. They lie quietly in their cots for months, planning their escape route down to the final detail. The time of the first successful escape attempt varies greatly from child to child, and from cot to cot.

No matter how energetic and ambitious the young child may be, he is unlikely to scale a high side that has no horizontal stepping bar from which to take off. The first effort usually ends in a hard fall, as he finds the climb up considerably easier to control than the journey down the other side. Some children never consider climbing out of their cots at all and would probably remain there happily until school age.

Parents often ask at what age the child should be moved from a cot to a proper bed. This often happens precipitantly when a new baby arrives, but on other occasions it is a well-planned move. If the child has a good sleeping pattern, little harm will come from the change. The trouble comes with the child who sleeps poorly in his cot, and parents misguidedly think that the move to a bed will help. All it does is transfer the bad sleeper from one mattress to another with no attendant benefit. I am all in favour of toddlers remaining in their cots at least until well into their second year. There seem to be few advantages in an early release programme.

When the toddler starts climbing out of his cot, parents are usually terrified that he will fall and hurt himself. At this point, they have to decide whether to leave the side of the cot down or put him in a bed, both of which allow easy escape and will possibly lead to night-time problems. If they leave him in the cot, it should be situated against two walls with a soft floor covering under the exposed side. It may seem a rather callous thing to say but in my experience most young children who have a tumble from their cots usually have the sense to postpone further attempts until they have become sufficiently mature to guarantee a soft landing.

The nocturnally deaf husband

This is a fascinating phenomenon, which I have studied assiduously for years. My observations show that when the child cries at night, most husbands appear to become suddenly stone deaf, and thus their wives are forced out of bed to cope with the problem. I don't believe this is, in any sense, true deafness, but rather a conveniently learned response to an unpleasant situation. My wife claims that, when our children cried at night, she found that my hearing could be toned up with the aid of a sharp kick. Certainly in these enlightened days, I believe there should be more sharing of the less pleasant parts of parenthood, and if kicking is what it takes, then that is as good a method as any.

Fears

When a child starts to cry at night, many parents worry that he may be frightened and thus will not allow my firm methods of control to be used. Certainly younger children do have fears but when they wake once or more every night, that's a bad habit, not fear.

Separating from parents at night can cause anxiety in some toddlers, but it must be coped with if both parents and child are to get any sleep. To help with this separation, it is quite a good idea to use comfort items, such as a favourite teddy bear or a security blanket.

Fear of the dark is common among older toddlers, and indeed in quite a large number of adults. A dull, low-wattage light is a small investment that will relieve a great deal of stress. Some academics dispute the value of night lights, believing that the shadows they throw make the child even more frightened. This certainly doesn't seem to be the case with any of the children I have ever seen.

Nightmares

Nightmares are much more common at an older age, but they can occur in toddlers. As the child wakes from active dream sleep, he may still be in the midst of some alarming escapade. He has an unmistakable frightened cry and is easily soothed by the rapid appearance of a parent. He quickly becomes aware that it was a dream, not a real event, and in some cases he can even remember all the details. Nightmares may occur quite regularly, and although there is some association with stress and anxiety, it is usually the sort of normal stress of life that we cannot change. The most loving, attentive, angelic parents, who have the best possible relationship with their child, will find that the child still has nightmares. He's probably dreaming in this case that he has become separated from them.

The treatment for nightmares is simple. Go quickly to the child, hold him, talk soothingly and stay as the child slips quietly back to sleep.

Night terrors

These occur in a slightly younger age group. The child wakes from a deep, sound sleep in a state of utter terror. He sits up in bed, looking through glazed, staring eyes and cries profusely. His parents run to his aid and are confronted with a difficult situation, as the child seems almost paralysed and stuck in a different world that they cannot reach. The thing to do is cuddle the child, talk quietly to him and after a while the child will gently relax and go back to sleep. This can take anything up to twenty minutes. In the morning, the child will have no memory of the previous night's events, although the parents will find it much harder to forget.

Once again, there may be repeated episodes but it is extremely rare that any treatment is required other than letting time do the healing. As with nightmares, it is unlikely that there is any treatable anxiety-provoking event that causes night terrors.

Sedation

Sedative drugs are abused and over-used by many parents. In some families, they are almost a nightly routine, being used for sleep problems that could be more effectively and safely treated by simple behavioural methods. I disapprove of sedatives being used unnecessarily, but there are three situations in which I think their use is justified:

- in conjunction with my controlled crying technique;

- as a safety valve for fragile families to use in times of crisis when sleep is imperative to maintain sanity and stability; and

- to sedate the severely handicapped child who is extremely irritable by day and is awake crying all night.

The secret with sedation is to give the right dose at the right time. Most doctors quite gratuitously write the instructions 'to be taken at bedtime' on the bottle. It is, however, unrealistic to expect that a sedative given at 6 p.m. will miraculously ensure sleep right through until next morning. When I want a child to sleep, I give the drug, in its correct dose for the child's body weight, on the first occasion that he wakes in the night. This is more effective than administering it before the child goes to bed, because he was probably going to sleep perfectly well for the first few hours anyway, but when given later the effect will extend to protect those golden hours between midnight and dawn.

Over the years I have seen children who have never in their life ever slept more than six hours a day. With these and other families who are exhausted and fragile, sedation not only brings immediate relief but gives them the strength to see through one of my behaviour programmes. When parents are really shattered I may prescribe a few days' sedation for the child to allow everyone to get back onto an even keel before embarking upon a more permanent cure by more effective methods. There is no harm in having a sedative in the house as long it is used with sense and as a last resort when an unbroken night's sleep is vital for survival.

Sedatives are not without their problems. Some children become quite hung over the next morning whilst a minority may demonstrate some unexpected paradoxical effects. These children become irritable, overactive, unreasonable and poorly co-ordinated. They adopt all the worst characteristics of an obnoxious drunk, staggering around the house, slurring their speech and walking into door handles. Be careful before administering a large first-time dose on a car, train or especially a plane trip. The thought of being trapped at 33 000 feet with a drunk, belligerent toddler is somewhat mind boggling.

Sensitive neighbours

Parents with children who sleep poorly are often sabotaged in their attempts to implement controlled crying by complaining neighbours. I recommend the direct approach in these instances. On returning home from my office, the parents go straight in to see the neighbours and tell them that the child is now in the hands of a specialist doctor from the Children's Hospital who has designed a new treatment for sleepless kids. They explain that this is quite revolutionary and the doctor has insisted that they let the child cry a number of times at night, but that the cure will come inside a week. On most occasions this super-scientific approach, blaming everything on the doctor, has worked. So far I have had no reports of parents being set on by the neighbour's dog, but despite all my best efforts, some have been verbally abused and even reported to the police and welfare agencies.

12

What Should Toddlers Eat?

Food is the fuel that powers our young children. It makes them grow strong, gives them pleasure and provides them with many opportunities to wind up their parents. We can choose the healthiest designer diet, put it on a plate, even get it into the mouth, but if they decide that's as far as it is going: checkmate—the game is over!

When animals feed their young, it seems such an uncomplicated affair, yet humans, with all their nutritional advisers, find it is downright difficult.

As parents, let's aim to loosen up a bit, stick to realistic expectations of diet and never let food become a battle. We should also set a good example, and where better to begin than at the start of toddlerhood. There we have complete control over the available diet. After all, we are the ones who buy the stuff.

Occasionally an uptight parent tells me, 'My 2-year-old seems to eat nothing but chips, chocolate, chocolate biscuits and more chips.

What can I do?'. Is this parent telling me that junior gets up in the morning, takes the keys of the Volvo, drives down to the supermarket, loads up a trolley with chips and chocolate, drives home and eats them? I think there is a message in this somewhere.

What is a balanced diet?

Adults and toddlers need six different types of nourishment to survive: protein, carbohydrate, fats, vitamins, minerals and water.

Protein is present in meat, eggs and cheese; lesser quality vegetable proteins are found in beans, nuts, etc. In our affluent country we tend to eat considerably more protein than we need.

Carbohydrate comes in simple forms as glucose and cane sugar or the more complex form as the starches in cereals, bread, pasta, vegetables, fruit, etc. The simple sugars are easy to eat and quickly absorbed and it is not hard to eat too much. Not only do they come as refined cane sugar but they are also present in honey, ripe fruits and other natural foods. The complex carbohydrates are digested slowly so the energy they produce is sustained for a longer period. They have much more bulk than the simple sugars, which means it is not so easy to over-indulge and thus become overweight. Complex carbohydrate is the in food for today's athletes and in fact every one of us.

Fats are present in meat, cooking oils, milk, butter, cheese, nuts, etc. There are two types of fat, the saturated sort mostly found in animal products and the unsaturated type more often derived from vegetable sources.

Fats are an important source of energy, providing double that of the same amount of sugar and putting on twice the amount of weight if we are not careful. Though reduced fat diets are important for adults and older children, young toddlers burn up so much energy with their activity and growth that a reasonable amount of fat does not seem a problem.

Vitamins are required in small quantities if we are to remain healthy. Once we have the desired amount, doubling or trebling these levels does not make us twice or three times as fit; in fact it does nothing. There are various vitamins such as vitamin C which is found in fruits and juices, and vitamin D which is present in eggs and butter as well as being manufactured by sunshine acting on our skin. There is a great deal of misleading advertising about vitamins. Australian children who do not have some major bowel or other medical condition will be getting all the vitamins needed if they are given a half reasonable toddler diet. My understanding is that natural vitamins come from natural foods, not from a pill laboratory.

Minerals are required in small amounts. Iron and calcium are the two we think of most. Iron is found in large quantities in meat and lesser quantities in fortified cereals, bread and some vegetables. Toddlers who do not eat these can become short of iron. Calcium comes mainly from dairy foods and it may be low in a child who takes absolutely none of these in any of their varied forms.

Water is required in large amounts and what better way to take it than straight from the tap. In this form it has even fewer calories than Diet Coke and your dentist, no matter what his religion, will bless it. Most of our water is now fluoridated and despite various ill-informed pronouncements, this is safe. As for other pollutants we can protest about discolouration or too much chlorine, but the water we use must be purer and safer than that available to 90 per cent of the world's population.

He doesn't eat enough

So often parents tell me, 'Dr Green, he hardly eats a bite'. I look up and there stands an infant heavyweight about as puny and malnourished as King Kong. You cannot get this build from swallowing air. A few calories must have slipped down along the way.

Most children who seem to eat too little are in fact getting a very adequate and healthy diet, if only we realised it. When in doubt, note down all the food eaten as snacks, milk, juice and half-finished main meals. When this is added up you will be surprised at just how much goodness has gone down the big tube in one day.

If our children are growing well and are healthy, there cannot be too much wrong with their food intake. Health in a toddler means boundless energy and a mischievous zest for life. The healthy toddler has bright little eyes full of devilment that twinkle as if he is thinking: 'Let's go home and put a bat up grandma's nightie'.

The hunger striker—cracking the code

When parents say their child just won't eat, one starts to wonder how these little hunger strikers manage to survive. Over the years I have thought long and hard about this and now believe I have managed to crack the code. Children who eat nothing, usually eat plenty but it is just in an invisible form, taken as some inconspicuous nourishment.

The milkaholic These children bring joy to the dairy producers as they live and thrive on milk. Each day they consume litre upon litre which leaves no room for solid food. Milk is of course a good food but alone it does not provide a balanced diet for a toddler.

If our children are taking a reasonable diet as well as all this milk, then there is no cause for concern. If they are eating an inadequate amount of solid food and overdosing with milk, now is the time to cut the volume by half. This will produce some hunger and a renewed interest in other food.

The grazer It is not just Australian sheep that nibble away all day; whole flocks of little children also graze. They may not be eating three major meals a day but the food still seems to get in. Children thrive well on this regime as long as we ensure that the pasture they nibble is of reasonable quality.

Unorthodox eaters Often children eat plenty but it is not registered by parents as proper food. Toddlers can get an excellent, well-balanced diet without eating sliced beef, potatoes and two vegetables of different colours. Of course it is important to encourage variety, as long as our children get the right balance.

It doesn't matter how food is presented, as once it hits the stomach it is irrelevant whether the meat was lamb, pork or beef, whether it was minced or carved and how many vegetables were served. The body is more impressed by nutrients than Nouvelle Cuisine.

He won't eat his vegetables

Vegetables are a valuable source of fibre, complex carbohydrate and certain vitamins. There is still a myth that they must be of the green leafy variety as favoured by Popeye, or the orange coloured roots planted and protected by Elmer Fudd. But wait a moment, peas, beans and potatoes are also vegetables and what is more, most toddlers will try at least one of these.

Our generation believed that children must 'eat up all their greens', with a special interest in Sailor-man Spinach. Recent analysis has shown that this is not a particularly special vegetable, competition coming from some surprising quarters. The much-maligned baked bean now finds itself elevated to almost health food status. It has an amount of iron, protein and complex carbohydrate as well as all that natural gas! Maybe if Popeye had blasted around on beans, he would have been twice the hero.

When it comes to vegetables and toddlers, the story is quite simple. Try to introduce different textures, tastes and variety from the earliest days. If your little ones enjoy them that is great, if not don't force the issue. Experiment with the full spectrum of vegies, from greens to beans. If all this is a non-event, don't worry, our children will manage well without any vegetables as long as they take an ample amount of fruit. If they don't eat fruit, they will still thrive if they take bread, cereal and fruit juice.

He won't eat any meat

Parents often tell me, 'He won't eat any meat; he just eats chicken, hamburger and sausage'. We should remember that all meat does not come in a thick slice of cow or sheep. There are many other animals and presentations, one of which will usually tempt the appetite of the toddler.

The main need for meat is to give protein and iron. When the toddler meat embargo is total it would be extremely unusual for them to also refuse dairy products like cheese, milk and yoghurt. Eggs are always another excellent source of first-class protein.

Beans, lentils and nut products, when used wisely, can keep vegetarian children healthy, but usually those who refuse to eat meat will be equally militant when it comes to accepting these alternatives.

He won't drink any milk

Dairy products provide by far the most important source of calcium to the growing child. It is not uncommon for children to go off milk, but thank goodness they rarely go off all dairy foods. When milk is not being taken, cheese is the great standby. Cheese has plenty of calcium and protein and what's more is one of the more universally popular toddler foods. In fact some years ago we surveyed parents and found that cheese and chocolate were equal favourites behind the number one food, ice-cream.

If cheese is not eaten, there are other popular products such as yoghurt, dairy desserts, milk-based ice-creams and sweet flavoured milks. Come to think of it, they tell us that there is a glass and a half

of full cream dairy milk in each bar of chocolate. Presumably the calcium is absorbed and strengthens the teeth from inside, whilst the
stickiness and sugar rots them from the outside, the forces of nature
once again working in perfect harmony.

It is extremely rare for a child not to take some form of dairy
product and if this were a genuine concern, it would be wise to seek
some professional advice. There are times when there is a true milk
allergy and in these cases a calcium fortified alternative product
would be suggested. If you want to go the natural way you could
always try spinach and sesame seeds. They would be sprouting out
your toddler's ears before he got even the calcium of half a glass of
milk, but oh what a feeling!

A toddler relies heavily on the full cream dairy products that
would cause spasms in the adult heart watcher. At this young age
they need all those fats to fire up their furnace, to keep them going
and growing.

Healthy diet—healthy example

It is unrealistic to expect our young children to have a healthier
lifestyle than that of the adults whose example they follow. If
parents are chain-smoking, overweight and under-exercised without a sniff of self-discipline, then it is not going to be easy for the
next generation. Diet and healthy living are a family affair and
that must start with us, the parents, getting our act together.

The best way to start toddlers along the straight and narrow is to
try to introduce them to as wide and varied a diet as possible. They
need to be offered many different tastes and textures in the hope of
broadening their feeding horizons. This is the way to go but be
warned—some little militants will be immovable in their quest for
monotony. Another important aim is to avoid establishing foods that
are either too sweet or over-salty. There is nothing wrong with the
occasional potato chip or chocolate but when it becomes a regular
part of diet, this habit may be hard to shake.

The healthy diet of the nineties is not one of don'ts, nevers and
definitely nots. Some nutritional extremists forget that food is for
enjoyment and turn it into an unhealthy obsession. Our children
are just as entitled as we are to have moments of indulgence, as
long as the general balance is on track.

The aim for healthy eating in the nineties

- Increase the complex carbohydrate intake.
- Reduce all fats, particularly those which are saturated.
- Cut down on highly sweet and refined foods.
- Reduce salt intake.

In practice, this means maintaining a balanced diet.

- Eat plenty of pasta, cereals, bread, fruit and vegetables.
- Eat moderate amounts of lean meat, fish and, once past toddler age, low fat milk, low fat cheese, low fat yoghurt. (Toddlers should have full cream dairy products, the rest of us should not.)
- Eat small amounts of nut products, raisins, fried foods, sweet drinks, butter, margarine, cakes, lollies, honey and sugar.

The varied diet—often a dream

Some children take to new food like a duck to water; others are much more stuck in their ways. For this group the daily diet is: Weet-bix, Weet-bix, Vegemite sandwich, Weet-bix, a sandwich, then goodnight! This of course would never be a hit on the a la carte menu at the Ritz but some toddlers love it today, tomorrow and forever.

We should aim for variety but it is pointless fighting about it. It is better to introduce small amounts of new foods from time to time until a varied interest is achieved.

Another common area of confusion is toddler taste as opposed to adult taste. Parents may feel that toddler foods lack salt or have an unpleasant texture but that is none of our business and we must not pollute them to our palate. Likewise, parents who themselves dislike liver, beetroot and brains will never give these to their child. In fact the toddler may be quite happy with these foods, but parental hang-ups prevent them from being tried. Let's face it, adults have some pretty odd tastes of their own, such as oysters, anchovies and chilli sauce. Toddlers have a right to their own tastes.

Diet and teeth

Our toddler's teeth are calcium-filled pearls surrounded by a tough enamel shell. This protects them from almost everything, with one major exception: acid. Unfortunately this acid is never far away as we all have bacteria in our mouths which ferment any passing carbohydrate food to form enamel-eating acid. These bacteria are natural and otherwise harmless lodgers which we cannot get rid of. Two ways of protecting our children's mouths are to give fluoride to strengthen the teeth and to keep contact with acid-producing carbohydrates to a minimum.

When fluoride was added to our water supply the incidence of dental caries in children took a 60 per cent nosedive. This provides a good reason for fluoride to be given to all children. If it is not in your water supply, drops or tablets can be ordered from the chemist. It is now recommended that young children should also use a toothpaste with added fluoride.

Teeth should be brushed regularly. A soft toothbrush should be first introduced at the age of 2, with the parents guiding it around the mouth. The child could go solo about the age of 5. Toddlers should visit the dentist in their pre-school years, even if they do not have cavities.

Trying to keep carbohydrate from teeth is a pretty tall order. After all, food is not much use to us until it has touched the teeth on its way down to the stomach. The best protection is to keep the mouth free of carbohydrates for as much time as possible and this means that children should not be encouraged to eat sweet foods or drink sugary fluids non-stop throughout the day. Also beware the sweet bottle at night! The other point of protection is the realisation that certain carbohydrates appear to be enjoyed more by the bacteria while others seem largely left alone and produce little tooth damaging acid.

Everyone knows that sugar, lollies, sweetened milk, cakes and lemonade are bad for teeth. What is generally unrecognised is that some so-called health foods can be almost equally damaging. Honey would do as much harm as sugar, while many natural fruit juices are just as damaging as lemonade. The breads, vegetables, and some fruits are much less of a problem, but to some extent all carbohydrates can be fermented to make acid. Remember that it is the simplest sugars that make the biggest impact and the longer these simple sugars are in contact with the teeth, the greater will be the damage.

Some interesting recent work shows cheese to be one of the least damaging of all the carbohydrate-containing foods. Unsweetened milk and yoghurt are also thought to be reasonably benign.

In conclusion, don't be a party pooper and ban all sweet pleasures but if we cannot protect our children's first teeth for six short years, what hope have the second teeth in the seventy years that follow? Moderation is important.

Tonics to stimulate appetite

In Ireland, I trained in a hospital that was particularly sensitive to the happiness and well-being of its elderly patients. Each night a well-known black, alcoholic Dublin beverage was handed out to help wash down the hospital food. Some believed this helped to stimulate the old peoples' appetites; others were more realistic in thinking that it merely stimulated their feeling of well-being. I am often asked for a tonic to stimulate a child's appetite. It would create quite a stir if I were to prescribe the black Dublin 'medicine' but it would be just as effective as any other proprietary brand tonic. There is no such thing as an appetite-stimulating tonic for children.

Vitamins and iron

Children who are on any sort of halfway decent diet don't require any extra vitamins or iron. Though many parents swear by the beneficial effects of their favourite multi-vitamin preparations, there is really no scientific evidence to back up their claims. I recently read an article in which the author said he had gathered together all the papers ever published on the beneficial effects of vitamin C in preventing the common cold. For every paper that claimed it was effective, there was another that presented proof to the contrary.

Occasionally I prescribe a vitamin preparation when I am confronted by an over-worried mother who is sure her child is malnourished, sickly and in need of such things. As I write a prescription I smile as I tell the mum, 'You know this is not going to help your child in any way but my God, it is going to make you feel better'.

Diet and bowels

There is as much variation in the bowel habits of toddlers as there is in the bowel habits of parents. Some children seem to be born with normal bowel regularity; others have lazy bowels, and some are definitely overactive. We are stuck with the equipment we have been allocated, and it can only be regulated by introducing certain dietary changes.

Roughage is definitely an 'in' substance these days. It is said to exert a 'normalising' effect on the bowels, speeding up the sluggish and calming the hyperactive. When a child tends towards constipation, more dietary fibre is encouraged. This roughage can be increased with selected palatable breakfast cereals, vegetables and more fibrous breads and biscuits. Even the baked bean is an excellent form of fibre, having exerted a regularising effect on an entire generation of cowboys who won the west. Fruit and fruit juices provide a most palatable and effective way of giving the sluggish bowel a push.

The term toddler diarrhoea is applied to a condition where a healthy child tends to have a very active bowel. Parents worry over the apparent diarrhoea and, as the children are also generally very physically active, they put on little weight, which further concerns the parents. Gastroenterologists treat this problem by restricting the fluid intake to mealtimes and increasing the fibre and roughage the child eats. Sugars in the diet are reduced, fewer snacks are given, and the child is steered towards the adult pattern of three meals a day. Toddler diarrhoea is a temporary condition; these suggestions just keep it under some form of control until it is cured by time.

What makes a fat kid fat?

Children, like adults, become fat when they have a genetic tendency to lay down fat and then take in quantities of food greater than their body's needs. For years, the experts have debated whether it is the over-eating or the heredity factor that predominates. Despite years of discussion, no-one is any clearer about the answer.

Over-eating

Certainly the amount you eat has a significant bearing on weight gain. Overweight toddlers often have overweight parents as well, but whether this is hereditary or simply the parent inflicting the same over-eating habit on the child is unclear. A great many parents set a very bad example to their children with the type and quantity of food they consume. Others spoil their children with food, sometimes giving it as a poor substitute for proper love and attention. Some parents seem to take a delight in fattening up their offspring, like a cattle farmer preparing beasts for market. To parents, fat may be beautiful but when the competitive teenage years arrive, few children give thanks for obesity, and by that time it is often hard to do anything about it.

Heredity

No-one can become fat without eating but there is no doubt that all children and adults react differently to identical food intakes. Some could be locked in a chocolate factory all weekend and still come out looking like a famine victim. Others only need to see a Mars Bar and they have already gained a kilo.

The statistics relating overweight children to overweight parents are interesting. If neither parent is overweight, there is only a 10 per cent chance that the child will have a weight problem. If one parent is overweight, this increases the child's risk to 40 per cent. If both parents are overweight, the child's risk increases to 70 per cent. This would appear to give all the evidence we need to show that the child's weight is predestined by heredity. One humorous piece of research, however, has rather shattered this view. One group of researchers successfully showed that fat parents had fatter children. Meanwhile, another group came up with the added discovery that they also tended to have fat pets![12]. This rather threw a spanner into the works of the heredity lobby, and once again we are left in some confusion. In reality, both diet and heredity are important factors and still no-one is quite sure which plays the stronger role.

Do glands cause obesity?

Many children are referred to endocrine clinics of big hospitals by parents who are convinced that their child is overweight because of a glandular problem. This is a widely held view. This may be true but only to the extent that obesity is related to the salivary gland, with the child's mouth watering whenever he sees any food. Other than this, a connection between glands and obesity in children is extremely rare.

Puppy fat

At the end of their first year, babies have a very different shape from that at the end of their second year. Before children start walking, they usually have rolls of fat on their thighs, arms and abdomen, with few muscles visible. Once they start to exercise, the puppy fat generally disappears and the more grown-up muscular body proportions appear.

Many parents become concerned at about this time, being unaware of the different weight gain rates of different ages. The baby in his first year of life gains weight at a remarkably rapid rate but this reduces markedly after the first birthday, often becoming stationary for a period. At the same time as this fat starts 'burning off', many children become fussy, negative eaters, which causes even more worry about weight.

Over the past decade, numerous articles have been written expressing concern that fat babies become fat toddlers, who in turn become fat children and finally fat adults. The most recent work, however, shows that there is minimal connection between fat babies and fat adults. After the age of 1 year, there is an ever increasing relationship between the ageing child's weight and his adult build. For the fat teenager, it is far easier to put weight on than to take it off, which can be the start of a weight problem that will dog them all of their adult lives.

Special diets

Over the last 2000 years doctors have tried to relate health and behaviour to foods in the diet. Although you might think this is sufficient time to have gathered the evidence, I have to report that conclusive data is still not yet available. Certainly there are some specific conditions in which food causes ill health, for example, the allergy of wheat found in coeliac disease, but there is also a great deal of confusion between fact and theory in this matter.

Some children and adults have true allergies to certain foods. A child may eat eggs, seafood or oranges and then have an attack of itching and swollen eyes or diarrhoea. There is little doubt as to the offending substance, as the symptoms appear each time it is introduced into the diet.

There are, however, claims that milk, wheat, corn, malt and yeast are responsible for many conditions, ranging from asthma through to runny noses, dyslexia, sleep problems, clumsiness, and just annoying one's mother. Judging from figures released each year from the asthma clinic in my hospital, it is extremely rare for milk allergy to precipitate or worsen asthma. For most, therefore, this must be regarded as a myth. Our experts also dispute the claim that milk causes runny noses. Folklore has it that milk causes the human body to produce mucus, but scientific evidence to support this is scant.

Much of my work is with handicapped children, an area in which constant claims are made that diet improves intelligence and behaviour. I recently saw a mildly retarded boy whose parents had been assured that if he ate one kelp (seaweed) tablet a day his intelligence would rise to normal within six weeks. This would have been harmless enough, except that each tablet was about the size of a pigeon's egg and tasted like something found in a sewage farm. The child had the insight and was clever enough to remain mildly retarded.

Other parents have been told that a vitamin B preparation would cure dyslexia but while this preparation is of enormous benefit in the treatment of pellagra, beri beri and possibly even premenstrual tension, it has no beneficial effect whatsoever on reading difficulties.

I have been told that zinc cures autism, which is not true. It is also claimed that artificial colourings, preservatives and some natural foodstuffs have a major detrimental effect on the concentration and on behavioural problems of the hyperactive child. Occasionally this can be true but its effect is much less common than generally believed.

Parents are bombarded by the claims of special diets but it is wise to remember that real medical breakthroughs do not take 2000 years to gain acceptance. From the first dose of penicillin administered, there was never any doubt of its amazing effect. Kelp tablets, artificial colourings and milk, despite all manner of extravagant claims, are simply not in the same league. (See Chapter 17, The Hyperactive Child.)

Junk food is not all junk

Junk food is a term created by some media writers to describe all those fun eats like chocolate, soft drinks, lollies, thick shakes, sweet biscuits and fast foods. Now I am not the sort of killjoy who believes that strict avoidance of anything pleasurable is the only way to health and holiness. I do however worry that if taken in excess, these foods have far too much fat, salt and sweetener.

I am a great believer in the therapeutic powers of McDonald's restaurants. It seems to me that these are the best places for any demoralised mother to eat. You just have to walk in the door and immediately you know that there are other children even worse-behaved than your own. For many parents that trip through the golden arches brings the realisation that they are normal, which lifts the morale with probably as much effect as a year of visits to a psychiatrist and all for under ten dollars!

Health foods may not be all that healthy

I have to admit that I do suffer from an allergic condition. I am allergic to the advertising agents who promote health products. Bending of the truth with phrases like, 'no added sugar', 'naturally decaffeinated coffee', 'healthy, dairy-free milk', 'the vitamins to cure colds and stress', 'the magical properties of glucose and honey', make me go pale, cringe and start to stutter.

Don't get me wrong, I have nothing against health foods; in fact my family often eats brown rice, potatoes, vegetables, bread, fruit, baked beans and even drinks water. What is more, when weak and in that need of an occasional glucose lift, my health food is something nice that is sweetened by natural Queensland sugar.

My objection is not to the much needed promotion of healthy diets. It is just that trendy words and truth get somewhat tangled when financial advancement is a major part of the message.

Overdosed with orange juice As I see parents struggle out of the supermarket, weighed down with litres of natural fruit juice, I wonder if this is all quite necessary. Off they rush pouring glasses of it into the line of open little beaks that look over the edge of the nest as they get home. These juices have become almost a sacred part of life and you could believe that the mothers will be testing the teeth for the wobbles of scurvy if they miss a few days. If our children eat real fruit, of the sort that comes from a tree, fruit juices become nice but not necessary.

Orange juice is encouraged as there is still the belief that excessive amounts keep children healthy and fight off the common cold. Despite years of study there is no evidence to back up this idea. The body does not store excess vitamin C, which is flushed out the kidneys and down the toilet as quick as you can say ascorbic acid. It astounds me that some parents will give up to five glasses of orange juice a day to their children. If each glass were to contain three oranges, you have just seen fifteen oranges disappear. That would be enough to turn me inside out.

The perfectly balanced breakfast cereal It would be very smart to eat a low fat, low salt and low sugar cereal if our children were like battery hens who lived on nothing else. But for them this is only a part of a big balanced diet. It all seems a bit pointless, if this perfect product is then submerged in full cream milk and sprinkled with sugar until it looks like the alps in winter.

The juice with no added sugar So often the advertisement says, 'This juice has no added sugar'. The truth is that it probably doesn't need any more, it already contains quite enough sugar in its natural state. There are many ways of getting sugar into contact with delicate teeth other than spooning it in from sugar cane.

Sometimes juices have no added sugar but that is not to say that artificial sweetening and other chemicals have not been included.

Glucose, honey and health Glucose is a simple, highly refined sugar, similar to sucrose (cane sugar). Its absorption into the blood may be marginally more rapid but it is no more nutritious than its cheaper brothers.

Honey is a natural product which many believe has almost mythical properties. In reality it is just a blend of simple sugars refined by the intricate innards of a bee. Though it has a pleasant taste, it is less pure than glucose or cane sugar.

Glucose and honey have no special health-giving properties. As sweeteners they have no advantage over cane sugar and when made into a health drink they are no kinder to teeth than lemonade.

Health bars If health bars are going to be popular, they generally need to be sweet, fatty or full of fruit. The fact that the product gets its sugar from fruit, honey or glucose, instead of sugar cane, does nothing to promote health. There are of course some genuinely healthy exceptions but most children would not be tripping over each other in the rush to eat them.

Healthy natural vegetable milk I find it hard to come to terms with vegetable milks, as my old-fashioned mind believes that milk is something that comes from a mammal and not from a vegetable-processing plant. Cow's milk is good for little cows and not too bad for little humans either. Soy and other milks may be beneficial when our children have true milk allergies but for the average child they have no special health-giving properties.

Bran—good for horses Processed bran is popular with both health enthusiasts and horses but toddlers are not without wisdom, and dislike eating something that tastes like sawdust. If you want to get bran into little children, some of the high roughage breakfast cereals or fibre rich loaves are the best answer. For most young children it is better to leave bran in the stables and rely on the more enjoyable fibre that comes in fruit and vegetables.

Vitamin enriched health drinks Blackcurrant, rosehip and other syrups are advertised as a healthy way to tank up on vitamin C. They are no better than the cheap vitamin C tablet, readily available from your chemist. The main concern with these syrups is that some contain an unhealthy excess of sugar for safe, regular use.

Dried fruit and nuts Raisins, sultanas and dates are a popular form of toddler snack but they are sweet and stick to the teeth to some extent, causing the same sorts of problems as chocolates, toffees and other confectionery. Peanuts and toddlers are generally a bad combination. Peanuts are quite nourishing if eaten but hospitals spend many hours each year removing inhaled ones from little children who have sent them down the wrong tube.

An enormous industry exists out there producing health drinks, health bars and healthy breakfast cereals but these products bear some investigation. Certainly added roughage and complex carbohydrate is to be encouraged but if the product is then smothered in honey, glucose or some other high carbohydrate food then the benefit is lost. Some products are advertised as containing no salt and sugar, but these will only be of benefit if the child is going to continue on this diet right through the day. It is pointless if it is followed immediately by a highly sweetened milk shake and some salty salami. Health drinks that contain all natural ingredients may contain these in unhealthy proportions. Milk is a true natural food, if it is not tarted up with additives.

Perhaps I am a trifle cynical about the advertised advantages of health foods. A substance may be natural but this does not mean it must be healthy. You can rot teeth, become fat and poison your system just as well with natural substances as with factory produced ones. Tobacco and opium are two very natural substances.

Conclusion

There are many ways to get a good diet into our young children, it just takes a bit of ingenuity, calmness and commonsense.

Example is important and that is where we, the parents, need to smarten up our own act. Sensible parents who give a reasonably balanced diet have little to worry about. If the children are growing, healthy and happy—relax, you have got it right.

13

Feeding Without Fights

Parents use up an enormous amount of energy forcing stubborn but otherwise well-nourished toddlers to eat against their will. All these parental antics are a great source of mirth to the child but, when the final score is taken at the end of the meal, not an extra pea has been eaten. Playing aeroplanes, dive bombers, singing, dancing, crawling round the floor barking, and threatening that they won't grow up 'big and strong like daddy' are a complete waste of time. Just as adults don't eat bigger meals while being entertained at a theatre-restaurant, toddlers' consumption won't be improved by all this entertainment either. What they really need is gentle encouragement.

Some children take their food extremely seriously, never lifting their eyes from the plate until they have almost scraped the pattern from it. Others dawdle, play, and escape at the first opportunity, finding food a complete bore. Some children are thin, some are fat, some are fussy and some are walking garbage bins. Don't force. Remember, no child has ever starved to death through stubbornness. At a recent lecture I made this statement and almost before the words had left my lips a militant mum at the back was on her feet complaining. 'Dr Green, you are wrong. My child once went for twelve hours without food and if I hadn't forced him he would certainly have starved.' 'Do you know how long it takes the average hunger striker to die?' I asked. 'No I don't,' was the frosty reply. 'Well it's about sixty-eight days,' I said. 'Do you mean that at Sydney's Royal Alexandra Hospital, you recommend only feeding the children every sixty-eight days?' was the answer. With this, the dietitian sitting beside me could control himself no longer. 'If you are really worried in the future, how about giving Dr Green a call on the morning of the twentieth day?' I think she got the message.

Normal feeding patterns

Most babies in their first year are in no doubt about what to do with food. They don't mess about, generally getting the food to where it belongs with a minimum of fuss.

By 9 months, the food goes down with relative ease, and the chewing pattern becomes well-established. At this stage, the first teeth are just tiny, ornamental pearls that do little damage to the food as it hurries past.

By 1 year, the teeth are used more for chewing, and the child eats a diet similar to that of the rest of the family. Many children at this age undergo a dramatic change of attitude to food, halving their intake and becoming extremely fussy. At this time, too, the child's weight gain may slow up, stop or even go down, while activity burns up the puppy fat and stubbornness restricts food intake. From this age onwards the negative streak is always just around the corner, so with most children, forcing them to eat becomes unproductive.

At 15 months, independent children are keen on holding a spoon, although few can keep it level between plate and mouth—the contents usually slip off as the arm tries to negotiate the bends. Children will also hold a feeding cup and, after 18 months, most children will suck rather than chew the end of a straw.

At 3 years old a knife can be used by them to cut soft foods and attempts to butter their own bread will follow soon after. By 4¹/2 the child should be able to use a knife and fork in a sort of way, and it is just before this age that Chinese children generally learn to use chopsticks.

Feed—don't fight

Toddlers have minds and tastes of their own. The dining table must never become a battleground.

The eight-point plan for problem-free meals

1. Avoid disorganised, disturbed, noisy mealtimes. The toddler should sit and eat with the rest of the family, but if this is impractical then a parent should sit next to the child and feed him before the main family meal.
2. Although the toddler should ideally be given a variety of well-balanced foods, if he dislikes variety, then a repetitive but nutritious diet is perfectly acceptable. After all he's the one who has to eat it, not you.
3. Adult eating habits should be encouraged, but it is no disaster if a child decides to return to the main course after having polished off his pudding.
4. Use labour-saving cooking ideas, because it is hard to stay calm when the wilful toddler refuses a dish that has taken hours to prepare.
5. Gently encourage the child to eat, NEVER force.
6. Once it is obvious that the child is not going to eat any more, wipe his hands and face clean and allow him to get down from the table. Whether this is after five minutes or half an hour, don't worry about it. If the child is dawdling over his food, leave him to dawdle without an audience.
7. Display no anger if food is not eaten. Put the untouched plate in the fridge and bring it out later on request.
8. It is the child's right to eat or not to eat his food as he pleases. Parents have a perfect right to fight with their child if that is what they want, but they should have the sense to avoid battles over food. If a child refuses the meal, he must not be allowed to immediately top up on milk, chips and the like.

Make food fun

When serving fine food to adults, a chef prides himself not only on the taste but also on the presentation. The same should apply when feeding toddlers. For a start, portions should not be massive. Various garnishings should be used, such as a square of cheese, some raisins and a few fingers of fruit. Vary texture and colour wherever possible and make food look appealing. Bread can be cut into fun triangles and homemade biscuits can be cooked in animal shapes.

When feeding problems continue, then try varying the venue. Wonders can be achieved by transporting stubborn feeders to the balcony or the garden, where they can drink milk through a straw and eat little sandwiches out of a lunch box.

I think we have to rid ourselves of some of our rigid and old-fashioned ideas about feeding toddlers. Within reason, try to give them what they want, where they want it, and when they are hungry. They are going to have to learn adult eating habits sooner or later, but to begin with it is more important to get them enjoying the process of eating.

Nibbling can be nutritious

Toddlers have none of our funny adult ideas about food. When they are hungry they want to eat. When they are not hungry they don't. Rigid fixed mealtimes are more appropriate to top restaurants than to the toddler. We should encourage the main meal habit but when this is obviously failing, cut your losses and let them eat on the hoof. Now is the time for snacks.

Healthy snacks don't mean thick milkshakes, chocolate or salty chips. Ideally, they should include raw carrots and long bits of celery but few children have read that book and remain unconvinced. It seems that the 'in' food of the nineties is complex carbohydrate. Bread is pretty complex, especially if fortified with some extra fibre, so sandwiches are healthy. All that's needed is a bit of imagination with the fillings. Surprisingly, there are substances other than Vegemite to put on bread. What about egg, or peanut butter? Chewable meat or even baked beans are good too. Add a glass of milk to the baked bean sandwich and you'd have most nutritionists smiling.

Finger foods make ideal snacks for the busy toddler. Cubes of cheese, slices of fruit, sliced, cooked vegetables, can all be consumed on the move. Of course there is also banana and cold sausage, both of which are highly portable. Anything that you can both eat and poke the dog with has got to impress the average toddler.

We might as well face the fact that between-meal snacks are here to stay, so they should be treated as seriously as the main meals they often replace. Properly orchestrated, this 'alternative' diet can improve rather than damage children's health.

Labour-saving food preparation

I'm sure that at some time or other in your life you've slaved over a hot stove for hours preparing a delicacy for your dream child, only to find he takes one look at it and turns his nose up in disgust. Times like these tempt you to child abuse! Rather than taking this drastic course of action, may I recommend a bit of labour-saving cooking instead.

A liquidiser or food processor and a freezing tray are all that the parents of babies need for food preparation. In one morning you can cook carrots, cauliflower, pumpkin, steak, chicken, fish and apples, pop them in the liquidiser (one at a time), and then put them into individual ice-cube trays for freezing. When mealtime comes, all you have to do is look in the freezer and decide on the menu, defrost it, and there you have a small portion of an instant, but freshly made meal. This idea can be carried through to toddler-hood as well, using slightly larger containers and of course non-liquidised food. Food can be prepared as quickly as it takes an ice-cube to melt and, when refused, can be returned to the refrigerator (not the freezer) as quickly as you can say 'See if I care!'.

Feeding the militantly independent child

From their first birthday, some children are hell bent on feeding themselves without any outside assistance. Unfortunately the most independent children are usually the most impatient, which is a sure recipe for trouble. These children should be given a spoon large enough to allow them to load the food with some accuracy. To cope with the spillage on the long journey from plate to mouth, a 'pelican' bib, one of those strong plastic bibs with a large catchment area at the bottom, is recommended. As the drop-out food is caught in the bib, it can be quickly recycled, cutting down on mess and wastage.

To further help the impatient and hungry child determined to have a go at feeding himself, it is best to give him one spoon while feeding him with another. Finger foods are another good means of keeping little hands occupied.

The toddler who's hooked on bottles and baby food

If after 8 months of age the child's diet is still milk and bland, untextured baby foods, it may be extremely difficult to change him over to a proper mixed diet. Prevention is obviously better than cure, so parents must be encouraged to provide a variety of textured solids after 6 months, avoiding milk as the sole source of nourishment.

For those who are hooked on milk and refuse solids, it is hard to give effective help without cutting down dramatically on the milk intake. Some people are extremely tough on these toddlers and exclude all milk immediately, substituting less calorific fluids until the child gives in and starts taking a reasonable diet. I prefer a gentler approach, which in the end achieves exactly the same results. The milk intake should be reduced by about half and other fluids and a variety of interesting nibbly things introduced. This is usually all that is required, but if it does not work immediately then the milk can be further reduced. Like all such procedures, the parent must not weaken mid-way.

Firmness is also needed with toddlers who have remained on slushy baby foods for too long. These children often refuse to chew and the slightest lump causes them to gag. Somehow, however, they seem to exert some hidden strength when a piece of chocolate is popped into their mouths. Once again, prevention is better than cure, as these children will often put up quite a fight before you can get them onto a normal diet. To cure these children, I start again by halving the milk intake so that it cannot be used as a substitute food. Then I gradually start polluting tinned baby food with homemade liquidised products and, as the days go by, I make the food more and more homemade. Gradually a normal diet is achieved in a matter of weeks.

What is enough food intake?

Children have different food requirements. They eat like birds: some like sparrows, others like vultures. There is no correct amount of food for all children to consume in a day. Food intake and growth are not the only indicators of good health, energy is also important. If my car used only half the manufacturer's recommended amount of petrol to cover a given number of miles, I would not complain. I would be grateful that I had an efficient machine that was obviously tuned to perfection. Forcing toddlers to feed is futile. We need more sense and less food.

Consider the toddler's point of view

It is a very special occasion and you are booked to eat at the best restaurant in town. Out comes the food, immaculate with those cordon bleu sauces flowing off the meat. Your mouth is watering at the very smell.

Then up marches the head waiter, looks you in the eye and with a stern voice says: 'Just one thing, madam. You will not be leaving the table until you've eaten every bite. What's more there will be no dessert until your plate is completely clear.' Would it not make you choke?

A minute later there beside you is the chef, complete with beard and big white hat. He takes out a large carving knife and fork and proceeds to cut up your meat into little pieces, mashes it all up with the vegetables and then starts spooning it into your mouth.

Just put yourself in your child's place. Why should he like it any more than you would? Get off their backs and don't fight over food.

Conclusion

Most toddlers whose parents claim that they never eat are in fact getting a very adequate food intake.

If children wish to eat three good meals a day, that is highly commendable, but for those who don't, it is usually better to provide nourishing snacks rather than fighting with them. Time and peer-group pressures will eventually force the toddler into more traditional mealtime habits; in the meantime, be flexible and use your imagination.

Remember, food is not just for nourishment, food is for fun.

Nasty Habits in Nice Children

In those dreamy days before toddlers, I bet you never saw yourself reading and recognising your children in a chapter like this. Now you may well have found that the nicest of nice children can display some of the nastiest of nasty habits. Let's look at a selection of these.

Biting

The residents who man our hospital's busy Casualty Department once asked me if I would come and lecture to them, and I presumed they wanted to hear me expound on some high-powered medical topic. To my surprise, I found that what they wanted to hear, more than anything else, was how to manage children who bite! It seemed that in our city biting had reached almost epidemic proportions, which was upsetting not only our casualty officers but also parents, playgroup leaders, and any child or adult within biting distance.

In my experience, biting is purely a playgroup habit found mostly in the 1 to 2½ years age group. It is not a premeditated, spiteful act, just a symptom of this age of little sense. Your little biter doesn't get up with the lark, sit there and hatch a plot to get into playgroup early, hide behind the door and ambush Freddie Smith when he enters, sinking his teeth into his arm like a demented piranha. It's more a case of Freddie happens to be passing, your angel is a bit overexcited and not thinking. He bites him as an impulse. It just seems like a good idea at the time.

Experts who have written on this topic state that it is a symptom of a tense, anxious child and although this may occasionally be the case, in practical terms I find it a great deal easier to stop a child biting than to stop a child feeling tense.

Many babies in the first year of life suddenly sink their teeth into whoever is carrying them, unaware of the pain they may cause. Although this is not a malicious act, it is important that the baby be taught that it is not an acceptable form of behaviour. Rather than shouting, becoming angry or slapping the baby, it is preferable to put him down on the floor immediately. It does not take the average baby long to work out that, if he wants the pleasure of a cuddle, he shouldn't indulge in cannibalism.

With the toddler, it is usually a piece of brother or sister that finds itself wedged between the closing teeth and as this is a sort of family feast, it is much easier to discipline, as you own both the biter and the bitee.

When it is a neighbour's child that has been nibbled, the parents may expect you to instigate some sort of major retribution. If justice is not seen to be done, friends may ban their little children from your house and it can lead to family feuds more vicious than witnessed by the Campbells and the McDonalds.

How you react to a bite will depend on the circumstances. If just a minor nip in times of excitement, a gentle warning is all that is needed. If it is repeated, premeditated or major and a stern warning has been ignored, then use Time Out or a short sharp smack to register the limits of acceptable behaviour.

When your toddler bites another at playgroup, this is a different matter. Now you are in the full public view, without Time Out to fall back on and if you smack, half the audience will criticise. It is particularly embarrassing when your loved one has become known as 'Jaws' to the other mums. The best you can do is to watch carefully, warn firmly, divert when an impending attack is anticipated and then, if a bite occurs, ignore the biter and give the best toys and attention to the injured party. This may sound rather wishy-washy but when outside the home, your hands are tied and in truth your child probably has more teeth than any technique I may suggest.

Many parents view all this warning and diverting as pathetically weak. For them there is only one answer. If their child bites, they bite him back. This is the eye for an eye and a tooth for a tooth approach that was probably pretty modern 2000 years ago. I think that there are better ways of doing things now.

Don't despair—remember that biting is only a habit of the first 2^1/$_2$ years and be reassured that they will not be going round biting others as adults, unless they take up rugby league.

Finger up the nose

Little noses are to little fingers like a burrow is to a bunny. It is a comfortable place to explore when there is nothing better to do. Though most toddler fingers find toddler nostrils at times of tiredness or boredom, occasionally an older child with an easily baited parent will do it just to annoy.

Finger in nose—dad explodes. Finger up again—dad explodes again—great fun for child! Soon this little arm is going up and down like the first violin in the orchestra. When this happens, it is best to ignore, divert to something more useful and if you decide to take notice, don't make a game out of it, be 100 per cent firm.

The gentle poke of boredom is another matter. When recently I was on tour in the United States it seemed that every time I talked on air some parent asked about fingers up noses. Such was the concern, you might have thought this habit to be exclusive to North American nostrils, but it isn't; this is a universal toddler pastime.

The toddler watches the TV, is bored, his mind slips and with it a finger, ever upward and inward. You can only sympathise with the problem, such is the standard of today's television.

With toddlers, the aim is to divert them and keep those little hands and minds fully occupied. I believe we should not be too tough with our youngsters; after all we adults have some pretty nasty and not dissimilar habits ourselves. The next time you stop at a red traffic light, take a look at the car beside. You can see where one hand is, but you have no idea what is happening with the other. That's why film stars have tinted glass in their limousines.

Head banging

Head banging is a habit which can occur for one of two reasons. Usually it is part of a tantrum in the senseless 1 to 2-year-old, though it may be a form of innocent entertainment in the child of a slightly older age. Parents fear that a bit of banging will damage their child's brain but when you look at football players and boxers, you realise that even the most persistent toddler's efforts are pretty trivial by comparison. Other parents believe that this is a sure sign of retardation or mental disturbance, but if the child is normal in every other way, head banging is not a sign of significance.

When senseless young toddlers do not get their own way, they may fall to the floor and bang their heads. They rarely hurt themselves and if this does happen it is certainly not intentional. They are usually careful to seek out the surface with the greatest noise potential and the lowest pain-inflicting factor.

Head banging tantrums are short lived, as the child soon develops sufficient sense to realise that self-inflicted pain is a poor way of punishing others. It is as silly as a robber who enters the bank and says, 'Hand over the money or I will poke myself in the eye with this stick'. Head banging is quite self-limiting and all you have to do is divert attention elsewhere. If that's difficult, just let them go for it. Toddlers may have little sense but they are not stupid. Whatever you do, this habit will be well away by the age of 2 years.

Some children head bang when bored or tired. This is usually the speciality of active children who enjoy rocking and gentle head banging, particularly in the cot. They do it because it is enjoyable and sends them to sleep as reliably as counting sheep. Though it may be soothing for children, the rhythmic thump is far from soothing for the adults of the house. There is not much you can do about it other than padding the edge of the cot, or in extreme cases, putting a pillow under each cot leg to deaden the transmission of sound. This sort of head banging is not a sign of bad behaviour but a form of innocent entertainment that gives as much pleasure as thumb sucking or nail biting.

Breath holding attacks

These are among the most alarming of all toddler behaviour traits. Some children have been reported as having up to ten attacks a day, others one a month. Luckily the vast majority of toddlers never indulge in this nasty habit in their lives.

Breath holding comes in two forms, the more common cyanotic (blue) type and the rarer pallid (faint) type. With the cyanotic attack, the child voluntarily holds his breath to the point of passing out; it is a kind of super-tantrum used to stir up anyone preventing the child from getting his own way. Although less common, the pallid form is associated with a painful experience. For example, the child sustains a minor hurt and passes out rapidly in a form of fainting fit.

The cyanotic (blue) attack

These attacks most commonly occur from 18 months to 4 years, although they may occasionally be seen before the first birthday in the really negative child. This is not a new behaviour pattern brought about by the hectic life-style of the nineties. Hippocrates described something very similar happening among the terrible toddlers of ancient Greece.

What normally happens is that the child is thwarted in the midst of some action that is vitally important to him and, reviewing his repertoire of reactions, he decides that breath holding will be a more effective reprisal than one of his lesser tantrums. He then gives about three long cries, the last going all the way until his lungs are completely empty of air. The audience waits in anticipation for the next breath but the ensuing silence is deafening. No breath is heard. Over the next fifteen seconds the child voluntarily holds his breath, which inevitably leads to him going blue in the face and passing out. Once unconscious the child loses voluntary control of his breathing; the body immediately switches over to 'automatic pilot' and breathing restarts, with full consciousness returning about fifteen seconds later. Occasionally the episode may end in a minor short convulsion, leaving the parents even more upset.

Breath holding attacks terrify parents but do not harm children. Although the treatment is extremely easy for a doctor to prescribe, I realise it is very difficult for a parent to administer. If breath holding is to be stopped it must be viewed in the same light as a tantrum or any other challenging behaviour. It must simply be totally ignored, as making a fuss about it will only ensure that it is repeated.

Firstly the parents must be quite certain that this is a breath holding attack and not some quite different medical problem which they are misunderstanding. After this, the techniques of diversion and ignoring must be used. Diversionary tactics will usually fail, so when the child stops breathing, he must be left to his own devices. Difficult as it is to do, parents should watch carefully while the child is briefly unconscious but the moment consciousness begins to return, move away immediately. With this he will open his eyes and look around for the appreciative audience, but he has wasted his time because they have just walked out.

Some experts suggest splashing cold water on the child's face as he starts to hold his breath. This may be effective, but it will only work if done in that first fifteen seconds of voluntary breath holding. After that it is pointless and probably dangerous once unconsciousness has occurred.

I have no illusions that this is an easy treatment but I know that firmness and ignoring the child, although hard, are the only effective methods of curing this behaviour. After the child reaches the age of 4, breath holding becomes extremely rare.

The pallid (faint) attack

This is not the true breath holding attack, as it is more like a simple fainting spell than a form of attention-seeking tantrum. Children who have pallid attacks seem to be particularly sensitive to pain or fear, either of which may trigger off an attack. (They are generally thought to become the sort of adults who faint at the thought of a hypodermic needle or the sight of blood.)

A 2-year-old may be walking under a table when he hits his head hard on the edge. In the pallid attack, he would not cry out or hold his breath but will simply go limp and fall to the ground. His heart rate drops dramatically, and he looks very pale. This is the child's equivalent of an adult faint, and recovery is usually quite quick.

As for treatment, if the child is lying flat nothing else needs to be done and nature will remedy the situation. If the attacks are genuinely the result of some involuntary reflex in a sensitive child, then the child should be cuddled and fussed over upon recovery. Although this seems quite logical, most authors on the subject in the past seem to have doubts about whether or not there may be some minor attention-seeking component in this action, and it is suggested that the parents maintain a low profile and do not fuss too much over the child.

Let me reassure parents with children who suffer from breath holding attacks, however, that it is not a serious condition. It is the parents, more than the children, who need consoling.

Playing with their private parts

Most toddlers play with their genitalia at some time or other. They may touch, rub, rock or move their legs, all for the pleasurable effects these motions afford. It is normal toddler behaviour, and it has no true sexual overtones.

Historically, so much fuss has been made over children masturbating that even the most broad-minded parents still have a twinge of concern when they see their children doing it. Tales of how it would send you mad or deaf, or both, still ring in their ears. It was even claimed in Victorian times that it sent you blind. This of course is utter rubbish, but even if it were true most of our children would opt to do it a little and wear glasses.

These days, parents are encouraged to relax, ignore it and not let their own hang-ups get in the way. Playing with the genitalia occurs in both boys and girls. It starts in the second year when the nappy region is unveiled and a new area of discovery is made available. The treatment is to completely ignore what is, after all, a perfectly innocent habit.

Now it is all very easy for me to say ignore but what do you do when the child is standing in church with his hands down his pants, or when the maiden aunts are visiting? In fact it is probably more realistic to gently divert the offending hand or interest the child in something more sociable. I emphasise that at toddler age this has no sexual connotations and it almost exclusively happens when they are tired, tense or bored. Ignoring, diversion and keeping them active is the answer—not humiliation or punishment.

Sometime later in the pre-school years, children discover that little boys and little girls are not identical. This leads to a certain amount of innocent interest which is a quite normal and natural stage of development. This needs to be viewed with a broad mind and a relatively blind eye.

When I was recently in the United States one talk show host asked an off-the-air question about little boys and little girls. She was quite embarrassed, as her own 3½-year-old boy had the day before been found naked with the neighbour's 4-year-old girl. I said that this sounded all pretty normal to me and she agreed, but it appeared that the neighbour had taken it as a serious form of assault. I said it was not the children but the neighbour who had the problem and maybe she should consider seeing a psychiatrist. Quick as a flash my host replied, 'The trouble is she is one'.

Whingeing

Whingeing is one of the most parent-destroying activities that any child can indulge in. Naturally we expect children who are tired, sick or teething to whinge but there still remains a great band of healthy, well-rested children who continue to devastate their parents. As practised by some children, this habit is equal in potency to the Chinese water torture. In my experience, boys generally take the prize for overactivity and really bad behaviour but when it comes to whingeing, the fairer sex usually gets the gold medal every time.

There is a great variation in a child's ability to whinge. Some never whinge at all, others wind up to full volume at the drop of a hat, whilst some work their way up in fits and starts, prolonging the agony as skilfully as any torture in the Spanish Inquisition.

The trouble with whingeing is that we can unintentionally make it into a much repeated behaviour by the way we act. The 4-year-old is not allowed out to play because it is raining. He complains and whinges. This gets particularly painful after ten minutes so you repent in order to preserve your sanity. Now you have blown it. You have set a precedent that a definite 'No' can be turned to an equally definite 'Yes' if you whinge long enough. This is not a wise way to run things.

Skilful mothers can divert lesser whingers back to the straight and narrow by noticing something around the house or setting off on some interesting activity. This strategy can be of some benefit in the not-very-determined whinger.

If diversion does not work, the child must be ignored. Mortal man has only a limited ability to actually ignore whingeing, so pretending to ignore it is probably the best we can hope for. It still gives an equally strong message to the offending party. When the parents can no longer ignore the irritation, and the situation is coming close to a blow-up when somebody is going to lose control, this is the moment to employ the Time Out technique. This avoids a loss of control when everyone would become very unhappy, and little would be achieved.

As a last resort, when diversion, ignoring and Time Out have all failed, mother must sweep up the offending party and head for the great outdoors. Most children suspend hostilities as soon as they escape from the restrictions of the home battleground, and with the minority who continue, the whingeing never seems so bad when competing with bird song and noisy motor vehicles.

The absconder

Any toddler worth his salt, and who has read up on his child psychology, will realise that he is meant to be clingy and loath to be separated from his parents. A small percentage, however, seem ignorant of this fact, and they are forever running off and getting lost. Absconders are a real trial to their parents, who are forced to take part in high speed pursuits down the main street, hide and seek in the supermarket and the interminable wait for the voice to come over the loudspeaker informing them that the infant absconder has been corralled and is awaiting pick-up.

Luckily most absconders develop sufficient sense to stop the habit within a six month period but some may take years to grow out of it. I have little success in treating children who run off. I am able only to suggest that the parents remain fit and vigilant at all times, or resort to toddler reins. I have fitted reins to many children including two who had the curious habit of jumping on passing buses. The first did it as a form of attention-seeking but was always extracted before the bus started off. The second child managed to get as far as the terminus, his mother following in hot pursuit in a taxi.

Interrupting adults

One of the greatest sources of irritation with small children is their inability to refrain from interrupting when adults are talking. In some houses it is almost impossible for parents to talk to each other when there is an awake toddler around. Parents often find it hard even to communicate by cuddles and kisses without the star of the show trying to force his way in between them.

The child has three problems. He thinks his wise sayings are of earth-shattering importance and that everyone must immediately shut up and listen. He does not like others stealing his much enjoyed position centre stage, and he knows that if he does not say his piece immediately it will be forgotten and lost forever.

Some children become absolutely impossible when visitors call and want to talk at some length to their parents. The child interferes so much that tempers are lost or the visit becomes a complete waste of time for all concerned. Visitors who are real friends should realise that the toddler needs a lot of attention, and if they are not sharp enough to see this, their absence is probably not a great loss anyway.

Some children refuse to let their parents talk on the phone. They successfully prevent this by either making so much noise that reasoned conversation is rendered impossible, or create such havoc in the house that the call has to be abandoned.

Several years ago I looked after a young handicapped boy whose favourite trick was to wait until the phone rang and then set off at high speed round the house, turning on every possible electrical appliance he could before the call was terminated. When his mother got off the phone the house was buzzing with the noise of vacuum cleaners, food mixers, hair dryers, while lights blazed like a crystal palace on a Saturday night, and the electricity meter raced round and round like a Grand Prix car.

Now the bad news... I have no answers to help those whose children behave in this way, except to assure you that it is perfectly normal behaviour. I suppose that visitors who try to monopolise parents are pretty boring to a toddler, who tries to discourage them. Long telephone calls are fairly antisocial at the best of times and should be reserved for the evening. The constant interruption of conversations will resolve itself by the end of toddlerhood, by which time the child will have a better short-term memory, be less impulsive, and will have learnt to wait his turn.

Teeth grinding

The noise of grinding teeth sends a shiver down any parent's spine and conjures up all sorts of thoughts of madness. Grinding the teeth during sleep is a common, normal occurrence. It doesn't indicate that the child has worms or is suffering from any form of lunacy. There is little to be done to help the situation, although in very extreme cases dentists have been known to intervene.

Normal toddlers occasionally grind their teeth noisily by day but, in my experience, it is almost exclusively the behaviour of a child with a major handicap. Some people report success with these children, but it has not been my experience that any therapy has lessened the amount of nerve-shattering noise.

Bad language

Bad language is not a major problem in toddlers. Most of the obscene language they know is learnt at pre-school, along with all the other appurtenances of a normal education, and is regurgitated parrot-fashion at home. When a toddler swears or uses bad language, he is usually only copying someone he has heard at home or at pre-school. Toddlers are great mimics and they have mighty retentive memories. Just remember that the next time you hammer your thumb instead of the nail or express your opinion of someone else's bad driving.

Toddlers also have an extraordinary interest in 'lavatory' talk. Bottoms and bodily functions seem to make fascinating topics of conversation, probably because in the toddler's world of limited experience, these are subjects that they can talk about with real authority. The bodily function fascination usually disappears of its own accord before the age of 5, and before that it can be gently doused, generally by diverting the child's attention to something else.

When new, undesirable words come from the toddler, the chances are that he will not know what they mean but is aware of the interesting effect they have on his parents. In handling this problem some degree of selective deafness is suggested and a quiet caution, like 'we don't really want to hear that'. If the parents throw a tantrum every time the child uses a certain word, it again gives him a potent weapon to stir up the household any time life begins to look a bit boring.

Undesirable language shouldn't be allowed to upset the parents, but it should be gently moulded out of the vocabulary. A major confrontation will lead to nothing but trouble and will probably only suffice to implant the behaviour even more firmly.

If a household is run on democratic lines, it is only fair that if parents are allowed to use excessive bad language, then the toddler has the same right. If you don't want your toddler to use bad language, then watch your own words.

Stealing

To a child under 5 years of age there is no such crime as stealing. However, adults are obsessed with who owns what, and they spend thousands of dollars guarding, insuring and locking away all their treasures. Toddlers are fortunate in not having reached this stage of life; they are totally uninterested in all the hang-ups of possession, titles and deeds of ownership. Although they may collect items and money, this is not done with any malicious intent. All that is required, therefore, is a gentle reminder, when objects are taken, that they should really be left alone. Nothing more should be said. When out visiting, a slightly firmer line is required, more for the benefit of the person whose house you are visiting than as a genuine reprimand to the toddler.

Vomiting on demand

When I am feeling weak there is nothing I dread more then dealing with a child who vomits on demand. This problem certainly can be cured but the method of treatment can be extremely tough. Some children have a weak valve at the top of their stomach which allows them to regurgitate their food frequently and effortlessly. Others have completely normal anatomies but still find that profuse crying or coughing can result in a return.

The last, and luckily the rarest, is that group which vomits on demand for the sole purpose of manipulating and punishing their parents. These children present one of the greatest challenges that we behaviour experts ever meet.

Children of the first group, with the weak valve, need proper X-ray diagnosis, medical treatment and review. Those from the second group who find that coughing or crying leads to vomiting, need firm but sensitive handling. They may be left to cry but once this changes from gentle to upset and hysterical, you must intervene quickly if disaster is to be averted. With these children the controlled crying technique is useful (see Chapter 11) but the period of crying must be kept short and if vomiting is used to manipulate the parents, firmer action is needed.

I see quite a number of children in the third group who quite blatantly vomit when they don't get their own way. These children are usually in the 1 to 2½ year age group. A frequent problem is when parents need Time Out for discipline but it is sabotaged by vomiting. Without some form of 'safety valve' technique, the parents find it hard to control their children and are now left completely impotent.

With such children, Time Out can first be tried combined with my controlled crying method. They should be put in their room and allowed to cry for a brief period, then given a small amount of comfort to keep them very aware of what is going on but not good attention. If this gives an effective form of Time Out and there is no vomiting, that is great. If there is too much comfort for it to be an effective form of discipline, or if they vomit, you now have to be extremely tough.

When put in the cot, they vomit. You are upset and feel a heel, but today you must not give in to this form of blackmail. Calmly take the soiled child and place him in the bathroom. Close the door.

Quickly change the cot without the child being able to see you and your obvious upset. Return to the bathroom, remove the clothes without fuss, sponge off using cool water, then dry. Put the child in a nappy or pants and return him immediately to the cot. This must all be done in a matter-of-fact way, without anger, emotion or any good quality attention.

I must emphasise that it is extremely unusual to be driven to such lengths but when it is necessary, this method certainly works.

I recently worked with a brilliant mother and her 2-year-old twins. These little girls were unbelievably militant and unfortunately they could also vomit with the greatest of ease. One had quite severe asthma which required inhaled medicines and the other went hysterical when put down to bed. When either of these young madams was pushed, they didn't argue, they just threw up.

Fortunately, their mum was way ahead of them. When it was time for medicine, she handed this girl a bucket and then produced the pump. With the other the bucket appeared at bedtime after which stories were read, kisses and cuddles were given, but it was made obvious that vomiting was not going to be tolerated. Within two days, this awful problem, which would have floored many of us, was past history. In my job, I am constantly amazed by the strength and wisdom of the parents who find remedies for seemingly impossible situations, like this one.

Smearers

The unpleasant habit of smearing is mostly seen in young handicapped patients, although occasionally normal toddlers aged about 18 months will indulge in it. It is usually restricted to the early morning—the damage is done to the accompaniment of the dawn chorus. The toddler wakes before the rest of the household, is bored and has a dirty nappy, so to wile away the hours he engages in some 'finger painting' on the walls.

This ghastly behaviour pattern sickens and depresses parents, so we use two methods to cope with the problem. First, the parents must get up and change the toddler's nappy the moment he wakes in the morning. Second, the child must be prevented from getting his hands near the nappy area, which is achieved by dressing him in high dungarees or similar 'high rise' garments, fastened firmly in place with safety pins. If the right style of garment is used only the infant Houdini would be able to get his hand into mischief. And even then he couldn't extract it loaded! Luckily, smearing in normal toddlers tends to be a very short-lived problem.

15

Fears, Comforters and Security

All small animals know fear and small children are no exception. Some of these fears may seem quite 'off the beam' to parents, and some children's comfort habits may seem distinctly strange. Parents are never quite sure what is acceptable for well-adjusted offspring. In fact, it would appear that just about anything seems possible at an early developmental stage and in this chapter we look at some of these fears, as well as security and various methods of comfort.

However foolish a child's fears may seem to an adult, they are very real to the child, and they must not be put down or ridiculed. Talking openly about anxieties helps to keep in clear perspective the division between fact and fantasy. The best way to treat childhood fears is by good parental example, lots of support and comfort, and then gradual desensitisation. There is usually no reason to get too worried, as most fears at this age are temporary problems that evaporate with the passage of time. Looking back one year on, it is hard to think what all the fuss was about.

Different fears for different years

Children have very fertile imaginations that are capable of generating great uneasiness as a result of hearing stories or watching television. The result is that they conjure up visions of ghosts, long-legged beasties and things that go bump in the night. It's all part of growing up. At birth, babies are relatively immune to the fears that beset the rest of us. This is probably a mercy, when you think what the inside of a modern neonatal nursery looks like, with all that space-age gadgetry attached to the poor little, underweight scraps. The only things that startle the newborn are sudden movement and noise. Forty babies will leap in unison when a clumsy nurse drops a tray on the nursery floor. From birth to 6 months there is little progress in this department, until somewhere around the seventh month the baby suddenly becomes inseparably attached to his main caretaker, usually his mother. After this, any attempts to separate him from mum will precipitate distress and floods of tears.

At 1 year this separation is still a major problem, and the child will also often react badly to loud noises, such as doorbells, vacuum cleaners or food mixers. As the decibels rise, he will cuddle in tighter to his mother for protection. Strange people, strange objects and sudden movements can also cause him distress. At the age of 2 the fear of separation still exists but it becomes slightly less intense and more predictable than in the 1-year-old. Loud bangs still cause upsets, as will the unexpected screech of brakes, ambulance sirens or the violent barking of dogs.

Between 2 and 4 years that obsessively tight attachment to mum weakens further and a whole new package of fears starts to emerge; animals and the dark featuring prominently in this array. The fear of animals hits its peak around the age of 3; fear of the dark usually peaks nearer the fifth birthday.

Between 4 and 6 years the child develops a highly vivid imagination, with fear of the dark constantly worsened by regular visits from ghosts, bogeymen, monsters and travellers from outer space. After the age of 6 some children are said to worry about being injured, or they may even start to fear death, although they still do not have the adult picture of either of these possibilities.

By the age of 10, the child has been lumbered with most of the burden of adult fears, which he will carry for the rest of his life. These are compounded during adolescence with the major fear of not 'making it' as a fully accepted member of the peer group.

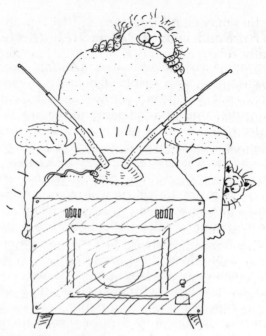

Some specific fears

All young children have one overwhelming fear in common: the fear of being separated from their parents. Other fears come and go and are either of the child's own making or instilled into him by transference of anxiety from the parent. Whether we like it or not, fear has always been a major part of life, both for adults and children, and nothing I can say is going to make it go away.

Separation

The fear of separation is common to all toddlers from the age of about 7 months, until it wanes by pre-school age. It is at its most intense in the early years, its ebb varying greatly from child to child and family to family. Initially, the child resents being handled by anyone except his mother, but this quickly eases to allow all the other members of the family and close friends in on the act. When playing, he is never far from mum, and if outside or playing in another room, he reappears every few minutes to reassure himself of her presence.

Most parents need babysitters at one time or another so that they can maintain some outside life. The ideal babysitter is a grandparent, other relative or close friend. Leaving the child with other babysitters may be difficult initially, with profuse tears being shed on departure and again at pick-up time. Between these times there is usually relative happiness which can be confirmed by one quick phone call. The child should be accompanied by his cuddly toys and security items, and he should never be left in a great rush, preferably being given a little time to acclimatise, after which the parents should leave decisively, not weakening to his cries when halfway out the door.

Although most toddlers do well in the care of a good child minder, a few are immensely unhappy and never really settle. If this happens, the parents must ask themselves if separation is really necessary and if it might not be kinder to wait several more months before continuing. Of course, in our modern world many parents are forced, for a variety of good reasons, to leave their child with a babysitter whether they like it or not. But some parents seem particularly blind to what they are doing to their children. An intelligent mother recently asked me for advice on a problem that was worrying her. For the past 6 months she had attended church each Sunday morning, placing her toddler in the church creche, where he cried inconsolably throughout the entire separation. What could be done to make the child less unhappy? I explained that I was certain that an understanding God would probably much prefer to see a happy child than a pew occupied in his church.

By the age of 3 most toddlers are able to separate and settle quite happily at pre-school. As this is his first major separation, the child must know what is going to happen to him when he is left, and he should be gently introduced to his new surroundings before being abandoned. Parents are never sure, when they bring their child for the first time, whether it is best to sit with him for an hour or so or leave immediately. This advice is probably best left to the individual pre-school director, who has a great deal of experience with this problem. What I do know is that once the parents have made up their mind to go, then go they must, decisively, without lurking in the bushes to spy on the child.

Occasionally the child will not settle happily, nevertheless parents will insist on his going, believing that non-attendance will cause him to miss out in the warm-up heats for the academic rat race. Once again, where the child is very unhappy, there is little point in forcing him to go on. Better to wait 3 to 6 months and then try again.

A band of philosophical child raisers believe that it is important to rush through the stage of separation, to prepare a child for schooling and later life. I believe that toddlers were designed to remain close to their families for a number of years and in a normal 70-year life span, rushing a child out into our far-from-perfect world any earlier than is necessary seems rather unkind and pointless. When I am irritated by bureaucrats, bullied by bank managers and forced to read continuing evidence of man's inhumanity to man, I secretly would love to regress to those blissful toddler years with a loving mother to protect me from all this stress.

Baths

Most babies like water and enjoy splashing in their baths. But for unknown reasons, after their first year some take a strong dislike to this and the very word 'bath' or the noise of a running tap will set them to arching their backs, crying and complaining bitterly. Once again you must use the technique of gradual desensitisation and reintroduction to the bath.

A good start for the toddler who absolutely refuses to bath is to stand him in an empty basin in front of the fire and sponge him with warm water. After a time of this, some water may be put in the basin and, when he is rather braver, he can be sponged in a bath with a maximum depth of water of two or three centimetres at the deep end. From here he will sit down, and you can start increasing the water level until you have a child who baths in the right place, at the right time, and with the right attitude.

To prevent bath refusal, it is important to avoid frightening the young child with such things as spluttering taps, gurgling plugs and slippery baths. Place a rubber mat in the bottom of the bath if there is any chance of the child slipping and losing his balance. The bath can become one of the best playtimes of the day, and this should be actively encouraged, filling the bath with boats, submarines, rubber duckies and discarded detergent bottles, which double as excellent water squirters. A bubble bath is always fun and is easily provided by a quick squirt of dishwashing liquid, if you don't want to go to the expense of commercial preparations. Be warned, however, that happy aquatic toddlers and carpeted bathroom floors do not go well together—a tiled floor with a big drain is definitely preferable.

Once again fears of the bath are generally short lived and, if handled sensibly with gentle desensitisation, they are quickly overcome.

Genuine fear of the bath should not be confused with the theatrical antics of a manipulating, attention-seeking toddler, who, out of principle, refuses to bath when told. Recently I saw a 3 1/2-year-old girl, who greatly upset her mother by refusing to do anything she was asked whenever her father was home in the evenings. She would never bath unless the water was turned on by her father, and she had to be carried to the bathroom and undressed by him as well. When father was out, the child would never take a bath, because her mother thought it was never worth the fight.

This situation was cured in a rapid, though slightly devious, manner. Father continued to show great love and attention, running the bath, undressing his daughter and putting her in the water, but one minor adjustment was made to the routine. 'Absent-mindedly', he consistently forgot to turn on the hot tap when he was running the bath with the consequence that the water had an Arctic chill—the balance of power was immediately redressed. Mother's care at bathtime was once again in equal demand.

Toilets

Some children are afraid to sit on the toilet, which obviously makes toilet training well nigh impossible. This fear may arise from a number of causes—maybe the association with a severe pain when passing a particularly hard motion or fear of being sucked into the toilet when it is flushed and being washed out to sea down a big pipe. Some children are frightened of gadgets, like the extractor fan in some bathrooms that starts automatically when the light is switched on and which, in a confined space, may sound like a jumbo jet about to take off. Other children refuse to sit on the toilet purely out of attention-seeking, toddler stubbornness.

I recently saw an irate mother who complained that her 3-year-old daughter had lost all her previously excellent toilet training skills as the result of a stupid action by the girl's father. Browsing through a shop one day he came upon a poster of a gorilla climbing out of a toilet bowl. So impressed was he with this piece of visual art that he brought it home and stuck it up on the back of the toilet door. Well, the little girl walked in, sat on the toilet, kicked the door shut and, after seeing this horrific vision, absolutely refused, not surprisingly, to sit there ever again.

With children who will not sit on the toilet for one reason or another, we once again must introduce gentle desensitisation. For the most resistant, they should start sitting on a pot with their nappy still on. There should be no forcing but lots of rewards given. From here progress to sitting without the nappy; sitting on the pot beside the toilet with mum close by; sitting on the toilet with mum close by; sitting with mum outside giving encouragement; and finally going solo while mum rustles up some interesting treat in the kitchen.

This may all seem rather cumbersome and excessive but often you will find that some of these steps can be bypassed. The important message is that children should not be forced; give them good security and gently desensitise them.

Noises in the dark, monsters and other assorted beasties

It is perfectly normal for toddlers to be frightened of a great variety of noises, even such common ones as household appliances. This does not mean that the child is hypersensitive or emotionally disturbed, and the phenomenon in any case is usually very short lived. Sensitivity to some noises never goes—dentists' drills and the screeching of car tyres are two that are guaranteed to make my hair stand on end, for instance. I presume that, although these noises worry me, the perpetrators have long since come to terms with them. Fears are very real to the person who suffers them. No amount of explaining will convince me that dentists' drills are a form of relaxation therapy. We must accept the fears of others, whatever the age, give comfort and not belittle their beliefs.

At an older age, somewhere between 4 and 5 years, fear of the dark usually hits its peak and then largely disappears by the child's seventh birthday. A low wattage light is much appreciated by many children at night. When the sun sets and darkness appears, this is the time when the older child's vivid imagination conjures up visions of robbers, monsters and other assorted bogeymen. It is popular for authors to attribute this to the 'junk viewing diet' that we feed our children on television but children have been terrified at night-time for centuries, long before Mr Logie Baird's ingenious invention became freely available.

Children listen to stories told to them by their parents, grannies or friends or read books full of varying degrees of mayhem, terror and violence. Ali Baba's offsider was so mutilated after his murder that they needed a leatherworker to sew him up for burial. Hansel and Gretel and Snow White were all taken to big, black forests and abandoned. Snow White was poisoned by a nasty old woman. In 'Struwwelpeter', the boy who sucked his thumbs had them cut off with a large pair of scissors. The Pied Piper took all the town's children hostage and never returned them to their parents. Humpty Dumpty had a most violent accident, relived in gory detail at a thousand breakfast tables daily, and what about those three mice who, despite severe visual disability, had their tails so cruelly severed from their bodies. Even the Bible tells us of some exceedingly nasty people and punishments. So let's not blame all these childhood fears on modern films, television, cartoons and comics. The element of fear in childhood upbringing is as old as childhood itself.

Imaginary fears are all part of childhood development and only too soon fears move out of the area of fiction into the realities of the adult world, fears that unfortunately will not go away. It does no harm, however, to be a little selective with the type of reading and viewing matter your child is exposed to, and constantly remind them of where fact ends and fiction begins.

Dogs

It is common for the under 4s to fear animals, especially dogs. Naturally, we don't want to encourage the toddler to poke passing German Shepherds or pat every surly mongrel in the street, but those who fear dogs are usually quite unselective, being terrorised by even the most benign ball of fluff.

Most commonly the child who fears dogs will sight the offending beast, stiffen, then hold on tight to his mother and start to bawl. Rest assured if your child reacts this way that it is a normal developmental stage for many children and, even if you do nothing, it will pass in a short time. One way of helping overcome the fear, however, is to talk quietly to the child about 'nice dogs' and introduce him to some of the gentler of the species.

Very few children have such great fear of dogs that they hardly dare go outdoors in case one appears. Once again, you should gradually introduce the child to dogs, possibly starting with a small, newborn puppy or a securely caged dog in a pet shop window.

Some therapists I know introduce stuffed dogs into their treatment, but I feel that once you go to those lengths you're only a hair's breadth away from turning serious therapy into a sketch worthy of Monty Python.

Whatever else you do, be confident, talk openly about the animals and try to get a toe in the door with some distant dog contact. From there build to full desensitisation and cure.

Doctors

As a paediatrician, I have learnt the hard way that busy days surrounded by anxious, crying, unco-operative children are extremely stressful. It is, therefore, important for our own sanity, as well as the happiness of the children we serve, that doctors' surgeries are made as friendly and non-threatening as possible.

As mentioned, most babies up to the age of 6 months don't mind being separated from their mum, so it is easy for a doctor to lift them up and examine them on a couch. From about 7 months until pre-school age, however, this separation is a problem, and I find that examinations are best done with the child sitting relaxed and secure on mum's knee.

Some parents—and doctors for that matter—are amazingly skilful at stirring up a child the moment they enter the office. The child is bundled through the door and not allowed to touch anything, move or even talk in some cases. A nervous mother will wrench the child's clothes up and twitter in his ear in an unnatural way like a bird warning of impending danger. Utterances such as 'doctor is not going to hurt you' are counter-productive, since the thought of getting hurt had probably never even crossed the child's mind.

Children should neither be restricted, nor over-stimulated by anxious parents when taken to the doctor. They should be allowed to sit quietly on mother's knee to allow the doctor to make the initial examination. As far as the doctor is concerned, the introductory touch is best with arms and feet being wobbled in a fun way, which introduces the doctor to the child as a human being and not an ogre. Thereafter, examinations should be quick and confident, accompanied by quiet, reassuring talk. The doctor should engage the child's eyes, communicating gently with him and watching carefully for those early signs of distress that appear in the eye seconds before the first tear is shed.

Painful and uncomfortable procedures, such as throat examination, should be left until the end, followed by a cuddle and release. Neither parents nor doctors should insist on things like painful blood tests unless they are of indisputable diagnostic and therapeutic value.

Doctors are really very nice people, as long as they keep their scalpels, syringes and tongue depressors away from the child. A visit to the doctor should not be a fearful experience for either child or mother. Most of us enjoy working with children, otherwise we wouldn't be doing it.

Hospitals

In the not too distant past, hospitals were places of dread, run purely for the business of curing the sick and without much interest in protecting the emotional well-being of the patient. This was particularly horrifying for children who had to go into hospital. Between the ages of 7 months and 3½ years the young child grieves deeply when separated from his mother and is too young to understand the reasons and temporary nature of the separation. The unhappy toddler may feel abandoned, as if his parents had walked off, leaving him on the steps of an orphanage.

Initially the child will protest, crying his little heart out as his parents leave. Usually he will settle within five minutes, only to greet his parents on their next visit with copious tears, giving the impression that he has been crying non-stop since they departed. Hospitalisation may be upsetting for toddlers, but it is often even more upsetting for the parents.

Generally speaking, hospitals are not places to be feared by children, and it is important for parents to talk openly about them should they pass one in their daily travels to let the child realise from an early age that it isn't some dreadful institution. Each day we have pre-schoolers from some of our city schools visit our wards, and they have a ball, realising that it is really quite a fun place run by 'good guys'!

In the last ten years hospitals and their routines for the care of children have changed greatly. Now if a child needs to be admitted, there is open visiting for the parents and in most cases some form of bed for the mother if she wants to stay.

If you get some warning that your child may have to be admitted to hospital, it is important to prepare him, discussing openly what is going to happen and encouraging medical pretend play with dolls and teddies. If you can, take him to visit the ward before admission and make sure that when he does go in he has all his favourite cuddly toys and comforters with him.

'Day only' surgery is encouraged now, so that the child can go home to the care of his parents as soon as possible. When the child goes to the anaesthetic room, he is accompanied by his teddy bear and his mother, and he will find both waiting for him in the recovery ward after the operation. Anaesthetists who specialise in children's anaesthetics have thrown out all those cruel, old ideas that children don't really feel pain. Now, in a good children's hospital, any child from birth upward is afforded the same, or an even greater, standard of post-operative pain relief than we might expect for ourselves.

In short, hospitals are no longer places for children to fear. Talk to your children freely and openly about them, for one day they may have to visit one.

Comforters and security blankets

Children are not the only ones to enjoy comforters. Adults enjoy them too, relieving their tensions by sucking on a cigarette, a cigar, chewing gum or their fingernails, or holding on to a can of alcoholic beverage. Toddler comforters are probably a great deal less harmful to health, generally consisting of thumbs, dummies, teddy bears and security blankets. There's nothing intrinsically wrong with any of these, as long as the habit does not last too long.

Thumb sucking

Despite Sigmund Freud's inevitable emphasis on the sexual connotations of sucking one's thumb, modern thinkers believe they are sucked because it seems a natural and good thing to do at the time. If there were not some comfort and satisfaction in sucking the thumb, I doubt whether children would bother to do it. Thumb sucking is a worldwide phenomenon, although some writers claim it is less frequent in some races; apparently little Eskimos hardly ever do it at all, but I presume this is a practical move on their part, keeping their hands in mittens to prevent their digits falling off through frostbite.

Children certainly seem to suck their thumbs more when they are either tired, bored, frustrated or tense, and it is a good way of getting to sleep, particularly for those children who have not yet attained the mathematical skill to count sheep. In times of stress, and particularly when a new baby arrives, many toddlers regress to this old habit.

By the age of 3½, most children have spontaneously removed their thumbs from their mouths, although some studies suggest that up to 2 per cent still have this habit in their early teens. Most experts now believe that there is no harm in the habit.

It is not a sign of a scarred psyche or emotional insecurity. Little children do it for only one reason: they enjoy it.

If there is even a smattering of justice in this adult-run world, before any thumbs are plucked from the mouths of innocent infants we should first get our grown-up act together. For a start, cigarettes should be totally taboo, adult nail biters should be kept in mitts and those trendy gum chewers should be viewed as a trifle retarded. Once the big people have set the example, it would then be time for the young to follow.

The only worry with thumb sucking is that it can cause teeth to become displaced and stick out. This is of particular importance to today's parents who seek the perfect alignment of a Colgate commercial, yet know that getting wired up with an orthodontist comes mighty expensive. Certainly before the age of 6, thumb sucking does not damage permanent teeth and after that, it takes more than just a few minutes of thumb in mouth at bedtime to cause harm. There appears to be only a very slight risk of the continuing habit altering the position of children's teeth.

Kicking the habit

Thirty years ago, splints were attached to elbows, mittens put on hands, and the fingers dipped in bitter substances to prevent children from putting their thumbs in their mouths. Some dentists, fearing a misshaped bite, used dental plates, which blocked the ability to suck the thumb. For a child's emotional well-being, there is much to be said for leaving nature to cure this habit rather than engaging in these antisocial activities.

Below the age of 4 years I believe that sucking should be totally ignored. After this, hands can be subtly diverted and bodies can be busied onto something more productive. Rewards for 'grown up behaviour' can be given, but whatever happens it must never become the cause of a fight or the child will continue it, just to annoy.

Before 6 years of age thumb sucking cannot harm the permanent teeth as they are still busy burrowing their way up to the surface.

After this I don't mind a little gentle sucking to help soothe to sleep but if it is more major, you should discuss it with your dentist.

It is hard to know whether protruding teeth were caused by thumb sucking or just designed to be that way. Some parents believe that their own teeth were displaced by sucking but I often wonder if this had nothing to do with the thumb. Maybe they were born to have horizontal teeth and as the thumb slipped in and out so smoothly they decided to garage it there permanently.

Dummies, pacifiers and comforters

Most doctors have an inbuilt dislike of these plastic or rubber devices, but no-one has ever found any evidence to indicate that they really do any harm. Objection to them is more on aesthetic grounds than medical ones. It is fashionable in some quarters to claim that they are unhygienic, but so for that matter are the ten dirty fingers that would be inserted in the mouth if the dummy was not there. Many parents who are determined never to resort to these pacifiers relent when confronted with an extremely irritable, difficult child. If the dummy helps in those situations, then good luck to them.

I dislike the way a dummy can make an intelligent child appear dull, delayed and a dribbler. I also worry about them being used at bedtime because, although they undoubtedly precipitate sleep, they also have an unfortunate habit of precipitating wakefulness when they become disengaged in the early hours of the morning (see Chapter 11).

Kicking the habit

There are no long-term side-effects from sucking these comforters, as long as they are not of the sort that has a built-in bottle which constantly irrigates the teeth with a sweet tooth-rotting solution. When the time comes to discard the dummy, it is usually best to be brave, throw it away, and then brace yourself for the repercussions. There will inevitably be some hours, or even some days, of trouble but the dummy will soon be forgotten. Those who do not have the courage to discard it so abruptly may try a gradual withdrawal by losing it, damaging it, or letting it become slightly scorched when the sterilising saucepan accidentally boils dry! After 3 1/2, the child may well be reasoned with and the dummy given up after some hard bargaining.

Although I do not like dummies, I assure parents that they do not cause any harm. When a child is under stress for any reason he has the same right to his dummy as his parents have to their cigarettes—the difference is that thumbs and dummies are not proven health hazards. When the time is right, preferably before 2½, discard the object nevertheless. It has to go some time.

Teddies, cuddlies and security blankets

Most youngsters have some object that they seek out and cuddle up to when tired or upset. This can be some exotic imported stuffed animal, mum's own battered but much-loved teddy, a sheepskin rug or even a rapidly disintegrating bit of old fabric. Whatever the 'real-world' value of the object, in the eyes of the child it is priceless. These items are often referred to as 'transition objects'. They give security, continuity and comfort to a child when the environment and those in it are changing. At the day-care centre, at granny's, in hospital, although the environment has altered and mum may no longer be there, the child has a beloved familiar object to hold on to. It is his link with his home base; without it he feels a stranger in a strange world. No wonder ET wanted to go home.

As the child becomes more and more attached to his 'familiar', greater is the distress when it falls apart or is mislaid. To the toddler, this is a disaster of major proportions, not unlike a death in the family. But surprisingly, despite the great attachment, a bit of high-powered salesmanship from an enthusiastic parent will steer a toddler towards another, reserve comforter.

Security blankets of the type favoured by Charlie Brown's friend Linus get progressively grubbier and grubbier, until eventually they simply must be washed. This needs to be planned with all the precision of a military operation to ensure that they are in and out of the washing machine and returned dry to the owner with the minimum if discombobulation.

When a blanket is wearing out, it may be wise to remove a part of it to keep in cold storage until the fateful day when the original is in irretrievable tatters. Even without this foresight, a minute, disintegrating patch of material may be reincarnated if clever mum sews it onto the corner of some new material. This is rather like the horticultural grafting of roses and, when properly achieved, ensures years of continuing pleasure.

Comforters and transition objects are normal, natural and healthy. They promote, rather than postpone, security. Like Christopher Robin and his trusty bear, Pooh, the young child armed with his 'familiar' can accomplish many a daring feat that would never have been possible alone.

16

Sibling Rivalry

Sibling rivalry refers to that competitive streak which makes children squabble, fight and accuse their parents of impartial treatment. I do not see this as a pathological condition but just as a very normal human trait.

Probably the greatest problem our children have is that they are too like the grown-ups they live with. If you come to think of it, adults are remarkably competitive and jealous beings. Most humans seem to have a strong drive to get more and do better than their mates, even if a few people get trampled along the way.

Imagine the secret elation if we were awarded a 20 per cent pay rise and our colleagues got none. Then think of the disappointment if we unexpectedly were granted a 100 per cent rise and everyone else got 120 per cent. If adults are competitive to the point of starting wars and taking advantage of their fellow man, then what's wrong with a toddler having a few skirmishes and shows of strength?

All little animals love to taunt and fight. This builds up their bodily reflexes and muscles, while it drives their mothers mad. In

common with most child care experts I find it easier to philosophise about sibling rivalry than to come up with sure-fire ways to
stop our children fighting. Anyway for what its worth, here are my
ideas.

Two toddlers—double trouble

When the Greens had just one toddler, I thought I knew all about
children's behaviour. When we had two, I realised how little I knew.
Two toddlers are never difficult when separated by a distance of at
least a kilometre; it is when they come together that they set each
other off.

The creative genius of such young people is always astonishing.
A duet of toddlers can devise ways to get into mischief well beyond
the imagination of any adult or child alone.

When we talk of sibling rivalry in the toddler, the presentation
depends very much on the child's age. The very young are keen to
protect their home pitch from interfering intruders. Older toddlers
have a different but equally difficult style—they squabble. The
young behave badly when their toys are touched by brothers, sisters
or visitors and they hate anyone monopolising their mum's attention. Older ones just bicker, bait and complain of inequality. This is
a strange age where they can't bear to be apart but when together,
they show their affection in a very odd way.

True equality—fine for fairyland

We all know that each of our children must be treated with equal
love, limits and discipline. We also know that this admirable goal is
often quite out of touch with the reality of life in our own homes.
The discipline and expectations may be equal but the children we
discipline are not.

It seems to me that there is little true equality in our adult
world. He who is strongest and shouts loudest generally gets the
most. Parents of twins are often the first to realise this. No matter
how high their ideals at the start, the docile may miss out while
the difficult noisy half hijacks an unfair slice of the action. Time
and attention may not be divided fairly but our love is still transmitted with complete equality.

Try hard to be totally fair, but when this is sabotaged by two
children with dramatically different temperaments it may be necessary to tone down our demands for once, steer round trouble and

not force unwinnable issues. I apologise about this apparent double standard but if you are going to survive at the front line of child care, you have to be a realist.

Taunting

By the second half of toddlerhood our children start on the school-age special of taunting, squabbling and grumbling. There are of course great differences from child to child. Some are so good that you wonder if they are training for a place in the Peace Corps, while others could start a fight in an empty room. The most skilled taunters will always appear innocent, it is just that a trail of trouble seems to follow in their wake. Their brother's homework book mysteriously falls to the floor. The TV channel changes in the closing minutes of the movie. While all this goes on, children are poked, tripped and insulted.

Boredom brings out the worst in a taunter as they pace around the floor like a hungry lion on the lookout for a Christian. At moments like this it is best to keep them occupied and divert their attention as they position themselves for the pounce. Try to keep out of children's squabbles and if you do intervene, lay down the law quite firmly. There is no place for debating and democracy and, if they are unhappy with your decision, let them take their case to the Human Rights Commission.

Fighting

Fighting between our young is one of those universal but irritating parts of family life. Over the years I have talked to hundreds of parents trying to find some foolproof peace-keeping methods but so far they remain elusive. I do have, however, some suggestions that may help to secure an uneasy sort of truce.

- Turn a deaf ear and a blind eye to as much squabbling as you can.

- When siblings start to spar, divert them onto something more innocent and interesting.

- Bundle squabbling children into another room or banish them out the back door. Fighters like an audience.

- It would take a team of detectives to find who started the fight. Don't waste your time. It is usually the one who protests loudest who is most guilty.

- At the first grunt don't rush in like the United Nations keepers. Children have to find their own equilibrium.

- It becomes a different matter when one child is being unfairly and continually victimised. Now firm action is needed.

- When we do intervene, it must be decisive, without debate and with 100 per cent firmness.

- When all else fails, separate the squabblers with a brief period of Time Out in different rooms.

The main mistake we parents make is to get drawn into our children's battles. If they know that you will always intervene, you may still be intervening when they are 18. If the moment they start you rush in like the anti-terrorist squad, gas grenades and guns at the ready, soon they will squabble just to see you in full action.

Another observation I have made is that few fights take place without an audience. Can you imagine Ali, Tyson or other boxing champs, holding the World Title in their back room, watched only by the cleaning lady and her dog? It seems to me that if there is not an interested audience most fights will fizzle out. When our children squabble it is best to either move away from the ringside, or move the ringside away from us.

If you are eventually forced to become involved, do so properly. Don't hold an enquiry into who fired the first shot as, at the height of any conflict, it is peace not recrimination that is needed. Don't enter the squabble yourself. Pull rank, say 'that's it!' and leave them in no doubt that you are not going to take sides or tolerate any more. When this fails it is time for the warriors to be separated then banished for a while to their different rooms.

The toddler and the new baby

The way our families seem to happen, there is usually a gap of about 1½ to 2½ years between our first and second child. Now you don't need a degree in psychology to know that this spacing spells trouble. The unsuspecting baby is going to drop in on top of a self-centred toddler at the peak of his militancy.

If you pause to see it from a 2-year-old's view, he thinks he is the most important person around. He likes having his mum's and dad's undivided attention. He doesn't understand the meaning of

the word share. Anyway, no-one asked his permission to bring that thing into the house and in fact it should be sent back to the hospital with instructions to reinsert it.

I have to admit that despite all this potential for problems, if the toddler is handled sensibly, few will occur. We do however need to be careful. With the arrival of the new baby, the toddler has been provided with the most potent weapon he has ever held in his armoury. Before long he discovers how sensitive and overprotective his mother has become. For some reason she cannot accept that a grubby, accident-prone 2-year-old should be allowed to manhandle her newborn piece of perfection.

When life becomes boring, all that is needed is for the toddler to walk a few paces and poke the baby. The result is quite dramatic, but even this effect can be surpassed by jumping on the infant or tipping up the pram. The *pièce de résistance*, however, is reserved for very special occasions: a dirty digit is poked within a few centimetres of the baby's eye, which is usually quite close enough to guarantee an emotional eruption from one's mother.

If parents have been strong enough to get rid of other antisocial, attention-seeking behaviour, there is no reason for them to surrender now to strong-arm toddler tactics. It is important to protect but not overprotect the baby. If the toddler is scolded for going near the baby, who then receives cuddles and comfort, this is the surest way to sow the seeds of an unhealthy sort of sibling rivalry.

I believe that in general babies are pretty unbreakable. Within certain limits the toddler should be allowed to play with the new arrival and poke him just as long as he does not cause significant hurt. While all this is going on the parents must try to act nonchalant and keep off the stage. It is best to stand a short distance away and out of the corner of one eye to watch that the baby suffers no harm.

As for putting fingers near the baby's eyes, I don't believe that this is often done with any malicious intent. It may be done to reward an over-fussy parent who jumps every time a finger starts to move. More often it is just an innocent exploration; after all, the eye of an infant is a beautiful and fascinating structure. It interests me, so why should it not interest a toddler?

Making the right introductions

- When pregnant, talk to the toddler about a new brother or sister and how mum will need a little helper if she is to cope. Discuss possible names for the baby. Mention the impending arrival of all those dirty nappies. Toddlers can relate to this, as they are world experts on bodily functions.

- When mum is in hospital, leave the toddler with someone he knows well, where he will feel secure, e.g. dad, grandma or a good close friend.

- These days toddlers are encouraged to visit mothers and new babies in the post-natal ward. It should be a fun time with lots of fuss over the toddler and a few little presents on hand to sweeten the occasion.

- Visitors who come to see the baby must first fuss over and notice the toddler. After all toddlers see themselves as the main attraction.

- Though tired and overprotective of the new infant, try hard to give the appearance of equal attention. This can be achieved by what I refer to as 'sidestream attention'. As you feed the baby, use the toddler as mother's little helper, talk or read a story. If you don't do this they will hijack your attention by demanding to latch on to the unoccupied breast, or stalk away and do such demolition that you have to give in.

- Of course mums are sensitive and highly protective of their new-born infants, but this must never be permitted to put a wedge between the toddler and baby. If you cuddle the baby and scold the toddler every time they come together, this is the surest way to create resentment and unhealthy rivalry.

- If handled well, most toddlers will accept their baby brother or sister without the slightest hiccup. A few will accept initially but when the baby is around the age of 6 months, there may be a backlash. At first new babies are seen as interesting animated dolls but at 6 months, when they sit up and start to do other clever things, they then become a great threat to the balance of power.

- Be reassured that most new babies and toddlers will come together well if we parents are sensible.

Conclusion

- Rivalry and competition are to be expected in both big and little humans.
- All young animals squabble and fight. It improves their reflexes and tones up their bodies, preparing them for a 'grown up' life.
- Our children are going to fight whether we like it or not, and it is best to keep out of their battles.
- Keep taunting toddlers occupied.
- Divert impending trouble.
- Don't take sides.
- Put little skirmishers in another room or out the back door. They can fight but they cannot expect an audience.
- When forced to intervene, use few words and the gentle tones of a regimental sergeant major.
- When all else fails, separate the two fighters with Time Out in different rooms.
- Life is much easier if we introduce toddlers to babies carefully and, give attention to both in a way that appears to be equal.

The Hyperactive Child
(Attention Deficit Hyperactivity Disorder)

When planning the first edition of this book, I deliberately left out any mention of hyperactivity, as it was surrounded by so much professional disagreement and confusion. But it occurred to me that if my highly trained colleagues were confused, how much more so must parents be? This persuaded me to include my own views on the subject. These days, hyperactivity is more correctly called Attention Deficit Hyperactivity Disorder (ADHD), or Attention Deficit Disorder (ADD); different names for the same thing.

There is great variation among children. At one extreme is the quiet, controlled, compliant child with a good attention span; at the other end is the negative, noisy, overactive, impulsive, disorganised child whose mind flits from topic to topic with all the skill of a drunk at a cocktail party. At what point normal activity merges with hyperactivity is anyone's guess. There is no clear dividing line, and it depends to a large extent on the tolerance of the observer. I do not think it matters what you call the condition, be it 'classic hyperactivity' or simply 'difficult overactive behaviour'. What is important is that the child's very individual package of problems is recognised and acted on accordingly.

In this chapter I describe the picture of the full-blown hyperactive. Many readers will have children who display only a few of these features, so they should not become alarmed. These behaviours are only important when they cause a child to underfunction academically and behave much worse than expected for the standard of parenting they receive.

The full-blown hyperactive

The most widely known name is 'hyperactivity' or the 'hyperactive child syndrome'. Although we know the condition we are talking about, it seems that whatever label we use it will be deemed wrong by the academic nitpickers. Although a high level of activity is usually present, other behaviours, such as poor concentration span, poor impulse control and poor social skills can be far more damaging to the child. If activity level is not the major problem, many people resent the word 'activity' appearing in any form on the label. A 'hyperkinetic' child is just a pseudo-scientific way of saying exactly the same thing as a 'hyperactive' child. It is a clever piece of medical mumbo jumbo but it is no better.

Many behaviours make up the condition,[13] so a less specific title is often favoured. One of the oldest of these is 'minimal brain damage', but this is disliked because it incorrectly indicates that something has damaged the brain. As this is unlikely and can never be demonstrated, it seems an unnecessary diagnosis. A more popular title is 'minimal brain dysfunction', which indicates that there is a minimal difference in the functioning of the normal brain. It is as if the television is working well but the fine tuning is slightly out of calibration and this gives rise to the minor differences that make up the syndrome. I used to favour this label to describe this group of behaviours, but it's now out of date. As already mentioned, the titles which are now used are 'Attention Deficit Disorder' (ADD) or 'Attention Deficit Hyperactivity Disorder' (ADHD). This places the main emphasis on a lack of concentration, which is associated with a troublesome cluster of other behaviours.

I urge the reader not to get bogged down in all the finer points of terminology. My feeling is that as long as you recognise that there is an imprecise group of behaviours which cause difficulties, and require treatment in a certain way, then the precise label is unimportant. For the purposes of this chapter I am simply going to use the blanket term 'hyperactive'.

How common is it?

These problems are about six times more common in boys than in girls, which is, incidentally, the same male predominance that is evident in cases of dyslexia, autism and certain language difficulties. Owing to the vagaries of definition, it has always been difficult to know the exact incidence of this condition. We know that it has been described much more frequently in the United States than in England. This may be explained by British doctors' reluctance to diagnose the condition unless the 'human tornado' is seen in full flight before their very eyes. We doctors are strange people. We diagnose epilepsy based on medical history without actually seeing the child having a fit before us. Why not hyperactivity? Americans are, apparently, more prepared to believe the word of a shattered parent or the child's edgy teacher. As hyperactive children fluctuate greatly between their good and bad days, and as they may demonstrate little classic hyperactive behaviour when unstressed in the quiet of a doctor's surgery, the American view has to be correct.

I believe that about 10 per cent of all boys show a mild form of these behaviours. Most will pass unnoticed, though they will be more sparky to manage and may underachieve in terms of intellect at school. About 2 per cent of all boys have a major degree of hyperactivity and whatever we do, parents, teachers and the child himself will feel the impact. As one English expert recently told me: 'Maybe the most useful skill we can teach this 2 per cent is how to talk themselves out of trouble. They will need this every day as they pass through childhood.'

Hyperactivity is not just a Western diagnosis of modern trendies, it is universal and age-old. When a group of Beijing children were assessed equally with their American counterparts, the incidence was very similar.

History is full of hyperactives. I believe most of the greatest leaders, generals, dictators and despots came from this group. I can't believe that Caesar or Napoleon went off to bed at 8 p.m. each night with a warm cup of Ovaltine. I bet that they were busy, driving people.

When the Viking longships were loading up ready to sail to Britain, I expect the 'hypers' of the day were lined up on the quay hoping for a place. Sitting at home quietly weaving rugs was not their bag, whilst a bit of looting and pillaging was much more in tune with their temperament.

The cause

The main cause of 'busy-ness' in these busy little people, I believe, is not diet, or the decadence of the nineties, but heredity. Most of these children have at least one close relative, usually the father, with a similar make-up. Children of hyperactive parents adopted by average parents are often hyperactive, despite calm parenting. Children of non-hyperactive parents adopted by hyperactive parents rarely become hyperactive.

It is fascinating to look at the temperamental make-up of hyperactive relatives—doctors, bricklayers, expert mechanics, prime ministers and self-made business tycoons—who have many behaviours in common. As children, they were often like their own 'difficult' child. They were often either school drop-outs or late starters. They may still find it hard to sit quietly and relax, or stop fidgeting at home, except in front of the television. They are impulsive, often socially inept, and not all that easy to live with. Even those who seem academically brilliant still have some attention problems; they are often substandard in spelling and not avid social readers, for instance. Winston Churchill, Albert Einstein and Leonardo da Vinci are often quoted as people whose drive and other skills overcame some degree of 'hyperactive' handicap.

Studies that blame hyperactivity on parental handling usually fail to take heredity into account. The hard-to-live-with characteristics of a parent, which render the environment less than ideal, are often passed down by heredity. The result is a complex mix of heredity and environment which is never easy to untangle. Certainly poor parenting does cause behaviour problems but it is my belief that most true hyperactives were destined to be that way, long before their parents had even held them. Of course the way we handle these children will either ease or exacerbate that predetermined problem.

The features

Although no two hyperactive children are identical, a group of common features will, to some extent, appear in most.[14] Some have a 'full house', exhibiting every possible problem, others have a smaller selection. The effects they have depend on the specific features involved, their severity, and the ability of the parents to cope with a child who is often far from easy.

At birth

Many hyperactives are easy babies, but some make their presence felt from the earliest days. The worst are extremely irritable, hard to comfort, and cause difficulties for the new mum and everyone else with whom they come into contact. Every hospital nursery for the newborn has at least one of these noisy little people, who often find themselves exiled to a far corner for the protection of the other babies and the staff. I believe that this behaviour is part of their tense temperamental type but in the nineties, it is often fashionable to diagnose these children as suffering from oesophageal reflux. The belief is that the acid stomach contents leak out of the baby's stomach. This burns their oesophagus, it hurts and they become irritable and scream. I accept that many of these babies do reflux milk out of the stomach but so do a high proportion of normal, relaxed babies. I believe that the tense temperament is common but an irritated oesophagus is more of a rarity. I have seen many babies called reflux who later went on to be diagnosed as hyperactive. Other hyperactives at this age tend to sleep poorly and respond slowly to comfort.

The first year

Though many hyperactives may initially behave well in the maternity hospital, some start to show their true colours soon after they arrive home. Sleep patterns tend to become erratic, there is more irritability and crying, and the frequent appearance of the 'evening colic'.

Even as babies, hyperactive children tend to have very little patience, disliking such things as long car trips or stops for a good gossip in the supermarket. They are not the sort of children who enjoy lying on their back contemplating the ceiling all day, and they inevitably become the sort of adults who are unlikely to sit on mountain-tops contemplating their navels. Being propelled down a busy street in a fast-moving baby buggy is their idea of fun. They can't wait to get up on their feet and become less frustrated and irritable when this is achieved. 'Baby walkers' are often condemned by physiotherapists and child safety workers but they often give these children a degree of mobility that suits their level of impatience.

As well as this, sleep problems often continue, as does a dislike of sitting on anyone's knee and in some, a reluctance to be comforted. Surprisingly most children later diagnosed as ADHD started off as remarkably easy babies. Perhaps they were saving themselves!

The toddler

Hyperactives don't have to walk, run and climb earlier than other children but one thing is certain, once they are mobile they all have an incredible facility for 'getting into things'. Cupboards are ransacked in the twinkling of an eye, and mess quickly replaces the order that existed in the days before they found their legs.

Towards the age of 2, activity often increases, accompanied by an intolerable volume of high spirited noise. The general behaviour has much in common with that of the average toddler but it is amplified to be many times worse. The hyperactive child has a low threshold of tolerance when things do not go according to plan, and restricting his environment will cause problems; his behaviour will be particularly bad if he is stuck indoors on wet days. He likes to be busy outside, which he finds infinitely preferable to sitting quietly doing puzzles, pencil work or following some early-reading programme. Attention is limited, and the child will flit butterfly-like from task to task. Sleep often shows a special pattern; the child may rise early in the morning and find it almost impossible to settle at night if excited. Despite what is written in many books, these children generally sleep well once they have managed to calm down. Many of these children are also compulsive 'touchers', handling everything they pass, a characteristic that frequently leads to multiple breakages and a trail of debris. You don't bring these toddlers through the china department at your local store.

Despite all these difficulties, the hyperactive child is generally a loving and often immature and very sensitive child who needs a structured, calm environment and parents with unlimited patience.

School age

As a toddler, the behaviour that causes most concern is all the incessant flitting about. Once the child reaches school, he is confined to a classroom and made to conform and mix as an equal. School reports state that he is easily distracted, disruptive and inattentive. He fidgets and finds it hard to keep quiet or sit still. He disturbs others, goes walkabout and is slow to get work finished. He will be easily distracted, turning when a pencil drops or an aeroplane flies by. He maintains his work performance only if stood over and given great encouragement.

It is the problem of concentration that caused the hyperactive condition to be renamed 'attention deficit disorder'. This is always present in toddlers but it is only at school age that its full destructive power is revealed. Luckily, attention usually improves in the first three years at school, although in many it continues to be a significant problem throughout life.

The attention deficit surprises many people, as it is highly selective. The child may play a favourite video game with great accuracy but when asked to learn spelling or perform some reading, interest disappears within seconds. This attention deficit also shows in speech patterns. Some children will ramble on at length, or lose track of what they are saying in mid-sentence, owing to lack of concentration. Others will rudely interrupt your conversation because, unless they say their piece immediately, it will be lost forever.

Impulsiveness is another big problem and leads to a child who invariably 'leaps before he looks'. This is particularly dangerous on busy roads but it can also land the child in all sorts of playground trouble when he impulsively punches the boy who's teasing him without first checking if a teacher is looking. Many of these children are already clumsy, and impulsiveness contributes to this as the child trips and bumps into things because of lack of planning and forethought. There is often a genuine element of poor co-ordination, poor 'flow of movement', and a difficulty in performing two actions at the same time. Many are somewhat disorganised, having difficulty in discriminating right from left, tying shoelaces, putting on clothes the right way round and planning ahead. A few are so disorganised they are walking disaster zones. As one mother described her son to me: 'He's so disorganised that I believe he could eat a Mars Bar and brush his teeth at the same time'.

These children are hard to satisfy. They interrogate their parents mercilessly when they want something, never knowing when to give up. Give them one chocolate and they'll want six. They'll go on and on until those around are ready to scream. For some of their parents, life at home is about as relaxing as living in the midst of the Spanish Inquisition.

Specific learning problems are unfortunately very frequent with many of these children, who perform much more poorly at school than their intelligence scoring would indicate. The difficulty in concentrating reliably is the major problem but specific weaknesses in spelling, reading, comprehension and mathematics are also common.

A degree of social handicap is also common. Like most children, hyperactives crave other children's friendship and attention. Sadly they are often unable to achieve this and will resort to hopping around outside a group of playing children 'acting silly', poking and annoying them in an attempt to be noticed. Play is always much better with one good friend rather than in a group. With the concentration, learning, clumsiness and social problems, it is little wonder that many of these children receive a severe battering to their already weak self-esteem. Low frustration tolerance and overexcitability are very common, and their moods tend to swing rapidly—some days are excellent and others a complete write-off.

The attention deficit, social problems and specific learning problems often pass unnoticed at school and the stressed child resorts to bad behaviour as a cry for help. I believe all children basically wish to succeed, to be popular, and mix well with their mates. When a child has difficulties in academic, sport and social areas, there may be little left to excel in but nasty, naughty behaviour.

I have described the wide behavioural spectrum that may be seen in the hyperactive child, and in his lesser cousins, the minor fidgets, fiddlers and non-concentrators. Whatever the label, many of the problems described are common and respond best to special methods of treatment. I have described them in detail not in an attempt to label normal children hyperactive but rather to explain to worried parents with unhappy, under-achieving and undiagnosed children that there may well be something more than simple bad behaviour at the root of it all.

CLASS OF 1993

Symptoms of hyperactivity

The older hyperactive child may have many but not necessarily all of the following symptoms.

Poor attention
- a poor listener, forgets instructions, lists or messages, is easily distracted
- visually inattentive, blind to changes, skips paragraphs when reading, blind to oncoming hazards
- absorbed in own thoughts, a dreamer, spaced out

Impulsive
- leaps before he looks, mouth is in motion before mind is in gear, hits before he thinks and is consequently often branded as aggressive, easily led

Never satisfied
- interrogates parents mercilessly, gets stuck on one idea, gets a reward and immediately wants more, doesn't learn easily from experience

Overactive
- irritable baby, likes to be on the move
- overactive toddler, almost motor-driven
- fidgety, disruptive, easily distracted schoolchild
- prefers to be outside, worse with noise, tension or crowds

Variable performance
- behaviour fluctuates from day to day, some days does well at school, on others might just as well have stayed at home

Disorganisation
- right/left confusion
- late in learning to tie shoelaces, puts clothes on back to front, messy eater, poor flow of movement, finds it hard to perform two actions at same time, messy, finds it difficult to do things in sequence

Social handicap
- wants to mix as an equal but can't bring this about, speaks without thinking, a poor loser, low tolerance of failure, will act silly to gain attention in a group

Clumsiness
- is particularly clumsy

- impulsiveness causes accidents

Poor self-esteem
- probably present early on, exacerbated by social and academic failure

Language problems
- forgets what he's saying in mid-sentence

- interrupts others due to impulsiveness and fear of forgetting

- gets confused over yesterday/tomorrow, earlier/later, etc.

Others
- specific learning problems: probably half will have some degree of weakness, for example, reading, spelling, maths, etc.

- sleep problems: can find it hard to settle at night and will be a restless sleeper

- touchy, rarely satisfied, irritating yet very sensitive

Treatment—better everyday management

All toddlers should be receiving clear, uncluttered messages from the mouths of their parents. This is particularly important for the hyperactive, who has not only a major concentration problem but also one that especially affects the listening memory.

Communication

Before talking with the child it is advisable to cut down as much extraneous noise as possible. Turn off the television, radio and food mixer, and wait for the dog to stop barking. First call the child's name clearly and enthusiastically to engage eye contact. Once looking eye to eye, give a clear message using the utmost economy of words and communicating with all modes, such as hands, eyebrows and body. Many parents bury their children under a mass of monotonous, unenthusiastic verbiage and then wonder why they don't listen. Good communication is not only vital for hyperactives but also highly desirable for all children and adults.

Structure and organisation

Hyperactives are, by nature, extremely disorganised, and they tend to spread a trail of disorganisation around them. Paradoxically, these children do not fare well without structure and organisation and it is in everyone's interest to introduce routine into their lives.

The child needs to know when it is time to get up, what he will have for breakfast, the days he is to go to school, and if any major happenings are going to take place that day. Problems arise when the child is faced with the unexpected, like friends dropping by, dad going off on a trip, or a very late bedtime one night. For the good of the child, it is best to run a tight ship, with life aboard as well-controlled and organised as possible.

In the older toddler or school-age child, I would make out a list of tasks for him to do each day around the house. These would be his sole responsibility, such as making his bed, feeding the cat, tidying up his toys or getting the mail. All this helps to give structure and responsibility to his life and encourages a greater awareness of what is going on in his environment. When out shopping, he should be encouraged to make purchases from friendly storekeepers, while mum waits outside to check that all goes well and the verbal messages do not get confused. This has the benefit of providing therapy for listening memory, responsibility and creating a feeling of usefulness and importance.

Behaviour modification therapy

As the child hurtles noisily around the house day in and day out, parents' patience eventually wears a bit thin. In spite of the best intentions, it is all too easy to slip into a negative rut, handing out punishments left, right and centre, instead of thinking up positive ways of altering the child's behaviour. Hyperactives get wound up by tension and agitation, so this worsens their already difficult behaviour. They are sensitive children, and they will soon get the impression that 'nothing they do is right', which will eventually lead to loss of all self-esteem and much long-term sadness.

To guard against this, the child's behavioural antics should be viewed through the proverbial rose-tinted glasses. When good behaviour seems almost extinct, the tired parental brain must try to focus on any behaviour that is nearly good and then build on that. The danger with hyperactives is that they generate a great deal of negative tension as they storm around the house, so that when that brief moment of peace and quiet occurs, parents are tempted to give a sigh of relief and sit down and relax, thus ignoring the highly desirable behaviour instead of encouraging it.

Under the age of $3^1/_2$, praise and attention are good rewards when the child is constructive, helpful or tries hard. After this age, stars, stickers, stamps, sweets and small plastic toys are extra boosters.

Secure, childproof house

With all small children, a secure, childproof house leads to fewer anxieties and thus less attention being given for the wrong reasons. With the difficult hyperactive, this is even more important, as careful planning is needed to reduce the negative 'vibes' and increase the positive messages.

The school-age hyperactive

It is a sad fact that many happy little hyperactives lose much of their 'sunny disposition' once they go to school. Restrictions like having to sit still and keep quiet cause problems, which are greatly exacerbated when the children try to compete academically using their easily distracted, poorly concentrating brains.

These children fluctuate from day to day, and teachers often tell me that on bad days they might as well stay at home as they are impossible to work with. They also fluctuate from year to year and although maturation and environment have some role, I place part of the blame squarely on their teachers' shoulders. The punitive work-to-rule, rigid teacher will get nowhere with one of these children and, even worse, he has the power to destroy any vestige of self-confidence the child may have, as well as the will to learn. The enthusiastic, sensitive teacher who shows interest and gives as much one-to-one care as possible will boost the child's self-confidence and do well.

Hyperactive children often have to invest twice the amount of effort to achieve half the success of their classmates, because of their concentration and specific learning problems. If this is not recognised and the teacher looks only at results rather than effort, the child will cease to try and, let's face it, who would blame him? I don't believe that schoolchildren set out to be lazy, badly behaved or nasty. I am certain that if given the chance to be top of their class, socially popular and good at sports, they would grab the chance at once. Sadly, when none of these attributes seems available, the child has the option of either plodding on in the hope of getting some sort of recognition one day, or throwing in the sponge and becoming the class clown.

Both teachers and parents must recognise that these are special children who often have unrecognised problems of learning, concentration, mixing, staying still, frustration, impulse and emotional control. One could write a whole book on this subject but my main message here is to 'get off the child's back'. Stop focusing on failures; build up the child's success both in school and in outside activities.

The Feingold diet

Dr Ben Feingold, a former professor of allergy in San Francisco, first suggested a relationship between diet and hyperactivity in 1973. He noted that our diet contained over 2700 'intentional' food additives and as the quantity of these substances had increased over the years, so had the reported rates of hyperactivity and learning problems. His criticism was not solely of artificial preservatives, colours and flavours; he also blamed many natural substances usually considered part of a normal healthy diet.

He claimed 'rapid dramatic changes in behaviour, sleep and school work' in over 50 per cent of children put on his special diet. His ideas were soon headline news, and his diet spread like wildfire.

In the 1990s, it is so firmly accepted in the lay press that our preservative filled diets cause hyperactivity, that what I am about to say seems almost indecent. Despite this acceptance, ten years of worldwide research has only shown that a small minority of hyperactives get any benefit from this diet. In making this statement, I am all too aware of the multitude of parents who swear by the diet. When I talk to them, they are adamant that their child's behaviour 'blows apart' soon after any dietary indiscretion. I also know of many studies that report behavioural improvements when the parents know their child is on the diet. I do not dispute reported improvement, but I question whether this is due to the diet itself, or simply to the more disciplined lifestyle that is needed to implement the diet. Or is it simply the placebo effect? For instance, it is known that if simple distilled water is injected into a patient, instead of a pain-relieving drug, up to one-third of them miraculously lose their pain. There are many other such examples in medicine, ranging from patent cold cures and appetite stimulants to elixirs of youth and a whole panoply of tonics.

To ensure that the placebo effect does not influence the parents' assessment of their child's behaviour on the diet, the only reliable trial is one that is 'blind', in which the parents do not know when the diet is or is not being taken. Following Feingold's publicity in the early 1970s, concern regarding food additives was expressed by many agencies from Congress down to the Federal Drug Administration. This led to a number of well-constructed trials[15] to test the Feingold hypothesis. The children studied were all claimed by their parents as being greatly helped by the diet. Each child was assessed to ensure that hyperactivity was indeed the correct diagnosis. At this point, it was found that many of the claimed hyperactive responders had been misdiagnosed and were not hyperactive children. Before starting each study, the children were carefully assessed both on and off the diet, to give an

accurate baseline reading of behaviour from which to study possible changes once the diet was challenged.

To challenge the diet in a way that was completely blind to
parents, the child, and the independent observers, posed great difficulties. One group overcame this by arranging for all food to be
brought to the home on a sort of 'meals-on-wheels' arrangement.
This gave the trial organisers the power to secretly tamper with
the diet at will. Other groups placed the children on a strict diet,
and each day gave one additional item, which could be secretly
modified when they wished. One trial gave a daily capsule that
usually contained an inactive liquid but about once a week it was
heavily laced with the incriminated artificial colouring. Another
gave odd-looking cookies, which were usually as pure as if straight
from grandma's oven but occasionally were peppered with all manner of additives. One group gave a daily bottle of an odd-looking
homemade soda pop. Usually, this was pure and natural but once a
week was peppered with all sorts of hidden 'nasties'. As all this
secret modification of diet was going on, the behaviours, concentration, activity, and performance of certain tasks were being
assessed by teachers, parents and various other experts. Those
assessing the children had no knowledge of what diet the child was
getting, until the code was broken at the end of the trial.[16]

Feingold diet conclusions, 1996

When Dr Feingold first popularised his diet he said that 50 per cent
of hyperactive children would be helped. Now, seventeen years on,
this figure is still true, albeit only partly.

If parents know their child is taking the special diet, 50 per cent
see a significant improvement. If one then takes these improved
children and, unknown to the parents, secretly challenges them
with food additives, the figure goes down. Studies of these secret
challenges show that in only one in ten cases can the observers tell
whether the child is on or off the diet. This one in ten of the 50 per
cent who had been seen to respond represents only 5 per cent of all
hyperactives.

The 5 per cent figure may seem very low but it has been confirmed by many good studies from around the world.[17] With such
conclusive evidence that should, by rights, be the end of the debate,
but I still have my doubts. I find it hard to believe that so many
sensible parents could be so wrong. I am also aware of at least one
study which claims a much better response rate.[18] I note that most
workers looked at school-age children but there is evidence that
pre-school children may be more diet responsive. There is also evidence that when psychologists, teachers and parents all observed a

child's behaviour, the parents were more sensitive to realising behavioural change than those professionals who ran the studies.

My present stand on diet is that it certainly helps a proportion of children with behaviour problems. I don't believe it provides a cure, more a percentage improvement. The internationally accepted figure of 5 per cent response is, I am sure, too low. However, in reality, I cannot see the true figure rising much above 15 per cent.

If diet was really a dramatic cause of behaviour problems in children, I cannot see such confusion still remaining after seventeen years of debate. Let us hope that by the next edition of *Toddler Taming* things will be clearer.

The diet

There is a popular belief that this diet is all about cutting out lollies, lemonade, junk foods, artificial colourings and preservatives. Sure it discourages these but that is only half the picture.

Many natural substances and health foods must also be considered. For example, oranges and apples are high in nature's preservatives and should be avoided. Honey is under slight suspicion, yet pure Queensland sugar or syrup is safe.

To adhere strictly to the diet, care is needed with certain household substances. Toothpaste, dishwashing detergents, aerosols and perfumes should all be avoided initially.

Dietitians reviewing the composition of Feingold's original diet have come up with some considerable ambiguities. For example, Feingold banned orange and apple juice, relying on pineapple juice instead. Now we find that this has just the same unwanted natural chemicals as the other two.

All this just adds to the confusion, so if you're considering the diet, I advise you to use a modern, updated Feingold version, or better still go for a strict exclusion model devised and supervised by a qualified dietitian.

So should you bother to give the diet a go? I think there's no harm in having a try, all I ask is that you view the results with your eyes open and stop if there is no definite and sustained benefit. In my experience the greatest culprits are natural salicylates (e.g. orange and other juices, berry fruits, tomatoes and even Vegemite). Then there are the preservatives as found in some packaged foods and cordials. Further down the list come nitrites (e.g. ham, bacon, etc.) with the artificial colours and the amines (e.g. chocolate) at the end.

Be sure to get a proper diet and stick to it. I might further suggest that it is only fair for the whole family to go on the diet together, thus avoiding discrimination against just one child. You never know, your partner might just suddenly become easier to live with.

Medicines

Medication is rarely needed in the preschool child with ADHD, but some 3- to 5-year-olds with major problems dramatically improve.

Suggest that a hyperactive child be treated with stimulant drugs and howls of disapproval will be sent up from Ayers Rock to Yellowstone Park. I find it quite amazing that while the Feingold diet still remains scientifically unproven for all but a minority, it is nevertheless fully accepted. Meanwhile the use of medication, which has been shown by much scientific evidence to have advantages, is dismissed. How perverse human nature is.

The problem is that the drugs used are relatives of amphetamine (Methylphenidate-Ritalin and Dextroamphetamine) and, tarred by this association, they catch all the flak levelled at the 'speed' and 'purple hearts' abuse of twenty-five years ago. Having combed the international literature on the subject, I am assured that, when properly used in childhood, these are not drugs of addiction.

We often forget that amphetamines were first used on hyperactive children in 1937 and Ritalin has been widely used since 1958. Yet there is still no evidence of major side-effects and no increase in the incidence of the abuse of any drugs at an older age.

The problem with medication is that it may be overused. Medication is far too often given to a child in place of simple behavioural advice or facing up to a family problem.

Research papers from many centres now show that 80 to 90 per cent of school age children with a major degree of ADHD will respond to medication. Most preschool aged children are managed without medicines and when used the success rate is slightly lower than for the older child.

The short term benefits of stimulants are proven without doubt. The long term benefits have not yet been researched. After forty years of use these drugs are seen as safe and certainly not addictive when correctly prescribed in ADHD.

Other treatments

Such is the frustration and ill-founded feeling of guilt experienced by the parents of hyperactive children that they will grasp at anything that offers some chance of help. It is a long, difficult course they tread, often a steep, uphill one with little help from either doctors or educationalists. It is, therefore, little wonder that they open their wallets and throw their money to all manner of people who claim that they can provide miracle cures.

It is fashionable these days to state that hypoglycaemia (lack of sugar in the blood) or hyperglycaemia (too much sugar in the blood) both upset the hyperactive. Once again, there is absolutely no evidence to back this up, although it is a view held most adamantly by some parents. Equally, vitamin therapy, particularly with the B group vitamins, is claimed to help specific learning problems and many of the associated behaviour patterns. Once again, this is completely unproven.

Hyperactive children tend to be clumsy and poorly co-ordinated, so occupational therapy should be given to improve their motor skills. This must be viewed in the same light as giving remedial teaching, as both may improve only one specific area, leaving many others untreated and giving little general improvement in the condition as a whole. What occupational therapy may promote is improved self-esteem and better physical abilities, which help social mixing and leisure-time activities. Remedial teaching may have benefits as the child functions best in the one-to-one environment, and any gains may help his happiness at school, which has inevitable repercussions on his behaviour.

Other children are hung in nets and treated with swinging, movement and stimulation of the vestibular apparatus in the middle ear. Claims are made about the benefit of this treatment but, once again, there is no conclusive evidence that it works.

Whether your child has devastating hyperactivity or is just a small-time fidget, help is needed in many areas. No single treatment by itself is enough. They need sensible behaviour management, self-esteem boosting, help with social skills, some remedial work, with the possibility of some medication in the older child. Children with minor problems do well with a little treatment, while those with major problems cause much heartache and concern for most of their childhood years.

I do not agree with the view that major hyperactive features resolve with age. They change and mellow but many are still there in adulthood. The difference is that once out of school, we are permitted to camouflage our frailties and promote our strengths. We also learn how to get around problems, while determination does much to help concentration. I believe this hyper type temperament is often in evidence from the cradle to the grave. Many who have just read this chapter will see this not only in the child but possibly in themselves or their partner.

Happiness and self-confidence are important, not only for the child but also the parents. Both need support and encouragement, never criticism.

18

Playgroups, Pre-Schools and Early Learning

Eighty years ago children lived out their earliest years in an extended family of mum, dad and grandparents. They watched, listened and learned as they served a sort of apprenticeship for adulthood. Nowadays, in our more mobile society, there seems to be a move away from this natural approach towards formal, structured learning. Children from the earliest days attend day care, playgroups and pre-schools.

Obsessive, driving parents arrange swimming and gym then cram in reading, number work and music lessons on top of all that.

Is this really a great step forward, or is it a misguided stagger to the side? As a doctor who spends much of his time trying to support extremely sad parents with handicapped children, I admit I am heavily biased. I think that those of us who are privileged enough to have normal, healthy children should give thanks for what we've got, give them the best love, attention and example we can provide, and not seek to turn them from normal children into something super-normal. Happiness and success in life depend on many things other than academic tutoring. These efforts often do more for the givers' own egos and hang-ups than help the child to cope better with the real, harsh world they will have to live in.

Playgroups

Here young children come along with their mothers, play, attempt to mix with each other and, while all this is going on, the mums chat, socialise and watch. This has advantages for both children and parents. The toddler experiences a little bit of independence yet is never far from mum. Although he is too young to play with other children, he plays happily alongside them and generally enjoys their company. Often children have strange ways of showing their enjoyment, as this is the peak age for biting, kicking, pushing and not sharing. They are also directed in some simple structured play and get their sticky hands on a multitude of new toys.

By attending playgroup the isolated mum avoids becoming entombed in her own home. She hears what problems other mothers are experiencing, then sees she is normal and not alone. Playgroups are great places to compare notes and pool resources with one's fellow toddler tamers.

Pre-schools

Pre-schools take children from about 3 years old until school enrolment. The child stays at the centre, where all care and teaching is in the hands of the pre-school staff. The directors of our pre-schools are constantly being sniped at by pushy parents who think that they provide too much play and not enough 'learning'. Despite this, the staff hold firmly to their beliefs that this is the time for the child to enjoy and to develop a wide spectrum of skills needed for life and school. They provide an opportunity for gentle separation in a child who has previously been close day and night to his parents. They also give a quality of child care that is in most cases as supportive as the child would receive at home, thus making the transition a bearable one. This is particularly reassuring to those families who by necessity, or through choice, have to leave their children during the day while they work.

The best way to describe the activities of pre-school is 'learning how to learn'. The child is taught basic skills necessary for life at school. These include sharing, mixing, sitting, settling, listening and sticking to a particular task. Many children find this immensely difficult at first but the skilled, trained teachers know how to hold a child's waning interest and encourage him to sit and finish a task, bringing some structure and gentle discipline into the child's life. The skilled teacher builds on the child's natural curiosity to develop an enthusiasm for learning and a quest for knowledge.

In pre-school, the child learns to communicate not just in speech but in all sorts of other ways. Using imaginative play their little bodies tell stories just as skilfully as their mouths. Speech accelerates at pre-school, as all those busy little beings chatter among themselves. By speech, I do not mean that regurgitated, parrot-like repetition of clever sayings and nursery rhymes they will come up with, but the organisation of thought to produce appropriate original expression. I think that pre-schools provide some of the best speech therapy available in the Southern Hemisphere.

The child also mixes, learns to share, to take turns and to respect other people's property and wishes. He learns much about structure and discipline, which will prove invaluable when he enters school. As he separates from his mother, he starts to experience a little independence.

The child is not the only one who benefits from pre-school. At last mother has some time to herself to 'recharge her batteries'. If there is a younger child in the family, he will now receive some valuable one-to-one care, which he deserves without competition from the older child. Not only does pre-school prepare the toddler for the separation of going to school, it also prepares the mother for her feelings of separation when she views the 'empty nest' after the child has flown to school, never again to be a toddler.

Hints for starting pre-school

Usually by the age of 3 years and certainly by 4 years our toddlers are ready for pre-school. At such a young age there is however a great variation in each child's ability to separate. Some who are militantly independent will cut loose from mum at the gate leaving her empty-handed as they target in on the main action. The majority will be more tentative, being more clingy and cautious for the first week or so. Then there are a few for whom the start of pre-school will be very stressful.

Whatever sort of child you have, separation will be smoothest if you prepare in advance and don't rush the first day. When you leave, do so decisively and if in trouble listen to the advice of the pre-school director.

In the months before, talk about pre-school, visit, walk past and mentally prepare. Get them used to their new gear, the rug, the kindy bag, the lunch box, etc. Be sensible with clothes, taking care to avoid those high fashion designs with stiff belts and buttons that take on the style of a straight-jacket when toilet urgency is at its peak.

The food you send should be simple, nutritious and easy to eat. You don't have to compensate for your guilt about leaving your child at pre-school by giving out chocolate and other unsuitable pay-offs. Make sure that it is clear which packet is for playlunch and which is for the main sitting. Food should be packed in an easily opened lunch box with the child's name clearly marked. Don't triple wrap in some film that may be environmentally friendly but even the infant Harry Houdini could not find the opening.

On starting day set out in good time, don't rush and try not to transmit your uneasiness to the toddler. It has to be a bit stressful for them. Remember how you felt the last time you changed jobs or came cold into a party to face thirty complete strangers? If we big people get tense, it is likely the little ones will do the same.

Go in with purpose, hang up the bag and take a tour of the premises. The toilets should be first stop as these will be much used in the year that follows. Many little people find the lack of privacy and so much collective flush a bit mind boggling but will get used to it. On the subject of toilets, don't worry if there are a few wet pants. The pre-school staff will have been there many times before; they know that recently trained toddlers are prone to leak in times of stress. Put a spare pair of pants in the bag and leave the staff to do the worrying.

Don't rush your departure on the first day. Sit and play and give them time to settle. If a working mum, arrange some cover for that day so as not to drop off and rush away. When it is time to go, be sure they have your contact number, say goodbye and then leave decisively.

Like General MacArthur, say 'I will return,' and like the General, keep the promise. Explain, 'John, you will play, have lunch, a little snooze, more playing and then I will be back'.

Don't use transparent untruths like 'I am just going out to move the car'. Even a 3-year-old knows it's a mighty poor car that takes five hours to move!

If leaving does pose a problem, ask the director for advice. Most children will settle well, though for a few it sometimes becomes necessary to postpone pre-school for a few months. Some will settle well but after a couple of weeks they start to drag their feet as the novelty wears off. This is rarely more than a minor hiccup.

At home be prepared for a tireder toddler. In some instances their behaviour may be worse as they use their mum as a whipping boy to work out their tensions of the day. Beds that were dry may become temporarily wet but this is usually only for a few days. Generally, pre-school brings a maturity and better understanding of sharing, mixing and living at peace with one's fellow man and that includes mothers and fathers, though possibly not brothers and sisters.

Producing the infant Einstein

The word 'advanced' means different things to different people. Playing the piano at 4, or being two years academically superior to one's peer group at 5 are all signs of being advanced. But will this necessarily continue and be a help in later life? Being a vivid communicator, resourceful, reliable, sensible, determined, proficient at sport, popular with one's peers, and a keen observer and lover of life, may be much more desirable qualities to help a child struggle through his three score years and ten in a difficult world.

Children who enjoy learning should be encouraged but not pushed to ridiculous lengths. Parents must also be cautioned that many apparently clever tricks are in reality much less spectacular than they would appear.

Rote rituals

Rote learning (learning by memory) has some benefits but it does not always indicate brilliance or academic success. I often see a child whose parents ask him to stand up and count to a hundred for me. As these are rote learned skills they cut little ice with this singularly unimpressed doctor. The child may sound very impressive until asked the simple question: 'If you pass a field in which there are two cows and open the gate and let one out, how many cows would now be in the field?'—Silence! Rote learning is of no benefit in answering real-life problems unless you can think laterally.

Other parents ask their child to recite nursery rhymes, which is promptly done with all the skill of a trained parrot. Having heard about the three blind mice, I might then ask how many tails were cut off by the farmer's wife. Again rote skills are seen to be 'all show and no action', when it is obvious the child does not know what I am talking about. This lateral thinking is important in becoming a creative, intelligent person.

By lateral thinking I refer to the ability to be given one piece of information and use it to generalise for other situations. It is like a dog I know. Now Jake is a mad Rhodesian Ridgeback who has no lateral thinking, that is if he thinks at all. Last year poor Jake ran out on the road and was hit by a bus. He was badly hurt but recovered. Recently I asked his owner, 'Is Jake now more sensible on the road?'. The answer was that he was terrified of the spot where the bus hit him but was just as mad on every other road. Jake is a rote learner, he doesn't use his knowledge to generalise.

One 6-year-old autistic boy I work with has no speech, lives in a world of his own, and is severely and permanently handicapped. Despite this, each time I see him he takes a sheet of paper and as I talk to his parents he writes down with complete accuracy the name of every street he has passed on the way from his home to my clinic. He has an astonishing photographic memory but sadly this is no compensation for the multitude of real-life skills he does not possess.

General knowledge is another skill, most valuable for television quiz shows or to be dragged out as a party piece to impress, but it is more often than not rote learned information. For example, the child can be programmed to learn that there are seven days in a week, fifty-two weeks in a year, and 365 days in a year, but will he understand why his birthday was on a Tuesday last year and is on a Wednesday this year? Has he realised that all those figures don't add up and that there is one more day than fifty-two weeks in each year, which makes it a whole new ball game? And as for leap years, he has really started to think when he understands them.

Our aim in life must be to teach children the basic skills of learning, then encourage and enthuse them to work from there. Computers may indeed store an amazing amount of information but the human brain is infinitely superior when programmed in the right way.

Flash cards, sight words and early reading

Some parents with a certain upbringing and philosophy of child rearing can't wait to secure a place for their children in the academic rat race. Reading is one skill they wish to promote, and although they generally receive little encouragement from pre-school directors or infant teachers, they undertake the task themselves.

This generally does little harm, and although there is no doubt that at the age of 6 some of these children read much better than their 'uncrammed' contemporaries, there is little evidence that at the age of 8 or 10 these gains will still be apparent. There is also the very real danger that being forced to read and pushed too hard at too early an age can turn some children off the whole idea, and a definite resistance will appear which might hinder an otherwise normal approach to the subject.

In many cases, it is just about impossible to teach active young toddlers to read anyway, as their interests lie more in the areas of running, playing, helping mum or dad, and just enjoying the fun life of being a toddler. Let them have that time, it is all too short as it is.

One may ask why giving a 4-year-old the reading skills of a 6-year-old wouldn't be beneficial. Once again, it is because it is a photographic memory, rote learning exercise, which does no long-term good. These skills can be left until a much later date.

Some young children may be taught to recognise 'sight words' at the age of 3. This is a skill that greatly excites most parents, who are convinced that their child is a reincarnated Einstein. In fact, this skill can be imparted to any child who is prepared to settle and concentrate and has a good photographic memory for differences in patterns. This is the same skill that is used in recognising trade names or a favourite chocolate bar. To encourage this skill, flash cards are used (little cards on which the words are written), and when the appropriate response is given the child is immediately rewarded. Pigeons and chimpanzees have been taught to recognise shapes using very similar techniques. Of course the animal experiments can only reach a certain point because, although it is possible to reward a pigeon for recognising certain shapes, it is impossible to teach it to use its knowledge to work out unfamiliar shapes not previously encountered.

To read properly, recognising patterns is only the beginning. The real skill is in being able to look at a word, sound out its letters, apply a multitude of rules, short cuts and exclusions, and then come up with the right pronunciation. Once this skill has been mastered, words never seen before can be read with ease. Coupled with good reading comprehension, this is the real adult reading skill. Unfortunately, the human brain is not sufficiently mature to handle all this computation before the developmental age of 6, and it is then that we see who are destined to be the good or the bad readers. All this will probably have little relationship to the number of sight words the child could recognise at the age of 5.

Teaching a child to recognise words is not the same as teaching a child to 'read'. I believe that early reading is little more than a clever trick, but research could well prove me wrong. In a large group of toddlers, some are destined to do well academically, some will be average, and some will underachieve. It is known that parents who care and spend much time with their children will usually produce better academic results in their children than those who are uninterested. It is also known that the child who settles, concentrates and is receptive to learning at the age of 4 is more likely to succeed academically than the disorganised, over-active, poor-concentrator.

Although statistics may show that the recognition of sight words at an early age is associated with future academic success, I believe that teaching reading has nothing to do with it. To read successfully at pre-school age, you must have some basic academic ability and be encouraged by an enthusiastic teacher. This pre-requisite immediately excludes all those with a degree of dyslexia, developmental delay and children from non-reading households. Once these are screened out, it stands to reason that the academic future of this group must be more successful. Early reading is an imprecise indicator of ability, not the reason for that ability.

Swimming

Swimming is very good for toddlers, not only for obvious safety reasons but also because it provides a valuable and enjoyable form of exercise and family fun.

A 1939 study looked at the reactions of forty-two infants when put in the water. In the first four months of life, a reflex swimming pattern was observed with the child moving his arms and legs in a rhythmic manner, with vague similarities to freestyle swimming. At 4 months, this reflex disappeared, and the child started to show totally disorganised movement in the water. This is the stage when little children splash and enjoy water but do little more than that with their arms and legs. It was well into the second year that the first, feeble attempts at real swimming, some voluntary semi-purposeful movements, were noted. From here it was only a matter of time, brain maturity and practice until the little children swam.[19]

Swimming from the earliest days of life is to be recommended, if it is used as a form of fun for the whole family to enjoy together. The little baby holds tight to his mother or father with one hand, and the other splashes in the water. Later they paddle by themselves under close supervision before being fitted with some sort of flotation device that gives them more independence. A form of 'dog paddle' swimming develops somewhere between the third and sixth birthdays, depending on the child's determination and the practice he gets. Swimming for older children provides a healthy sport, which children of all physical and intellectual abilities can enjoy equally.

There is a modern trend, perpetrated in the name of early swimming, to toss babies into the water soon after birth. This, like early reading, has little long-term advantage; a communal family 'splash down' is many times more therapeutic.

Child wonders: who are we trying to help?

All good parents want the best for their children and put a great deal of effort into encouraging and helping them to achieve. This should, of course, be supported but it must never be allowed to progress to unhealthy extremes. Unfortunately, the efforts of some parents soon escalate from an admirable action into an obsession, and academic goals blind them to the realities of life. For some, this is a gradual and unintentional progression but for others, showing off a brilliant child is a crutch to prop up their own crumbling egos.

Recently I talked to a journalist who had just researched an article on teaching youngsters to read at an early age. In the process, she had come up against some amazing parents and their children. One 6-year-old boy was so advanced that his parents insisted that he was bored with school and arranged for him to be promoted to a class with 8-year-olds. Dad installed a home computer for his personal use and then arranged for extra home tutoring in the hope of widening the gap even further. Music lessons were also arranged and the child was largely withdrawn from activities that involved mixing with children of inferior abilities. Certainly he had become an academic genius but, as he had little exposure to anything that might loosely be termed 'fun', he was a pale, indoor child who was socially and physically backward. He was viewed by the school and his parents as an interesting showpiece and by his classmates as a boring nerd. To a sceptic like myself, it seemed that these parents were hiding from their own hang-ups in their obsessive crusade to produce a 'superchild'. Sadly, the other children in the family, who were 'only normal', were to a large extent ignored in the process.

Another family had a 3-year-old boy who was doing remarkably well in the second year of a reading programme. As this was so time-consuming, the parents hired an interesting lady from overseas to teach the child. Her daily task was to tutor the boy in reading, then to talk away to him in her native tongue so that the child would become at the same time academically advanced and bilingual. You might ask, where were the parents while all this was going on? Well, being busy professional people, they were out at work all day.

Just because pushy parents engage in these programmes, all you normal well-adjusted parents must not let yourselves be made to feel either inferior or guilty. Reading and jabbering away in a foreign tongue at the age of 4 may satisfy some parents' egos, but I can assure you children much prefer to learn through love and living.

Learning through living

The greatest educationalists our children will ever meet in their lives are their parents. The value of watching, listening, playing and just being around them must never be underestimated.

During the average day all manner of adventures take place in a toddler's life. A fire engine clattering by or a big, barking dog will spark off his imagination and he will want to verbalise his experiences to anyone who will listen. On the way to the shops he might recognise an advertisement previously seen on television, or he may want to talk about the shops, the cars and anything else of interest that passes. In the supermarket, he counts out the oranges, gets the bigger, not the smaller, packet, and learns to spot subtle differences on the labels. Once home, he will start matching and sorting as he helps to put away the groceries—all accompanied by non-stop chatter. In all this, the toddler looks to his parents for reassurance and guidance.

He listens to mum and dad, copying their sayings and asking innumerable questions. With this, his verbal abilities increase, and so does his general knowledge. He helps with the household chores, learning to run simple messages and generally being 'mother's little helper'. Unbreakable dishes are washed in the sink and helping with the cooking is a particular favourite. Pastry is rolled, cut and shaped and his rather grubby effort at a jam tart is ceremoniously placed in the oven alongside the family meal. While all this goes on, he feels very important and loved, and he develops a great interest in life.

He builds up his muscles, not in gym but on the arduous walk up to the park, sitting on swings, ascending the climbing frame and the sprint to chase some unfortunate pigeon foolish enough to land within a hundred metres of this active little bird scarer. Much of the day is spent in play, not with those expensive computerised inventions produced in Silicon Valley but with natural raw materials, such as boxes, chairs and paper.

Improvisation and free play produce an extremely inventive brain which is often lost in the 'spoon fed' child. One minute the chairs are all lined up, and money is collected and counted by the toddler conductor; minutes later he is piloting an amazingly noisy jumbo jet down the middle of the lounge room. The cardboard box becomes a garage for toy cars; later it is a rocket base from which the cardboard innards of a toilet roll blast off into space.

Academic education, like sex education, can be acquired in a number of ways. The child may be summoned to a room, alone with his father, and given a formal lecture on the facts of life. The relaxed parent usually abhors this approach, preferring to answer questions as they arise in the course of daily life. Similarly, toddlers may either be sat down and taught formally, or allowed to be apprentices to their parents and learn through the activities of everyday life.

Good parents must not let themselves be browbeaten by their friends who have adopted the role of high powered educationists. Being good, loving, caring parents, who teach their children through practical living, is to be commended above all. When viewed over a seventy year life span it seems pretty irrelevant that a child reads at the age of 4 or 6. Better by far to start life with a healthy, happy, balanced outlook. The trials and tribulations will come soon enough.

19

Working Mother—
Effective Parent

Books about child care often censure mothers who have young children and yet go out to work. In an ideal world they might have a case but the world we all inhabit is far from ideal. What's more, though many have tried, no-one has yet shown that children of good, working mothers are damaged or disadvantaged in any way.

Today in Australia 51 per cent of mothers of under-5s will be back in paid work. For an ever-increasing number, there is now no choice, if there are not two wages the mortgage cannot be met. Others have trained hard to attain a responsible position and with prolonged absence they lose skills as well as prospects of promotion in a competitive workplace. There are quite a few mums who find that they were just not made to be 24 hour a day mothers and no matter how they try, the role does not suit. It is all very easy to criticise but in these times of supposed sexual equality, it seems to me that few men would be prepared to be 24 hour a day parents.

Though I accept the inevitability of the current trend and the complete absence of evidence of harm, I still wish the percentages could be lower. I worry that young mothers *and fathers* are both so busy in these fascinating early years. It is only in later life that one can see how quickly this time has passed and once gone, we cannot ask for a re-run.

Guilt

If mothers who either wanted to work or were obliged to work could just get on with it and stop feeling guilty, their lives would be much happier. Recently I attended a pre-school parents' meeting where a bevy of home-based mums turned on the working mums in the group telling them that they had no right to have children if they didn't want to stay at home and care for them. Even without this unwarranted assault, most of those mums were feeling guilty at short-changing their children.

Let me reassure working mothers by quoting from the internationally respected writings of Michael Rutter: 'Although frequently blamed for their children's troubles it is now apparent that working mothers have children with no more problems than the children of women who remain at home. This has now been shown in a wide range of studies using different measures of children's behaviours'.[20] So there you have it. What is important, however, is that there is good child minding care and extra attention given to the child when parents and child are together.

Choosing child care

Those lucky enough to be surrounded by family are fortunate indeed. If this help is not available, day care can be arranged, using either high quality approved centres or a local mother, authorised to take in three or four children in her own home. With these official carers you certainly will not go wrong, but there are at present only half the places needed and even then they prove too expensive for many parents.

With a private arrangement, the minder must be chosen with great care. You must have complete confidence in her ability so that you can relax when at work and concentrate on the job in hand. When choosing a care giver, it is wise to watch how she relates to your little one. Does she talk, listen, play and share genuine mothering gentleness and care, or is it a relationship based on an adequate injection of money? When the child is first left with a minder, enough time should be allowed so that this isn't done with a great rush and fuss.

The child should be clearly told where you are going and when you will be back to pick him up. Despite the explanation, the young toddler will not understand and may shed copious tears on your departure, as well as probably punish you by doing the same when you return.

The minder should be left with a contact telephone number and told to telephone you if she has the slightest worry. This will help ensure a better standard of care for the child and some early warning for you if anything goes wrong.

Illness and child care

After a year of living in the relative isolation of home, our children have little immunity to all the bugs that cause colds, coughs and fevers. When they start in child care they are at their most vulnerable and they seem to catch everything that is on the go.

Child care is not designed to cope with unwell toddlers and this puts a great strain on the parents and their employers. Some firms are reluctant to employ mothers with young children as they expect so much adult sick leave to be taken on account of childhood sickness.

There is no easy answer to this. It's only right that close family have to be there to comfort children when they are unwell. I should, however, mention that mothers do not have the monopoly when it comes to taking time off work, fathers should also shoulder some of this responsibility.

A fair deal for the child

The mum who works must make sure she gives good attention to her child in the time that they are together. The work-tired mum feels little enthusiasm to start washing, cleaning the house and cooking, let alone talking and playing with a toddler. But, however good day care is, it is only acceptable if accompanied by good night care and weekend care. Shopping, cooking and housework must not be allowed to consume all the parent's and child's time together, although if handled properly these can be a source of fun and education. If money allows, shop well ahead so that only occasional topping up from the corner store is needed. Prepared frozen foods are a good standby diet, but rather expensive and monotonous on a regular basis. Exotic, time-consuming dishes must be deleted from the menu and replaced by nutritious, easy-to-prepare meals. For those with big freezers and an organised brain, there is much to be said for a weekend cooking binge, in which dishes are mass-produced and frozen in meal-sized portions. This allows good food to appear with all the speed of melting ice. A weekly visit to the local restaurant or hamburger joint will give the cook a welcome break and provide great excitement for the toddler.

Working mums and a 'Home Beautiful' are not a compatible combination. Cleanliness, hygiene and relative tidiness are desirable but obsessive house pride is out. Family fun comes first. It is hard to communicate with a child over the roar of a vacuum cleaner and difficult to have a good, fun-filled romp around the house when an obsessive mother resents the slightest disturbance to even a cushion.

A fair deal for working mothers

Working mothers are often expected to do at least two full-time jobs, and only one of which receives pay or thanks. All husbands are generous to a fault. They give with absolute equality at the time of conception but, unfortunately, for many that's where all giving and equality seems to end. For some fathers, you might well ask, 'Is there life after conception?'.

In these days of contraceptive choice and the increasing need for mothers to work, discussion of shared care would seem sensible before, not after, the act.

When two tired parents and an excited child get home each evening there must be a fair division of labour and the child must not miss out. Weekends can have one parent shopping, cleaning or taking the toddler to the pool or park, while the other irons and prepares for the week to come. If fathers can have a night out with the boys or go off to soccer training, mothers must be afforded the same opportunity. Husbands have no serious form of impairment that prevents equal sharing of home and child care.

Conclusion

The trend this decade will be for an ever-increasing number of mothers with young children to return to work. Now these mums have taken on two full-time jobs, one at home and one at work, and without help the stress will start to show.

It seems only fair that if children are planned and conceived together, then care should continue together. In the nineties, there can be no place for a sleeping partner in a two-wage family. Husbands must wake up to this reality.

Though many mothers worry and feel guilty as they leave their young, it must be stated that there is no evidence that working mothers harm their children in any way. Of course day care must be good and parents must not short-change their children after work and at weekends. In parenting it is not the amount of time, but how we use that time that matters most.

20

In Praise of Grandparents

Grandmas and grandpas are some of our most valuable, and least utilised, natural resources. Over the last fifty years, as a result of better housing and what is called 'progress', families have moved apart to live in relative isolation. This has brought with it all manner of problems. Mother-in-law jokes keep countless comedians in business but this brand of humour is lost on the toddler, who is not interested in squabbles about his grandmother's interesting, irritating ways. He just enjoys being in her company. I write here in praise of the older generation and their great value to us and our children.

Benefits

Historically, in families that lived together, the younger members would call upon the experience of the older ones for advice. Owing to the often self-imposed isolation of modern-day living, however, parents lack easy access to that sensible advice as well as that much-needed extra pair of hands in times of stress. Other young parents view the older generation as past it, out of touch and incapable of offering anything. This is a strange attitude, when you think that up until recently the world's most powerful countries were all ruled by people who are themselves grandfathers or grandmothers.

Life is lived at a more realistic pace as we get older, and it is viewed with that mature, 'been there, done that' approach. Most older people have lived through wars, financial deprivation and all manners of upsets, so they are in a better position to view the relative futility of the minor irritations that get blown out of all proportion in our day-to-day lives.

The older generation often has a more infectious, quiet gentleness that our fast-moving younger generation has not yet developed. Children who won't sit still are often quietened, as if by hypnotism, when in granny's care. Grandfathers may not be able to engage in high energy rough and tumbles, but they are streets ahead in other areas. The youngster will sit and listen to all manner of stories, viewing grandpa as the world's greatest wit and raconteur. They go out together on exciting safaris around the garden or the neighbourhood, and although perhaps never more than a hundred metres from base, there is so much of interest to see when helped by someone who can slow down for long enough to point it out.

There is no better form of temporary child care than that provided by good grandparents. This is really an extension of the parents, not least because genes and twenty years of brainwashing by grandma are bound to ensure that one parent will have much in common with her. Day care when the parents are at work, babysitting, care when sick—all these valuable services can be provided by grandparents. Some parents organise a regular afternoon or day a week when the child stays with grandma. Some take the occasional weekend mini-break, leaving their child with her, or take the grandparents on holiday to share the child care load. There are tremendous benefits for the parents, the child and the grandparents with this shared care.

Isolated mums should not be backward in befriending elderly

neighbours, a good move for the old folk and also enriching for the young ones. This can provide much needed foster grandparents.

Laying down the ground rules

The main cause of friction with grandparents is when it is thought that they are interfering and criticising. Their interference is perhaps understandable, because they find it hard to sit back quietly and watch their own children stumble through life making all the same mistakes that they themselves made and later regretted. A forewarning of one's errors is often greeted with either a deaf ear or much resentment. Many fights occur over trivial matters, which are irrelevant when viewed against the background of the great benefits of care-giving that grandparents can provide.

To ensure a good relationship, the rules have to be set down, and both sides have to accept that the other has rights. When the child is in the care of the parents, then the parents are in charge of the show, and although advice may be tactfully given, it does not have to be accepted. When the child is being looked after by the grandparents, then they are in charge and should not be forced to adhere to the parents' often obsessive and irrelevant ideas. A child is like a chameleon, who can match in easily with an ever-changing environment.

Within reason, grandma should be allowed to feed the child whatever she wants and if, for example, the parents believe the sugar content will damage the child's teeth, this can be remedied with a quick brush of the teeth on returning home, rather than a family feud. Grandparents should be left to discipline the child in a way that feels best for them, and this should in no way damage the overall behaviour and discipline of the child. The parents are the main caretakers, and they cannot go through life blaming grandparents, schools or other children for their offspring's shortcomings. What shortcomings there are must be laid fairly and squarely at their doorstep to remedy.

Conclusion

It would be foolish to suggest that all grandparents are interested in being closely involved with the toddler. Come to think of it, some have had little enough time for their own children and, having screwed them up, should not be afforded the privilege of doing the same to the next generation.

But most of us under-use our greatest resource, tending to keep grandparents like Christmas decorations, to be brought out and shown only on high days and holidays. Both children and parents have much to learn from the older generation, whether it be grandma and grandpa or the old couple living next door.

For a happy partnership there are some simple rules. The younger generation must have some respect for age and maturity. They must not fight over pointless trivia, nor interfere with grandma's care, and they can, therefore, expect the same non-interference when the child is in their care.

21

Sole Parent Families

Today's statistics show that over one quarter of our children can expect to be part of a sole parent family before the end of their school years.

In my more philosophical moments I despair over us human beings. We can split atoms, explore space and create computers but often we can't chose a compatible partner and live in peace together. It seems that as science races ahead, human relations lag far behind.

There are a number of reasons for sole parenthood but sadly for most people the end result is much the same. Isolation, loneliness, little social life, money worries and frequently, aggravation from the absent partner.

It may be tough for us adults but usually we had some choice in the course we took, whereas our children are not so fortunate. They had no say as to whether conception or contraception was advisable and once born they are stuck with a situation outside their control. Adults can separate but children often have to live with arguing, unstable and unreasonable grown-ups, as so far, divorce of one's parents is not a legal option.

The sole parent situation is difficult for both parent and child but not impossible. If the custodial adult can remain strong and emotionally together the outlook for the children is excellent.

Special situations—their problems

Each sole parent situation comes with its own special package of problems. How these evolve and affect the child will depend on three things: the warmth and resilience of the custodial parent; the amount of support or destructive interference from outside; and the circumstances that led to the sole parent state.

When two parents are committed to separating in a responsible and amicable way it results in a totally different situation to the angry aftermath of a bitter break. The sole parent shattered by the death of a much loved partner is again in a very different state to that of the isolated teenage mum, hardly more than a child herself.

Separation and divorce—sole parents

This is the most common 'solo' situation I meet. Though these parents have many worries, the greatest influence on the household happiness is whether there was peace or continuing hostility after the split. (See Chapter 22 Tension in Families—Spare the Children.)

No matter how unhappy life was before the break, most parents find the final separation an emotionally shattering watershed. Studies show the next twelve months is a most difficult time, as parents readjust and toddler behaviour is often at its worst. Many questions deserve a mention.

Custody and access rights I may have an oversimplistic view of the law but I see little point in parents fighting over custody and access. In my experience, if the mother wants the children, she will be granted custody, unless she has some very major emotional or addictive problems.

Access may occasionally be restricted but rarely is it totally blocked. I have been subpoenaed as a reluctant witness in a number of access cases and in all of these the infrequent successes could never justify the great emotional and financial costs.

Housing After separation, many families gather up their belongings and move home. This may be for financial reasons or as a result of an unconscious need to flee from a house full of bad memories. A word of caution: if possible make no hasty decisions. While the life we knew is falling apart, we need to grasp tightly to familiar places, people and routines. The house is like a nest which we can fly home to each night so we can feel the security of a place we know. Children are much the same, they have just lost one parent and if they lose their own home, this can add insult to injury.

Money For most mothers the solo state brings a drastic drop in their standard of living. This is all the more galling if they see their husbands parading around in relative abundance. When he visits, children may be feted and feasted, and then returned to the care of a mother, scratching to make ends meet.

The present pension is designed to support life but could never be classed as generous. Returning to work does much to boost a mum's flattened esteem and identity but by the time child care has been funded and the pension foregone, the job needs to pay well to be worth pursuing.

Fathers have both a moral and legal duty to support their young but often their contribution is unreliable if not non-existent. The courts have legislated but they seem powerless to police these payments. Life goes on—but life is not fair.

Family and friends

Where a close network of family and friends exists separation is so much smoother for both adults and children. An on-side grandparent provides all the security of a safety net, there to catch the children when the parents let them slip.

Though there may be great benefits, it is not easy for a mother to return home to her own parents. It is not just the loss of an independent life, it is also the subtle admission of failure. This however is not a time to be difficult or choosey. The advantages of a return to a familiar friendly patch, with help in child care and an emotionally secure environment for children, makes diplomacy a course to consider.

After a marriage break-up it is never easy to get back into the social set you knew before. Friends have divided loyalties, they do not know who to support, so often they support no-one. Married couples cope well with other married couples but may feel uneasy with a single in their midst. Some keep their distance almost as though they see separation as some sort of contagious affliction.

Parents who have lost a partner and now have no close friends or family tread a very lonely road. They are emotionally most vulnerable and in this state it is all too easy to rebound straight into another unsuitable relationship. It never ceases to amaze me how so many wives escape from one alcoholic or uncaring husband and by year's end have sought out and married another the same or worse.

Access visits

Whether you like it or not these visits are going to happen. You have the option to be stirred, which also stirs the children, or take it like a Swami, with a divine aura of acceptance.

Of course it hurts when your children are out with your ex and his frumpy new friend. Of course it hurts when you don't have a cent to spare and they live in relative affluence. Of course it hurts when you wash, feed and care all week, while they come and go taking all the rewards, with none of the responsibility. That's life. No-one pretends it's fair but that's the rotten way it is.

Behavioural backlash

Children are not marriage guidance counsellors, and have no idea or interest in the rights and wrongs that led to the split. Little children cannot grasp the permanence of the situation and no matter how obnoxious and unreasonable the absent partner has been, they still wish to see them.

Due to the peak time that most marriages break up, pre-schoolers represent the main age group involved. Their problems vary in intensity but usually show up as insecurity, regression of skills and difficult behaviour.

Insecurity hits with a bang. They have lost one parent and are sure they are not going to let the remaining carer out of sight. They cling like a limpet and are reluctant to move far away without checking that their parent is still around. Day care and pre-school may be difficult, with them protesting loudly when left and settling poorly through the day. Try to spend more time before leaving them and let the director know the situation so they may be even more supportive. Sleep may become disturbed as they wake at night demanding comfort, to check the remaining parent is still there. Many slip into the parent's bed, which is not a problem now but if a new relationship develops, it may pose quite an impediment.

Behaviour often takes a turn for the worse. They are angry at a situation they do not understand and they take this out on those nearest to them. They feel the sadness, confusion and tension in the air but are not at an age to tread gently, so instead they stir. For parents, bad behaviour is hard to take when in an emotionally weak state and feeling flat. We tend to forget that our little ones are also upset. They feel let down and need gentle guidance, not heavy and punitive discipline.

Mums and mental health

Although at the time of separation there may be a distinct feeling of relief, the year that follows will be one of confused emotions. Often there are regrets, doubts about self-worth, sadness, anger and confusion about whether the current difficult situation is any improvement on the one left behind.

I am not a psychiatrist but I believe that many mothers are pathologically depressed at this stage and the mental health of the caring parent has an immense effect on the children. When we become sad, isolated, immobile, without drive or enthusiasm and emotionally flat, it is time to seek professional help. It is always easier to struggle on but this is not good for either parents or the little people who depend on them.

Remember, it is not only the grown-ups who are unhappy, the children are also confused and upset. Our emotional batteries may be depleted but our little ones are more than ever in need of an emotional jump start to keep them going.

Life will be easier if you accept the inevitable and don't waste energy on futile fights. Access, inequality of responsibility and general injustice are par for the course, whether you anger yourself into a stroke or accept it.

Try to get out, to walk, to play in the park, to meet other mothers. Work hard to keep both body and brain in shape with regular exercise and interest. Remember, one emotionally together mother is more important than having distant parents who happen to live together.

New relationships

Sole parents are in a social straight-jacket. It is extremely hard to get out to meet interesting people when tied to the home with small children, no baby-sitters and a limited budget. If a new relationship gets going, this for many is where their toddler troubles seem to start.

See it from the child's point of view. They have just lost one parent and though there may have been a divorce, he's still my dad. They have been upset by one parting and don't really want to start down the same track again. Most have become extremely close to their mother and they don't want anyone coming between them—thank you very much. Then there are those who have squirrelled themselves into the family bed to sleep with mum and any suggestion of eviction would warrant a protest rally.

In any new relationship the secret is to be conscious of the child's feelings, to move gently and not force the issue. At first it is best to keep the initial action outside the home, as it takes time for children to adjust to one they see as an intruder on their own pitch. Don't be punitive when they stand up for their rights or are downright unfriendly.

With new relationships often step-children arrive as a sort of package deal, which can cause additional problems of personality clashes, territorial claims and divided loyalties. Again move slowly, be sensitive to children's feelings and give it time.

Finally another word of caution. Isolated, lonely people may crave adult companionship but rebound relationships are often fraught with difficulties. It seems foolish to enter any permanent relationship until quite clear why the last one did not work out.

This is not a caution without backing. The statistics show that over half of divorced parents with little children will have re-married within three years. Unfortunately over half of these second marriages will not survive a full five year term. A second separation causes a double dose of disruption that no child, and few parents need.

Sole parents through accident or illness

As caring humans we feel particularly sad when we read of the untimely death of a young parent. This is much more upsetting to us than would be news of an angry separation or a damaging divorce. Often these bereaved families tend to fare better than many other solo situations.

Life is suddenly shattered but there is a funeral and in the next year the events of the past are put firmly behind. While this goes on, friends, family and the community as a whole tend to rally to support. In this situation there is no bickering over property, access or custody. The wounds are deep but they are allowed to heal without unnecessary interference.

Little children cannot grasp that death is permanent and to them it is as though their dad had gone off on a long holiday. They usually need no counselling, play therapy or psychiatrist. They take their lead from those around. Their home has changed from fun and frolic to tension and tears. When the adults in their life get themselves together, the children will then follow suit.

One statistic always makes me sad. It has been shown that the young child whose father is killed in an accident stands to emerge emotionally many times sounder than the child of a long running bitter divorce. We humans have the ability to do much more harm to our children by our deliberate actions than through life's unavoidable accidents.

Teenage solos

It is not fashionable to talk frankly about teenage solos but few people who have a genuine interest in the long-term emotional well-being of our young, could be anything but concerned.

The group that worries me most are those children brought up in an unhappy, disturbed home, who have never seen a proper parenting example and have felt little warmth or love. Often the pregnancy for these teenagers is an attempt to find the love and purpose that life so far has denied them. Most cope reasonably well in the first year with a baby but often by toddlerhood they are in deep strife. The restriction to a life of 24 hour a day child care, the isolation from their young social scene, loneliness, poverty and for many the behaviour of a difficult, disturbed toddler make life far from happy.

Five years on, when I see these mums, some have done amazingly well, though I can't but worry that so many have had such a difficult and often deprived time. As the years go by and I get to know them better, it seems that with the hindsight that comes with age, many of these adults would have preferred to have done things differently if life would permit a re-run.

It is one thing mentioning this concern but what can we do about it? What is needed is support for the young parents of today and then to look at possible prevention for tomorrow. These young solos are extremely vulnerable and need a great amount of close, ongoing support. It is rare that the community can afford to provide this but bearing in mind the possible repercussions, one wonders if we can afford not to.

Prevention involves education and example.

Education is not just sex education. It involves the whole area of gaining a realistic perspective of relationships. This is hard to get across to the young who may see physical attributes and attraction as unreasonably important in having a close and continuing relationship.

Education also involves encouraging teenagers to choose the course of their life not through indecision but by active decision. Contraception, termination and adoption, whether appropriate or not, all require very active decisions. Conception and continuing with a pregnancy may also involve carefully considered decisions but in reality, many enter sole parenthood through never facing up to the events that were happening in their lives.

Teenagers need to be made aware of the restrictions and limits to life that comes with parenthood. It is hard to convince them of this; after all, most of us much older adults were never prepared for the change that our children brought.

Example It is easier to talk about setting an example than to put it into practice. However, example is vitally important to every child whether they are part of a one or two parent family. The number of parents is not the issue here, it is the warmth, peace and togetherness of a family that have the greatest bearing on the children. At this moment, our little ones are tuning in to the atmosphere of their home, storing it away in their memories to draw from it when they enter their own adult relationships.

It is quite a sobering thought that our behaviour today will have a considerable effect on how our children and even grandchildren may behave in the future. Whoever said parenting was easy!

Conclusion

It is a fact of life that many relationships will fall apart and many children will feel the repercussions. Life for the sole parent is not easy, with many upsets and injustices in their path no matter what they do. It is not the fact of being a sole or two parent family that affects the children but the strength and emotional togetherness of the main carer and the peace of the home environment.

22

Tension in Families— Spare the Children

Throughout the world today thousands of children live in the midst of war and conflict. We live in a lucky country where our young are presumed to be spared such traumas—but are they? You don't have to live in downtown Belfast or Beirut to know the full feeling of tension and hostility. You can feel it right here, not on the streets but where it hurts most—in many of our homes.

This year another 50 000 Australian children will witness the break-up of their parents' relationship but this is only a small part of the problem. A great many more continue to live unhappily with parents who are geographically together but emotionally and behaviourally a million miles apart.

It is not just the alcoholics, the psychopaths and the wife beaters who upset their children; it is also the thousands upon thousands of normal parents who bicker, nitpick, hold grudges, escalate events and make little effort to maintain their home as a happy and peaceful place.

Tension troubles children

Not a week goes by without some parent telling me: 'Dr Green, our relationship is a complete mess, but it's alright, the children don't know'.

Don't fool yourself for a minute, you can never hide tension and unhappiness from children. You may keep your disputes and disagreements behind closed doors but the chill that comes with them will permeate to every corner of the home. Whether we like it or not, our adult problems soon become our children's problems.

Tension makes parents irritable, unreasonable, and emotionally tepid. Children, when they feel these vibes, may become insecure, demanding or just downright difficult. Tension must be one of the main triggers of bad behaviour and child unhappiness in our peace-loving society today. Most of this is quite unnecessary if only we adults could act more like adults and less like self-centred, inconsiderate toddlers.

Bitter break-ups (legalised child abuse)

It is not the breakdown of a marriage that does the damage. Rather it is all the associated aggravation and hostility that upsets our children. We may not like our partners but they still should be treated with the respect and civility due to another human being.

Many parents are shameless in the way they abuse each other and then recruit their innocent children to become pawns in their battle. Soon these unwilling conscripts are being used as weapons to cause pain to the partner. Disputes on child management are heated and open. When one parent doles out the discipline, the other contradicts, just for spite. You can see how confused and bruised our little ones become.

Access visits are used as an excuse to gain entry and disrupt the happiness of the home. The visitor deliberately does not come when expected, is obtuse and inflammatory on arrival, vague about the time of return and then once more abusive.

Mothers tell children what a sick, no-hoper they have for a dad, while dads poison their young with equally spiteful untruths. Before long children dread the tension of the weekly visits as these become an endurance to be feared, not enjoyed.

Court battles are necessary to resolve genuine grievances. Sadly some cases are brought purely to cause prolonged pain to the other partner, and in this vindictive atmosphere there is no thought for the feelings of a child who is becoming increasingly disturbed.

It still seems strange to me that we, as intelligent, compassionate people, can so often set out to deliberately damage our children. These guerilla tactics, used both during marriage and through the break-up period, can keep tension and bitterness running high for years. I don't see this as a civil right of any parent. It is a form of legalised child abuse which would never be condoned in any country that genuinely believed in the rights of its children.

Amicable settlements (thank God for sensible parents)

Not only are amicable settlements possible between divorcing partners but thankfully they are also very common. Here parents split in such a way that they are both completely committed to cause the least amount of upset to their children.

In these families there will be no sabotage, no point scoring or trying to win affection over the other party. Discipline will remain consistent. Custody is not an issue, property is divided fairly and access is looked forward to and enjoyed.

Children of peaceful settlements usually bear no long-term emotional scars, a state of affairs greatly helped by close extended families, the support of good friends and the children staying in touch with those familiar faces and surrounds they know.

The toddler cannot be expected to fully comprehend the meaning of the separation but careful explanation is still important. This should be done using simple words, told without anger or blame. Words must be reassuring, as some little ones can feel they have somehow been responsible for spiriting one of their parents away.

Children must realise that though their parents will not live together, both still love them and will continue to care for them. They must know where they will live and it is advisable that they see where the absent parent will stay. This gives them a picture to store in their minds and assures them that their dad or mum has not departed from the face of the earth.

Access should be kept as flexible and peaceful as possible, with both parties committed to making it go smoothly. The best sole situations for our children are those where their parents, though they don't want to live together, can still be good friends when they live apart. In this amicable climate, peace is preserved while the children continue to have two caring parents who can work closely and constructively to ensure a secure present and future.

Conclusion: happy homes—happy children

It seems strange that most intelligent human beings tend to treat those near and dear to them with less civility than they would afford to those they hardly know in outside life. I find it hard to believe that the highly advanced ape called man is so often intellectually impaired when it comes to choosing a mate for life. Is this a human failing, or is our judgement quite sound, and our expectations unreal?

There are no perfect marriages, even the best will have their ups and downs. Don't expect roses and violins every day; in real relationships the roses go in and out of bloom and the violins slip in and out of tune. If it's going to work for us and therefore our children, we need to have sensible expectations and be committed to easing and not escalating the bumps.

All relationships will slip into a rut unless we work hard to keep them fresh and alive. You may be busy and tired but take time to notice, to encourage, to communicate and to cherish. A bunch of flowers given today is better than a whole shopful to put on a loved one's coffin. By then it is too late.

Tension and needless bickering are probably the greatest and most unnecessary cause of upset to today's children. Nothing I say will stop relationships running aground. What I ask is that some thought be given to the children before you hoist the battle-flags.

Settling our disputes in an amicable way may not be as satisfying to our adult anger but it is important to the emotional well-being of our children. While parents have the right to fight, children have the right to be spared trauma.

23

The Disabled Child:
Behaviour and Discipline

It is very difficult to define clearly the behavioural problems of disabled children, because there are so many different degrees of handicap affecting so many different children. There are a few generalisations that can be made, such as there being a somewhat higher proportion of restless, irritable, hard-to-comfort children among the disabled.

The best forms of behaviour and discipline techniques to use with disabled children are exactly those you would use with normal toddlers. The good is rewarded and praised. The undesirable is ignored, or pretended to be ignored. Time Out, where they are placed in their bedroom, provides a much-needed safety valve, to be used when everything else seems to have failed. The controlled crying technique is used with sleep problems, although sedation is more often needed in addition. One difference with all behaviours is that, try as we may, the cure rate is less spectacular than we would like. Part of the difficulty is that special children have special parents with special feelings. For many, it is hard to be as tough as is needed to get results. Another part is that many such children have bodies which are strong and advanced in their physical skills, while the brains which control all this power lack insight, sense and sometimes the ability to learn easily from experience. Bearing this in mind, it is often best to lower our sights and aim at first for a percentage improvement rather than the full cure. This is not defeatism, merely realism. Any small improvement will bring benefits to the tired parents.

As a general principle, each child should be treated with the discipline and management appropriate to his developmental (mental) age, no matter what the actual age may be. Despite this, however, you will find that outside factors can take charge and make treatment less successful. For example, children who have epilepsy that is poorly controlled are often more irritable and difficult than average. Their problems are often worse just before a fit and in the days that follow it. Some of the medications used for epilepsy can also worsen behaviour, and some doctors do not seem to realise that the drugs they prescribe, although giving perfect control to the fits, can make the child virtually impossible to live with.

Children with major expressive speech problems tend to get very frustrated and often display far from easy behaviour. Children born completely normal and later smitten by meningitis or head injury can develop many of the worst features of the hyperactive child. They may be of normal intelligence but so handicapped by restlessness, poor concentration and negligible sense that their parents are driven to distraction.

Autistic children tend to have very obsessive, repetitive behaviours and, hard as we may try, these can be very difficult to cure. We concentrate more these days on diverting these immovable problems to more socially acceptable presentations. The child who flaps his hands may be diverted to clapping, and the child who repeatedly flicks the light switch on and off can be diverted to a torch. Now that we have accepted our limited abilities we stop wasting time attempting the impossible and channel our full energies into what really matters—communication and socialisation.

Dealing with specific problems

Some severely intellectually handicapped or cerebral palsied children are extremely irritable by day. To soothe them, we use movement and other techniques, although occasionally we have to resort to sedation.

In the really difficult child, it is often necessary to provide care away from parents for one or two half days each week so that the exhausted parents have time to recharge their batteries.

Quite a number of handicapped children come to their parents' bed at night; others stay in their own but cry. Parents are often much softer with these children than their normal brothers and sisters, and they are reluctant to let them cry or to throw them out of the marital bed. The controlled crying technique can be used for many of these children although in some severely retarded children I have had no success with anything other than heavy sedation. If the parents are to survive the day, they cannot afford to be up all night with a crying child. The secret with sedation is to give the drug not at 6 p.m., just before bedtime, but when the child wakes up later in the night. This at least gives the parents some chance of gaining those golden hours of sleep between midnight and dawn.

Some young handicapped children can take an age to feed, and mothers often spend up to two hours at mealtimes, leaving little time in the day for anything else. The best that can be done is to engage in sensible experimentation. For example, the child who takes his milk painfully slowly from a bottle may be given it from a spoon or cup, or given more solids instead. For the child who has difficulty with solids or lumpy food, different textures can be manufactured, and there are ways a skilled therapist can desensitise the mouth and encourage swallowing.

Toilet training may be difficult and sometimes toilet timing is all that can be initially achieved. Some children, particularly those with cerebral palsy, may get quite constipated. In these cases, it is a good idea to introduce a simple laxative or a 'depth charge' extra fruit diet, which may ease the situation.

In the older handicapped child, all my greatest failures have been with those who have the major problem of 'little sense'. Day after day, year after year, the same behaviour happens with these children, despite my best advice. The problem is that these children, although they may appear quite intelligent on being tested, do not learn from their experiences. Their poor parents try their best but as nothing helps, they soon begin to feel quite impotent.

Unfortunately they may be further disadvantaged when advised by some newly qualified 'whiz kid', whose university education never taught him that a child may have the severe handicap of lack of sense. He will misread the situation, blame all the lack of success on the parents, and make their lives even harder than they already are. The parents should be given all the support and encouragement possible. If things are not going well, some temporary respite care should be arranged to keep the parents on the rails and to allow the other children of the family a more equal share of their parents' time.

Understanding and helping the parents of the disabled child

Many parents of a special child are determined to remain completely unchanged in their attitudes and expectations, but most do treat their child differently from his brothers and sisters. Many are overprotected, never allowed to cry, and usually given their own way. Behaviour techniques are often not seen through with determination, because parents find it hard to be tough on a child who has physical or intellectual problems. And even the most robust parent has considerable inner sadness and is under much stress.

I will digress for a minute and give a brief outline of the common reactions of the parent with a handicapped child. Once these are understood then it is easier to give them help.[21] Following the realisation that one has a disabled child, the parent may go through a form of grief reaction, not unlike the feelings experienced after the death of a loved one. Initially, when they hear the news, there may be a short stage where they feel stunned and disbelieving. This soon progresses to a long, painful stage where they try to come to terms with the situation they find themselves in. This may take months, years or even a lifetime. At this stage, the parents need to protect themselves from the harsh reality of the situation by closing the shutters of their mind and only letting a little of the realisation sink in each day. Denial, anger and activity are all methods they use to survive these difficult times.

With denial, the parents may refuse to accept the degree of the problem and shop around from doctor to doctor in the hope of hearing better news. Some deny they have even been told anything, and others embark on ill-proven miracle cures. Anger is a strange defence that we all use when under immense stress. It seems at times like this that displacing a bit of our anger onto those around us often makes us feel better. When the home football team has lost the grand final, you come home and kick the cat, not that the poor animal has done anything wrong but it just makes you feel better. Activity is a defence that we all engage in when under great stress. Sitting immobile and worrying only makes the problems seem even larger. The parents may take up a good cause, take on full-time employment, or work day and night for their special child. The activity will probably make them very tired but it does help them to feel better.

It is not clever for anyone to try to break through these defences.[14] Once the shutters are torn down and the full light of the problem hits the parents, they may be precipitated into that state of immobility, isolation and guilt called depression.

I believe that with time, talk, friends and good practical help, most parents get through this need to defend themselves in this way. They may still feel the hurt but they can look past it to talk realistically and plan constructively for the future.

How can friends help?

The reactions I have mentioned are all normal and healthy. With good friends and good time, the presence of these defences will become unnecessary. With denial, friends should not force the issue but equally must not be afraid to talk gently and openly about what has happened. Pretending that the handicap doesn't exist fools no-one and only serves to upset the parents. When parents are about to risk bankruptcy and destroy their other children's well-being all for the sake of some ill-proven miracle cure, they should be firmly encouraged to visit a top local expert beforehand rather than some dubious, expensive, overseas figure known to them only through the pen of a sensation-seeking journalist.

Anger is quite natural and may land on even the closest of friends. The anger is not really aimed at the friend; it is more a sign of the parents' tension and upset at their lot in life. Friends should be philosophical, and view it as a privilege that some of the anger that is probably levelled at the Almighty is landing on their humble shoulders.

Never criticise the mother who wishes to work or strive for some noble cause. She may well need this, and to suddenly remove it would be as ill-conceived as removing the crutch from a limping man. Activity is far preferable to immobility, isolation, guilt and the lack of enthusiasm that it generally replaces. Those who have

become isolated need great understanding. They need encouragement to get out and mix, as well as practical help with child minding. Last, but most valuable, they need your listening and
non-condemning ear.

The message is, stick with the parents. They may not say it in
so many words but they need friends and will be grateful, if not
openly then certainly in their hearts.

Conclusion

Such is the variety and degree of handicaps that there is no universal remedy for behaviour and management problems. As a general rule, use the same behavioural techniques with the
handicapped child as you would use with a normal child of similar
mental age. Bear in mind that other factors will sabotage your
best efforts, such as increased irritability, specific medical conditions, lack of concentration and lack of sense. Always remember
how stressed the parents of a handicapped child are, and how you
can help by sticking in there with them.

24

Common Toddler Illnesses

For the parents of a toddler it seems that hardly a day goes by without their child suffering from something, be it tonsillitis, an ear infection or the common cold. As part of growing up, the child goes through a whole series of illnesses, each one apparently more ghastly than the one before but nevertheless all quite common and in most cases nothing to be feared. To be forewarned is, as they say, to be forearmed. This chapter deals with the most common medical problems, and it is designed as a pointer to the parent. Naturally if you are worried by any of these symptoms, take your child to a doctor.

The common cold

Colds are caused not by one but by a number of viruses, which explains why one infection may follow straight after another, giving the impression of a non-stop nose run. As they are viruses, they do not respond to treatment with antibiotics but cure themselves, usually within four or five days of appearance. When the child first goes to day care or pre-school, he is coughed over by a multitude of virus-splattering infants, and this is frequently his worst year for infections. Eventually some immunity is acquired, and the number of illnesses gradually decreases each year until adulthood. Most of the natural immunity which a baby inherits from his mother is lost by the age of 6 months, and the first winter thereafter is often a prime one for colds.

Average toddlers will get up to nine colds each year, with six being about the usual number, which you may have gathered works out at about one every eight weeks. Colds are spread by playmates and other people with whom the toddler comes into contact; they do not come from getting wet or playing out in the cold, whatever the myths may be. Despite years of trying to prevent colds with various vitamins and other treatments, there is still absolutely nothing one can reliably do to help.

A further area of confusion arises because the common cold often starts with a sore throat, slightly pink ear drums and even a slight cough. When all these symptoms come together it shows that the child has indeed contracted a common cold; individually they indicate tonsillitis, ear infection or bronchitis. There is no specific treatment for colds, although paracetamol (Panadol) preparations may make the child feel more comfortable.

Tonsils

It is almost impossible to find tonsils in anyone over 25 years of age, because in years past they were whipped out at the drop of a scalpel, being regarded universally as useless appendages. Nowadays, removal of the tonsils is relatively rare, and the operation is not performed unless there are some major reasons for doing so. Tonsillitis is not the sore throat found at the beginning of a cold; it is rather the specific infection of the tonsillar tissues at the back of the throat and their associated glands at the angle of the jaw. The tonsils are not just red but 'angry' looking with flecks of pus, and is usually caused by bacteria. Antibiotic treatment is needed and is usually effective.

The decision for surgical removal is not dependent on the size of the offending part but the number of genuine tonsil infections and the chronically infected appearance of the throat. Tonsils are minute in the young toddler, reaching their peak size somewhere around the age of 7 years. Large does not mean unhealthy, and large tonsils do not cause feeding problems.

Croup

This is a juvenile form of laryngitis, usually caused by a virus, which creates an infection in the region of the child's voice box (larynx). Antibiotics are no help and probably the best remedy is the good, old-fashioned one of inhaling steam from a basin or kettle or sitting in a steamy bathroom. The child with croup makes a characteristic and often frightening 'crowing' noise when breathing in, accompanied by a cough like the sound of a sea lion. In its mild form, it can be easily treated at home with humidity. A small minority of children can become quite seriously ill, and if their condition deteriorates rapidly or there is any other medical concern, seek help immediately.

Bronchitis

Bronchitis is another viral infection, which will probably start as a cough and go to the chest. This ailment will not respond to antibiotics. Despite making quite a lot of coughing noise, the child should be relatively happy and show little sign of illness. When the coughing is associated with wheezing and shortness of breath, it may be wise to consider asthma as a possible cause. When fever and general sickness are also present, then it may be a more major chest infection and a medical opinion should be sought. Bronchitis may be the first symptom of approaching measles in some children, even before the very first spot has appeared.

Asthma

Asthma affects about 20 per cent of all children. Its hallmark is a musical wheeze that comes from the depths of the lungs, mostly when breathing out. It is made worse by exercise and viral respiratory infections, and it is often associated with periods of dry coughing in the middle of the night.

Many parents are obviously distressed when I diagnose asthma, thinking immediately of their schooldays when friends with severe asthma spent more time at home than at school, were excluded from sport, and were regarded as moderate cripples. This is not the case today. Most asthmatic children have the condition in a mild form, and they can live a completely normal, unrestricted life.

Treatment uses certain medicines to open up the air passages, and they are best administered as inhalants.[22] These products are now extremely safe and highly effective, and they do not lose potency with continued use. Allergy testing, milk withdrawal, chest exercises, antibiotics and restrictions of lifestyle are not prescribed for my patients.

Ear problems

At birth the baby is startled by loud noises and changes the pattern of his crying when comforted by his mother's voice. At 6 months, he will turn his head towards the direction of quiet sounds from objects he cannot see. Just before 1 year, there is much tuneful babble in some strange, unintelligible foreign language, which is soon followed by repeating appropriate words. At this stage we know there can be no gross hearing problem.

Hearing loss

Although most children who have severe hearing loss are now diagnosed between 6 and 9 months of age, I still see quite a few who have remained undiagnosed until 18 months. If the child does not respond to quiet, unexpected noises, if his speech development is slow, or if there is the slightest doubt in the parents' minds, a proper hearing test should be arranged.

The middle ear

The human ear is made up of an ear canal, which often contains some wax and goes from the outside to the ear drum, and inside the drum is the middle ear, which is a small chamber filled with air. In this chamber a number of delicate little bones transmit the sound waves from the ear drum to the hearing nerve and then the brain. This middle ear is connected by a thin tube (Eustachian tube), which communicates with the outside atmosphere through the back of the nose. This causes the 'popping' of ears associated with the pressure increase of a vigorous nose blow or when landing in an aeroplane.

For the middle ear to transmit sound efficiently it needs to be filled with air, which gives it resonance, rather like some musical instruments. When full of fluid, the tone and hearing volume is diminished much in the same way as filling a drum with concrete would affect its musical quality. Fluid gathers in the middle ear when the tube from the nose gets blocked, as may happen briefly during a heavy cold. If the fluid in the middle ear is associated with infection, this may cause an acute ear infection (acute otitis media). If the fluid is present but not infected, it deadens the hearing in a chronic manner, and the condition is generally referred to as 'glue ear'.

Ear infection (otitis media)

Following a cold, a swim, or diving into a pool, bacteria may enter the middle ear, and if the tube blocks, an infection can develop. The child becomes sick, irritable, has ear pain, partial hearing loss and, on examination, the ear drum looks angry and red. Nature will cure this condition either by re-opening the tube to the nose and releasing the infection or through a perforation in the ear drum. As the infection is usually caused by bacteria, antibiotics are given, along with the minor pain-killers, such as paracetamol (Panadol). Most doctors tend to greatly over-diagnose and over-treat ear infections, such is our concern to protect the young child's hearing. Even if the ear drum does perforate, this almost always heals by itself without problems, although, of course, prevention is a better course of action. Even if you don't halt the complaint in time, it is not the end of the world.

Glue ear

Sterile fluid may collect in the middle ear in association with a cold, flu or after an acute ear infection. This is most commonly seen in the early school-age child; a teacher will note that a child's hearing has deteriorated when he starts to talk louder than usual and ignores much of what is said to him. When glue ear is diagnosed, the parents must let the teacher know, so that the child may be brought nearer the front of the class to avoid missing anything that is said.

Pain is usually not a problem with glue ear, and there is no great urgency in treatment. With time, most cases will resolve themselves, although the process can be hurried along by a simple operation in which plastic tubes (gromets) are placed in the ear drum to let the fluid escape. The tubes drop out after a number of months and hopefully do not need reinsertion.

The insertion of these tubes has taken over from the tonsillec-tomies of earlier days as the most common operation performed in childhood. Studies showing definite long-term benefits are so far inconclusive, and it is uncertain whether this will prove to be a passing fashion or an operation for the future.

With the children I see, I steer a middle road, insisting that a proper hearing test is conducted, which must show definite hearing loss before surgery is contemplated. I also prefer to leave at least six weeks before surgery, since nature has an obliging way of resolving the situation.

Summary

- If a child does not turn towards quiet, unexpected sounds at 6 months, has no word-like babble at 1 year, and is slow to develop speech, a hearing defect must be suspected.

- If infected fluid is trapped in the middle ear (acute otitis media), it causes pain and fever and antibiotic treatment is needed.

- When sterile fluid is trapped in the middle ear it thickens and is referred to as 'glue ear'. This is not an acute condition. It will be cured either by time and nature, or by the insertion of tubes.

Vomiting and diarrhoea

These are both extremely common in the toddler. When vomiting and diarrhoea are present together this often means an infection in the gut (gastroenteritis); if vomiting occurs alone, it is more likely to be due to an infection in the body, possibly a cold, flu or occasionally some more serious problem. If your child is very sick and you have any doubts, medical help should be sought. If the child is not too unwell, however, and vomiting and diarrhoea are a problem, here are a few tips.

Children with acute gut infections need fluids, not solids. If they are going to be harmed, it is not through loss of body 'fat weight', but 'water weight' when too much water and salt have been lost. If vomiting and diarrhoea are caused by gastroenteritis, it is almost always of viral origin. They are not helped by antibiotics, which often have the side-effect of causing the diarrhoea to become worse.

I never cease to be amazed by the stream of odd cures I am confronted with by parents of vomiting toddlers.

'What's the problem?'
'He vomits everything up, doctor.'
'What are you giving him?'
'Oh, not much. A glass of milk with an egg and a little added custard just to keep his strength up.'

After all that, the parents are genuinely surprised when the child throws it all back at them.

The correct treatment for vomiting is to give *small amounts of clear fluids, frequently*.

Small means no more than one whisky measure of fluid at a time.

Clear means clear, not milk, not solids, not body-building protein, just fluid. The corner chemist will sell mixtures which, when added to water, are designed to replace all the water and chemicals a vomiting child may lose. Theoretically these should be given but in practice we often have to use a far simpler, and more readily available solution (e.g., diluted lemonade). Lemonade contains about 10 per cent sugar, which is too concentrated for a child with major gastroenteritis. The advice for the nineties is to dilute one part of lemonade with four parts water, which is still pleasant for most children to take. It seems silly to force nauseated children to drink fluids that they normally would not like, and you cannot go too far wrong with lemonade. You can even freeze it and make ice-blocks for the child to suck. Milk is best abandoned altogether, as it is less easily digested, and as every mother knows, it is very much more unpleasant to clean up than second-hand lemonade.

Frequently means each quarter or half hour during the day. Although this may seem very little fluid, you can in fact administer 1.5 litres a day in this fashion quite effortlessly.

When a young child craves for fluids and the parents give in to his requests on demand, this will probably result in vomiting. A simple way to overcome this excess intake is to set a cooking timer bell to ring every fifteen minutes. This will let the child know when his allotted fluid time arrives and, if treated patiently and not rushed, the vomiting will soon come under control.

Acute infective diarrhoea is almost always of viral origin, and antibiotics should only be used in some rare and very specific cases. If clear fluids are given, the bowel has little to discharge and the diarrhoea will come quickly under control. Chalk medicines to 'slow the bowel' are unnecessary in children and, as anyone who has tried to chew chalk when feeling sick will tell you, are far from pleasant. In the days that follow gastroenteritis, the child usually becomes extremely constipated. This does not need treatment and merely indicates that the bowel is quite empty and has nothing more to get rid of.

Summary

- Vomiting in toddlers is common and may accompany any childhood illness, even the most trivial.

- When the child has considerable vomiting and diarrhoea, the cause is usually viral gastroenteritis, in which case the child does not need calorific foods, milk, chalk medicines, or antibiotics.

- He should be given only clear fluids, in small amounts, frequently.

- If the child looks sick, 'distant', dull-eyed, weak and passes little urine, or if you are at all worried, get medical help at once.

Fevers

When the body is upset by an infection, whether it is a common cold or something more serious, the temperature will rise in response. Some illnesses, such as measles, can cause extremely high fevers, while others, which may in fact be more serious, may have quite low fever levels. The presence of a fever is merely an indication that the child is sick; the height of temperature is not an accurate barometer of the severity of the problem.

High temperature will upset the already unhappy child and make him feel even more miserable. His parents will start to worry since they know that some children with fevers are also prone to fits. For both these reasons, young children with temperatures tend to be treated more vigorously than their adult counterparts.

A feverish child must be dressed sensibly, not wrapped up in extra vests and woollens and put into a bed heaped up with

blankets. He should be given one of the commercial children's paracetamol (Panadol) preparations. Children usually find this liquid
pleasant to take, and it has few side-effects. Recent international
reports have strongly criticised the use of aspirin in young children.

Plunging the hot child into a bath filled with water straight
from the Arctic is not only exceedingly cruel but also counter-
productive. When the sizzling body splashes down into the icy
water the skin reacts by shutting off its blood supply and diverting
the blood to those warmer regions 'inland from the coast'. As a
result, little heat is lost by the child, despite the unpleasant experience. Being stripped and sat in front of a gale force fan is another nasty which will only cause the child to shiver and thus,
paradoxically, generate more heat.

The proper procedure is to strip the child down to his pants and,
if the temperature is still high, sponge him over gently with tepid,
rather than cold, water. This gives a gentle, cooling effect and does
not precipitate shivering or divert the blood away from the skin.

It seems a jolly unfair world for young children. When I have
the flu or a fever I go to bed, turn the electric blanket on to 'summer
Sahara' temperature, and sweat it out. But for the poor toddler it
is all stripping off and sponging down and general disturbance. Of
course the difference is that with the toddler, we have a great fear
of 'fever fits'.

Fever fits (febrile convulsions)

In some children, the developing brain seems particularly sensitive to temperature rise, and this causes them to throw a fit.
These fits are most common between the ages of 6 months and
3 years, and rarely happen after the age of 5 years. They are not
uncommon: 4 per cent of children in this age group will have a fit,
usually a febrile convulsion.

For most parents it is a frightening experience, and they can be
forgiven for thinking that their small child is about to die. The fit
can come on very quickly; many children are only slightly unwell
beforehand and give no warning at all. The victims will suddenly
go stiff, the eyes roll back, and breathing becomes laboured. They
will then start shaking or twitching, before relaxing to lie dazed
and confused. After this they become sleepy, and, having slept,
will appear fully recovered. Luckily most of these fits last for less
than five minutes, although to the watching parent it can seem
like an eternity.

If a child has a high fever, the cooling measures and medicines mentioned should prevent many febrile convulsions. If the child does fit, he should be placed gently on his side to prevent choking. Difficult as it may be, try not to panic. Young children do not die, nor do they harm their brains with short fever fits. Stay with him rather than running off for help. Don't force spoons or other objects into his mouth, as the apparently difficult breathing is not due to a blockage in his throat but rather a tightening of his respiratory muscles. If this is a first fit, or if it does not come quickly under control, take the child straight to a doctor.

A child who has a simple febrile convulsion does not have epilepsy, and these fits will not continue through his life. After one febrile episode, however, the child is much more likely to have another before he grows out of the convulsion-prone age group.

Summary

- The short fever fit does not damage the child, only his parents' nerves.
- Febrile convulsions do not mean epilepsy.
- Lie the child on his side.
- Don't force objects into his mouth.
- Don't panic. (That's easy for me to say!)
- Seek medical help when the child comes round or if still fitting at the end of five minutes.

Vaccinations

Toddlers should be given full immunisation against diphtheria, tetanus, whooping cough and polio, as well as measles, mumps and rubella. Lots of leaflets are available from your local health authority which set out the current vaccination procedures. All I will attempt to do here is set out the major illnesses and their risks. (See Appendix IV, Recommended Childhood Immunisation Schedule.)

Diphtheria

This is a particularly nasty illness in which bacteria produce a membrane which blocks the major breathing tubes, and a poison which can cause the heart to fail. Before the introduction of the diphtheria vaccine, it came in tragic epidemics and the gravestones of country churchyards list whole families of children and adults who were wiped out within weeks by it. Nowadays, thanks to modern vaccines, diphtheria is almost unheard of in the developed countries of the world. Immunisation for babies is vital and harmless.

Polio

As a child, I can remember my parents barring me from public swimming pools and keeping me away from other children as the summer polio epidemic swept into our city. My mother was terrified that I would join the children who filled the hospital wards, some in iron lungs, some with minor paralysis, and others crippled for life.

Across the water in the United States of America polio had, of course, come to prominence with the election to the presidency of Franklin D. Roosevelt, himself a sufferer of the disease which he contracted suddenly in his late thirties. Such was the panic over the illness, that even though the initial vaccines produced were relatively hazardous, mothers were prepared to take the risk. Now all that is past history. The vaccine is absolutely safe and doesn't even need a needle these days. It's as easy as swallowing a lump of sugar. But many mothers, lulled perhaps by the rarity of the disease today, just don't bother with it. Every child should have a polio vaccination.

Tetanus (lockjaw)

Tetanus is caused by an infection that enters the body through wounds that are contaminated, usually by soil. This makes every one of us susceptible and, since tetanus is a long, painful illness with a high risk of death, it is wise to be protected against it. Modern tetanus vaccines are completely safe and very effective.

Whooping cough (pertussis)

Although it is much less serious than the other illnesses mentioned so far, whooping cough follows a long, difficult course.
Death occurs about once in every 4000 cases during an epidemic.
It has been referred to as 'the cough of 100 days' and, although
this may be a bit of an exaggeration, full recovery may well take
three months. In the toddler, there are spasms of coughing, which
often end in vomiting and go on day and night. There is no treatment other than to provide good mothering and nursing care.

Pertussis vaccination rates were high until a much-publicised
scare about vaccine safety in the mid-seventies. It was reported
that the vaccine caused brain damage and following this, vaccination rates, not only for whooping cough but for all diseases,
dropped dramatically. Since then, some notable epidemics have
caused a number of deaths. It is now reckoned that this vaccination does have a minute risk of producing brain damage but the
risks are estimated to be at least one-hundredth of those of death
or brain damage occurring when the unvaccinated child actually
gets whooping cough. Vaccination is most strongly recommended.

Measles

Measles is not a life-threatening illness in children who are well-
nourished, although it causes very serious illness and death in
Africa and other parts of the world where children are underfed.
Measles is extremely infectious, and an unvaccinated child will
most certainly get it. It is a nasty illness which makes children
feel extremely sick, but this and other unpleasant side-effects can
be effectively prevented by vaccination. The vaccine should be
given after the child's first birthday, the illness being rare before
then because the baby still has immunity given by his mother.

Mumps

Recently a vaccine for mumps has been given along with the
measles one, and it seems to provide good protection. This is the
least severe of the childhood illnesses described but it is possible
for mumps to cause loss of hearing in one ear or even a viral brain
infection, and consequently it is believed that vaccination should
be encouraged.

The risks of vaccination

Nothing in life can be guaranteed 100 per cent safe but all risks must be balanced against the benefits. There is no doubt that with diphtheria, tetanus and polio vaccination the benefits are immense and the risks negligible. With whooping cough vaccination there is a definite but small risk, which must be balanced against the far greater risk of death or permanent handicap should the child contract the disease. Measles and mumps vaccines are not absolutely necessary but as the risk of contracting these diseases is extremely high, vaccination does stop quite a bit of needless suffering, and the occasional rare but serious complications the illnesses can produce. In short, the risks of these childhood vaccines are minute in comparison with those of the illnesses they prevent. I have had no hesitation in having my own children vaccinated against all these diseases, including whooping cough, and recommend the same for all children in my care.

The childhood illnesses

Having looked at vaccines and vaccination, let's look briefly at the common childhood illnesses themselves. In the days before vaccination, few of us would have escaped without having at least three of these four illnesses. Measles is so infectious that 100 per cent of all children would have got it, whilst 80 per cent of them would contract mumps and chicken pox. Rubella, or German measles as it is sometimes called, would have affected perhaps 70 per cent of children. So what are the main symptoms of these diseases?

Measles

Measles is a sick child with a red rash, a cough and sore eyes.
This is the most infectious of all the illnesses, and it takes ten to fourteen days to incubate. At first the child develops a high fever, a cough, and sore eyes, but not a spot is there to be seen. He has a runny nose, and as he coughs and splutters he spreads this highly infectious virus to all around, three days before anything is even suspected. About three days after the beginning of the illness the rash develops, which consists of many little red spots that cover the body. Many of us who have trained in children's medicine have

made fools of ourselves at some time or other in our early careers by admitting a coughing child with a high fever to a busy hospital ward, having diagnosed the condition as bronchitis, only to find next morning a rash of red spots and an irate ward sister wanting to know why a highly infectious child was sitting up in the middle of her nice, sterile ward!

Measles makes children quite sick but once over, will give life-long immunity.

Mumps

Mumps is swelling of one or both parotid glands plus a mild feeling of general illness.

Mumps is less infectious than measles and about 20 per cent of children will escape it altogether. It is caused by a virus, which takes two to three weeks to incubate. There is a mild fever and a swelling of one or both of the parotid glands, which are situated in front of the ear lobes at the angle of the jaw. Sometimes the child may have a headache and neck stiffness.

When the schoolchild contracts mumps and brings it home, most fathers get rather concerned as they have heard nasty rumours about what this illness can do to grown men. Orchitis (inflammation of one or both testicles) does not happen in the young child, and it is much less common in the adult than popular myth would have us believe. It is painful when it does occur but that other much-talked of complication, 'sterility', is exceptionally rare. Fathers can now uncross their legs and relax. Vaccination is now given along with the measles and rubella at about thirteen months.

Chicken pox

Chicken pox is an ugly, itchy rash with little fever or feeling of general illness.

This viral complaint takes about two weeks to incubate. It starts with a crop of itchy, raised red spots like flea bites, usually on the trunk. There are often little spots inside the mouth, which is well outside the normal chewing ground of the common flea. The spots enlarge, fill with fluid, and form vesicles (blisters), which eventually burst and are covered by scabs. The child may look awful and feel intensely itchy but he will only have a low fever and feel relatively well in himself. The old-fashioned pink Calamine lotion is probably as good as anything to ease the itching.

Rubella (German measles)

Rubella is a faint, generalised rash, with enlarged glands at the back of the neck in a child who does not appear to be sick.

This viral illness is completely different from measles. It takes from two to three weeks to incubate, and in the young child it is so mild it can easily go unnoticed. There is a fine pink rash, which may not be very obvious and lasts for about three days. This is associated with enlarged glands, particularly those at the back of the neck, on the lower part of the skull.

In young children rubella causes no harm and little sickness. The main danger is for pregnant women, as contact at an early stage of pregnancy can cause major abnormalities in the unborn baby. A vaccination is available and should be given to all children at about 13 months and again to girls in their early high school years to ensure they have good immunity before any thought of pregnancy. Any would-be mother can easily find out if she is immune or not before pregnancy by having a simple blood test.

Bow legs, knock knees, flat feet

Another area of the body that constantly concerns parents is the legs, including the knees and the feet. In the majority of minor leg and foot problems no treatment is needed. The days of night splints, irons and wedges for self-righting conditions have passed.

When the child first walks, his untried feet can be seen pointing in all manner of interesting directions. They usually right themselves within months, at which point you will notice that the child's legs are extremely bowed and he is walking around in his nappy with the posture of a saddle-sore cowboy. At about 2½ the legs will straighten, although this adjustment may be overdone and the child will then suffer from knock knees. By the age of 5, most legs are relatively straight and the feet point in the right direction. Some children continue walking with their toes turned slightly inwards and, if mild, this is of no great concern. In fact, one specialist colleague of mine sports the theory that these children may make the best footballers, being able to change direction and weave faster than anyone else on the field. There has to be some compensation for having feet that point in two directions at the same time.

All babies and toddlers have flat feet. It often takes until the age of 6 for the ligaments to tighten up and produce a proper arch.

This may never happen in some families where there is a history of flat feet. Some believe that the child should walk around without shoes and strengthen his ligaments; others believe that wedges in the shoes produce better arches. I believe that each year more and more are moving towards the 'no treatment' lobby.

Once again these are general observations. If the bends or postures cause any concern, a specialist opinion should be sought.

The sick child: when to panic

When teaching junior doctors I impress upon them that their greatest skill lies not in knowing hundreds of rare medical facts but in being able to reliably spot 'the sick child'. It is difficult and probably dangerous for me to try to express in written form what is essentially a 'gut feeling'. I believe that most of the clues are in the eyes and the child's alertness.

The child who has vomited all day may nevertheless appear alert, have bright eyes, and take a lively and keen interest when you walk into the room. If this is the case, he is probably safe. If the same child were dull-eyed, distant and at all confused, then medical help must be summoned immediately. When a child is pale, sweaty and looks anxious, it is a good idea to get help quickly. This is generally how a child will appear if he is 'shocked' and may have some major surgical or other condition. The child who has sunken eyes, a lack of elasticity in his skin, a dry mouth, and is passing little urine is also a worry. Any child with a stiff neck, which is painful to move or bend, needs medical examination, as does a child with panting, over-breathing or deep, rattling breathing.

When mum is worried, I worry. When mum is worried and grandma is worried, I worry a lot!

Medicines: how to give them

Doctors have no difficulty in writing prescriptions for children. The problem comes when it is time to force the strange substance down the toddler's throat. If an unpleasant-tasting medicine has been prescribed once, it is wise to let the doctor know, as often there is a more palatable alternative for the subsequent occasions. For the child who is a militant drug refuser, sometimes preparations that require fewer doses a day may be prescribed. With antibiotics, this is particularly useful, as often two-dose-a-day drugs can supplant the four-dose-a-day ones. I am all for using the purest and most modern preparation but if the latest no sugar, no preservatives, no artificial colouring product tastes like 'cat's wee', I feel that someone has missed the point.

Most drugs can be given in liquid form to toddlers, preferably slipped into the mouth on a spoon and chased down by a favourite drink. For the reluctant child, sometimes a plastic syringe is more effective. The medicine is squirted through a small opening in the mouth. Watch out for the fine aerosol spray which can blow around the room once the medicine has hit the child's tongue. If capsules or tablets are given, the mouth should be moist before their introduction, or the capsules themselves can be moistened before they are put in the mouth. These measures help to lubricate them on that short, difficult journey from the tongue to the throat. Little tablets toboggan down the throat with the greatest of ease when placed in a little ice-cream. Bigger ones may be crushed, placed on top of a thin layer of ice-cream, with jam or chocolate topping being placed over that, thus making a spoon-sized medicine sandwich.

When a child has an illness that is making his stomach delicate because of copious vomiting, giving medicine will be a far from popular exercise. Certain medicines have to be given but others are best omitted rather than vomited up. It seems pointless to administer a preparation designed to stop vomiting if all that is going to happen to it is that it is going to be thrown straight up again.

Bed rest for toddlers

In modern hospitals children who have undergone major surgery will be seen up and about the next day. Meanwhile, not a mile down the road, a child with a red tonsil will be confined to his bed by a worried mother for what may seem to him like an eternity. Bed rest is now an outdated practice reserved for children with pre-paralytic polio and other equally rare conditions. If the child feels well enough to want to be up, good for him. If he leaves his bed to lie on a rug by the fire, that's just as good. If he feels so miserable that all he wants is the peace and comfort of bed, that is when he will get bed rest.

There are no black and white rules. Sense and flexibility are the important things but you will usually find that, in these cases, the child knows best.

Toddler development worries

Books on child care usually list a multitude of clever developmental milestones for the child to attain at any given age. Few of these books, however, distinguish between the important milestones and those that are best termed interesting but useless. Looking at a child's developmental profile, one is interested in his gross motor, fine motor, hearing, vision, communication, social and play skills. When one has been working for some years in a developmental assessment unit, it soon becomes clear which of these have the most value.

The gross motor area—walking, running and climbing—tends to be of most interest to the parents. In fact, early walking bears little relationship to advanced intelligence and is much more likely to be an inherited family trait. Children who walk early often have a mother who was an early walker. When teaching psychologists, who have a great interest in motor milestones in young children, I cite the case of the greyhound, which is probably one of the most advanced 'gross motor animals' around. Any dog that spends its entire life chasing after a stuffed hare without suspecting it is being fooled is, to my mind at least, not very intelligent.

By far the most valuable skills are those in the area of communication. At 6 months, the child who communicates vigorously with his eyes, takes in everything in his environment, and 'doesn't miss a move' has a good start to life. In the second year, the child with good, appropriate, non-repetitive speech is likely to do well.

If the child has no speech, good comprehension is even more important, and the child should be able to point with accuracy to objects in pictures and books or to things in his environment. I learn much about a child's intelligence, when he is difficult to assess, by watching him play. I look for constructive qualities, where he uses the material provided in an intelligent way. I also look for imagination and pretend play. If these are present in the toddler, it is unlikely he has any major problem of intellectual development.

I worry when a child has little interest in his surroundings, walks around in a purposeless manner, and is slow to respond to sound. I worry when there is little understanding of simple messages and only parrot-like repetitive speech. I worry when there is apparently little understanding; for example, the child may flick through a book in an obsessive manner without displaying any interest or recognition of what is inside it. I worry when a toddler who does not talk to me with his voice does not communicate with his face or eyes either. I worry when the child has no pretend or constructive play and is stuck at the stage of throwing and banging toys together or running around the house aimlessly.

Many books are available on the developmental assessment of young children. My only aim here is to point out those general patterns that suggest success, and those which cause concern. (See also Appendix I, Meaningful Milestones.)

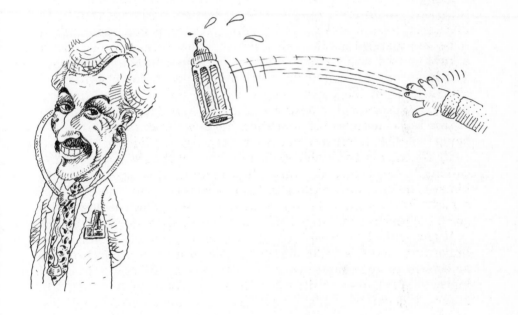

Meaningful Milestones

Note: There is a wide range of normal development, each child having relative strengths and weaknesses in the profile of abilities presented. If 1 or 2 items are delayed it is generally of little significance. If many items are delayed, and there is a lack of comprehension, disinterest in the environment and an absence of quality play, then an expert professional opinion should be sought.

Here is a guide to the general pattern of development at different ages.

1 year

- Walks reliably holding onto furniture.
- Some may be walking alone (average age 13 months—range of normal between 9 months and 18 months).
- Picks up small objects between the tip of the thumb and the forefinger.
- Understands the word 'No!' and at this age usually obeys it.
- Knows name and will usually turn when it is used.
- Babbles in a tuneful, foreign-sounding language.
- Understands 'Give it to mummy', but only if accompanied by gesture.
- Says 'Da da' and sometimes 1 or 2 other words with meaning.
- Uses a drinking cup with some assistance.
- Can hold a spoon but unable to load it at the plate and navigate without spillage to the mouth.
- Putting toys and other objects in the mouth is now on the wane.
- Waves 'Bye bye' and enjoys 'Peek-a-boo' games.
- Understands the permanence of objects. If a toy is hidden as they watch, they immediately know where it is.

CONCERNS   Be concerned when:

- No tuneful babble is produced.
- Hearing seems to be a problem.
- No interest is taken in the environment.
- Not yet standing upright beside furniture.
- Not using the finger/thumb grip.
- A child does not 'feel right' in any way or is significantly different to a brother or sister at that age.

18 months

- Walks reliably without any support.
- Squats down to pick up a toy.
- Pushes wheeled toys around the floor.
- Loves to put objects in and out of containers.
- Delicate pincer grip allows picking up of crumbs and other small objects.
- Holds a pencil like a dagger and scribbles without purpose.
- Talks tunefully to self in own language.

- Uses between 6 and 20 appropriate words. (Note: appropriate does not include repeats of what mother has just said.)
- Most start to show preference for one hand.
- Points to shoes, hair, nose, feet, on request.
- Responds to a simple one-part verbal command.
- Points to objects in a picture book, eg. dog.
- Holds a spoon securely and is reasonably reliable in feeding.
- Manages a feeding cup unaided.
- No longer mouths toys.
- Piles 3 blocks on top of each other.
- Starts to show discomfort when wet or dirty.
- Starts to go upstairs holding on tight.
- Fluctuates between being very clingy and resisting attention.
- Not the age of reason. Do not know what they want but know they want it immediately.

2 years

- Walks well. Runs reliably.
- Walks upstairs placing both feet on each step, holding lightly to a rail. Almost able to come down again upright.
- Enjoys ride on toys, pushing them along.
- Walks backward whilst dragging a wheeled toy on the end of a string.
- Attempts to kick a ball.
- Piles 6 blocks on top of each other.
- Removes a wrapper from a lolly.
- Holds a pencil almost correctly.
- Scribbles in a circular manner.
- Can imitate a vertical line.
- Enjoys looking at picture books.
- Turns one page at a time.
- Can usually point out 'Which boy is happy?'
- Hand dominance is established in most.
- Over 50 words in vocabulary and many more understood.
- Puts 2 and occasionally 3 words together.
- Refers to self by name.
- Joins in nursery rhymes and songs.
- Delivers simple messages, 'Daddy, come'.
- Chews food well.
- Spoon feeding a success.
- Usually dry by day.
- Usually tells when wants to go to the toilet.
- Imitates mother doing household duties.
- Will help tidy away toys.
- Real help with dressing.
- Demands mum's attention constantly.
- Plays beside, but not directly with, other children.
- Clingy—plays in another room, but checks every couple of minutes to ensure mother is still there.
- Rebellious when does not get own way.
- Possessive of toys and attention.
- Not a time for sharing and seeing another's point of view!

CONCERNS   Be concerned when:

- There is minimal or no speech. (In this case, check hearing, comprehension and other areas of development.)
- Toys are still being mouthed.
- Toys are being thrown in an unthinking way.
- Play is always repetitive—e.g. spinning wheels and banging blocks.
- Interest in environment is not being shown. Should be a real 'sticky-beak' at this age.
- There is a lack of 'body language'.
- There is unusual irritability.

2 ½ years

- Uses 200 or more words.
- Uses pronouns, 'I', 'Me', 'You'.
- Holds pen with a reasonable adult-type grip and imitates a circle and horizontal line.
- Builds a tower of 7 blocks.
- Pulls pants down for toiletting but usually unable to get them back up.
- Knows full name.
- May stutter in eagerness to get information out.
- Plays alongside in parallel to other children.
- Little idea of sharing playthings or adults' attention.
- Won't wait, expects everything immediately.

3 years

- Walks upstairs using alternate feet on each step and comes down using both feet per step.
- Jumps off bottom step with two feet together.
- Runs around obstacles with speed and accuracy.
- Pedals tricycle.
- Can walk on tip toe.
- Can catch a ball with arms outstretched.
- Threads large beads on a shoelace.
- Copies a circle and imitates a cross.
- Matches 3 primary colours, but still confuses blue and green.
- Cuts with scissors.
- Speech intelligible even to a stranger.
- Uses most plurals correctly.
- Will volunteer full name and sex.
- Still talks to self at length at play.
- Able to describe an event that has happened, simply but reliably.
- Questions start—'Why?', 'Why?', 'Why?'.
- Listens eagerly to stories and likes a favourite one repeated and then repeated once more.
- Recites several nursery rhymes.
- Rote counts to 10.
- Counts to 10, but only understands practical counting of 2 or 3 items.
- Washes hands but needs supervision to dry.
- Can dress self except for buttons, tight tops and shoes.
- Likes to help adult with home activities.
- Behaviour is less impatient and self centered.

- Able to wait for a short time before getting what wants.
- Understands sharing toys, lollies and attention.
- Plays directly with other children.
- Vivid imagination, loves pretend play.
- Separates reasonably well from mother, but this varies greatly.

CONCERNS   *Be concerned when:*

- There is an inability to communicate easily through appropriate speech.
- Body language is poor.
- Repetitive play shows little imagination, or richness.
- Behaviour is still like the senseless, sparky and unsharing 18-month-old.

4 years

- Walks and probably runs up and down stairs without holding on.
- Throws and catches well; starts to bounce a ball.
- Piles blocks, 2 to the side and one on top, to copy a bridge.
- Holds a pen like an adult.
- Draws a man with trunk, head, legs and usually arms and fingers.
- Draws a reasonable likeness of a house.
- Names 4 primary colours.
- Grammar and speech construction is usually correct.
- A few sounds still mispronounced and immature.
- Can describe an occurrence in an accurate and logical way.
- Can state address and age.
- Questioning is at its height. Constantly asks 'Why?', 'When?', 'How?'.
- Listens intently to stories.
- Tells stories, often confusing fact with fiction.
- May have imaginary friends.
- Understands yesterday, today, tomorrow, ie. past and future.
- Rote counts to 20 and understands meaningful counting up to 5 objects.
- Enjoys jokes and plays on words.
- Eats with skill and cuts with a knife.
- Rarely uses a knife and fork before age 4^{1}/$_{2}$.
- Washes and dries own hands.
- Brushes teeth with supervision.
- Blows nose reliably.
- Wipes bottom after toileting.
- Can fully dress and undress except for inaccessible buttons, bows and shoelaces. (Shoelaces are rarely tied before the age of 5 and with the advent of Velcro, for many children it is much later).
- Plays well with other children.
- Now argues with words rather than blows.
- Verbal impertinence and bickering are developing fast.
- Understands taking turns, sharing and simple rules.
- Starts to believe in justice and everyone keeping to the rules.
- Many like to be the king pin, 'bossy-boots'.
- Shows concern for younger siblings, playmates in distress.
- Usually separates well from mother.

Reference: *Children's Developmental Progress,* Mary Sheridan
(N.F.E.R Publishing Co., UK).

Hepatitis B Vaccine

The Hepatitis B virus causes hepatitis, an infective condition of the liver. This can vary in severity. At its worst it is a very serious condition and can sometimes lead to long-term liver complications. In many the illness passes completely, while others are apparently well, but still carry the virus, which is infectious.

This virus is carried in the blood and also in a less infective form in many body fluids. This puts at risk those who are intimately involved with any adult or child who carries the virus.

There is an effective Hepatitis B vaccine which is now relatively cheap. In a number of countries (e.g. New Zealand), this is now offered routinely to all infants and children.

In Australia, the present policy (as of October 1996) is to vaccinate only high risk groups, which would include those living with, or going to day care with, a known carrier. At this time routine immunisation of all Australian children is not advised, however this policy is currently under review. It would appear that immunisation of all infants and adolescents will be recommended within the next two years.

Miscellaneous Facts

- At the age of 2 years most toddlers have attained half their adult height.
- From birth till 2½ years every parent can expect to change between 7000 and 8000 dirty nappies.
- A toddler requires 2½ times more food to power each kilogram of body weight as would a mature 20-year-old. This explains why toddlers eat so much to keep their furnaces fired up.
- The average children of today will have witnessed at least 18,000 murders on television by the time they have left school.
- A toddler cannot comprehend the permanence of marriage break-up or death. To them both are reversible states.
- Religion has little meaning for toddlers, who follow without question the beliefs and example of those closest to them. Independent inner faith is first found in late adolescence.
- Home is a very dangerous place. Domestic violence is much more common than street violence.
- Five per cent of all adult Australians are true alcoholics with 20 per cent said to be problem drinkers. This has a devastating impact on their families especially the children. This 5 per cent figure would account for almost one million Australians who are, or will become, alcoholics.
- About 33 per cent of Australian men and 29 per cent of Australian women smoke. The number of young men smokers is reducing at present, the figure for young women smokers is increasing.

  Passive smoking is not without its problems. Adults can escape this, but our children are not so fortunate. They have to inhale whatever we put in their environment for 18 years until they are in a position able to make up their own minds on whether they wish to smoke or not.
- There is no necessity for routine worming of the average Australian family. Worms are incorrectly believed to cause abdominal pain, pallor and malnutrition. When worms are seen in the motions, or children have an itchy bottom, particularly at night, treatment is needed.
- Sun in excess is extremely damaging to skin, making young adults look prematurely old and wrinkled. The 1990s are a time of being sensible in sunshine. Hats, high factor sun screens and caution are needed from the earliest years.

Recommended Childhood Immunisation Schedule

(Recommended by the National Health and Medical Research Council in August 1994 and current at the time of publication, October 1996.)

At two months	Injection of diphtheria, tetanus, whooping cough and Hib (Haemophilus influenzae type b) vaccine, plus oral polio vaccine.
At four months	Injection of diphtheria, tetanus, whooping cough and Hib vaccine plus oral polio vaccine.
At six months	Injection of diphtheria, tetanus and whooping cough vaccine plus oral polio vaccine. Also Hib if using HibTITER or Act-HIB.
At twelve months	Injection of measles, mumps and rubella (German measles) vaccine. Also Hib if using PedvaxHIB.
At eighteen months	Injection of diphtheria, tetanus and whooping cough vaccine. Also Hib if using HibTITER or Act-HIB.
At five years or prior to school entry	Injection of diphtheria, tetanus and whooping cough vaccine plus oral polio vaccine.
Between ten and sixteen	Injection of measles, mumps and rubella vaccine.
Prior to school leaving (15 to 19 years)	Injection of diphtheria and tetanus vaccine plus oral polio vaccine.

APPENDIX V

Heights from 1 Year to 4 Years
Height in cm—girls (boys)

Age Yrs	Mths	Average height		Lower average 3% will be shorter 97% will be taller		Upper average 3% will be taller 97% will be shorter	
1	0	74.3	(76.1)	69.0	(71.0)	79.6	(81.2)
1	1	75.5	(77.2)	70.1	(72.1)	80.9	(82.4)
1	2	76.7	(78.3)	71.2	(73.1)	82.1	(83.6)
1	3	77.8	(79.4)	72.2	(74.1)	83.3	(84.8)
1	4	78.9	(80.4)	73.2	(75.0)	84.5	(85.9)
1	5	79.9	(81.4)	74.2	(75.9)	85.6	(87.0)
1	6	80.9	(82.4)	75.1	(76.7)	86.7	(88.1)
1	7	81.9	(83.3)	76.1	(77.5)	87.8	(89.2)
1	8	82.9	(84.2)	77.0	(78.3)	88.8	(90.2)
1	9	83.8	(85.1)	77.8	(79.1)	89.8	(91.2)
1	10	84.7	(86.0)	78.7	(79.8)	90.8	(92.2)
1	11	85.6	(86.8)	79.5	(80.6)	91.7	(93.1)
2	0	84.5	(85.6)	78.5	(79.6)	90.5	(91.6)
2	1	85.4	(86.4)	79.2	(80.3)	91.5	(92.5)
2	2	86.2	(87.2)	80.0	(81.0)	92.4	(93.5)
2	3	87.0	(88.1)	80.7	(81.7)	93.4	(94.4)
2	4	87.9	(88.9)	81.4	(82.4)	94.3	(95.3)
2	5	88.7	(89.7)	82.2	(83.1)	95.2	(96.2)
2	6	89.5	(90.4)	82.9	(83.8)	96.0	(97.1)
2	7	90.2	(91.2)	83.6	(84.5)	96.9	(97.9)
2	8	91.0	(92.0)	84.3	(85.2)	97.7	(98.8)
2	9	91.7	(92.7)	84.9	(85.8)	98.6	(99.6)
2	10	92.5	(93.5)	85.6	(86.5)	99.4	(100.5)
2	11	93.2	(94.2)	86.3	(87.1)	100.1	(101.3)
3	0	93.9	(94.9)	86.9	(87.8)	100.9	(102.1)
3	1	94.6	(95.6)	87.6	(88.4)	101.7	(102.9)
3	2	95.3	(96.3)	88.2	(89.0)	102.4	(103.7)
3	3	96.0	(97.0)	88.8	(89.6)	103.1	(104.4)
3	4	96.6	(97.7)	89.4	(90.2)	103.9	(105.2)
3	5	97.3	(98.4)	90.0	(90.9)	104.6	(106.0)
3	6	97.9	(99.1)	90.6	(91.5)	105.3	(106.7)
3	7	98.6	(99.7)	91.2	(92.0)	105.9	(107.4)
3	8	99.2	(100.4)	91.8	(92.6)	106.6	(108.2)
3	9	99.8	(101.0)	92.3	(93.2)	107.3	(108.9)
3	10	100.4	(101.7)	92.9	(93.8)	107.9	(109.6)
3	11	101.0	(102.3)	93.5	(94.4)	108.6	(110.3)
4	0	101.6	(102.9)	94.0	(94.9)	109.2	(111.0)

Reference: World Health Organisation Standards.

Note: The ideal relationship of height and weight is to be in proportion (e.g. if the child is of upper average height, his weight should also be upper average).

Note: 1 cm = 0.3937 inches   1 inch = 2.54 cm

APPENDIX VI

Weights from 1 Year to 4 Years
Weight in kg—girls (boys)

Age Yrs	Age Mths	Average weight		Lower average 3% will be lighter 97% will be heavier		Upper average 3% will be heavier 97% will be lighter	
1	0	9.5	(10.2)	7.6	(8.2)	11.5	(12.2)
1	1	9.8	(10.4)	7.8	(8.5)	11.8	(12.5)
1	2	10.0	(10.7)	8.0	(8.7)	12.0	(12.8)
1	3	10.2	(10.9)	8.1	(8.8)	12.3	(13.1)
1	4	10.4	(11.1)	8.3	(9.0)	12.5	(13.3)
1	5	10.6	(11.3)	8.5	(9.1)	12.7	(13.6)
1	6	10.8	(11.5)	8.6	(9.3)	13.0	(13.8)
1	7	11.0	(11.7)	8.8	(9.4)	13.2	(14.0)
1	8	11.2	(11.8)	8.9	(9.5)	13.4	(14.2)
1	9	11.4	(12.0)	9.1	(9.7)	13.6	(14.4)
1	10	11.5	(12.2)	9.3	(9.8)	13.9	(14.6)
1	11	11.7	(12.4)	9.4	(9.9)	14.1	(14.8)
2	0	11.8	(12.3)	9.6	(10.2)	14.4	(15.5)
2	1	12.0	(12.5)	9.7	(10.3)	14.8	(15.7)
2	2	12.2	(12.7)	9.9	(10.4)	15.1	(15.9)
2	3	12.4	(12.9)	10.1	(10.6)	15.4	(16.1)
2	4	12.6	(13.1)	10.2	(10.7)	15.7	(16.4)
2	5	12.8	(13.3)	10.4	(10.8)	16.0	(16.6)
2	6	13.0	(13.5)	10.5	(10.9)	16.2	(16.8)
2	7	13.2	(13.7)	10.6	(11.0)	16.5	(17.0)
2	8	13.4	(13.9)	10.8	(11.1)	16.8	(17.2)
2	9	13.6	(14.1)	10.9	(11.3)	17.0	(17.4)
2	10	13.8	(14.3)	11.1	(11.4)	17.3	(17.6)
2	11	13.9	(14.4)	11.2	(11.5)	17.5	(17.8)
3	0	14.1	(14.6)	11.3	(11.6)	17.8	(18.0)
3	1	14.3	(14.8)	11.5	(11.7)	18.0	(18.2)
3	2	14.4	(15.0)	11.6	(11.9)	18.3	(18.5)
3	3	14.6	(15.2)	11.7	(12.0)	18.5	(18.7)
3	4	14.8	(15.3)	11.8	(12.1)	18.7	(18.9)
3	5	14.9	(15.5)	12.0	(12.2)	18.9	(19.1)
3	6	15.1	(15.7)	12.1	(12.4)	19.1	(19.3)
3	7	15.2	(15.8)	12.2	(12.5)	19.4	(19.5)
3	8	15.4	(16.0)	12.3	(12.6)	19.6	(19.7)
3	9	15.5	(16.2)	12.4	(12.7)	19.8	(19.9)
3	10	15.7	(16.4)	12.5	(12.9)	20.0	(20.1)
3	11	15.8	(16.5)	12.6	(13.0)	20.2	(20.3)
4	0	16.0	(16.7)	12.8	(13.1)	20.4	(20.5)

Reference: World Health Organisation Standards.

Note: The ideal relationship of weight and height is to be in proportion (e.g. if the child is of lower average height, his weight should also be lower average).

Note: 1 kg = 2.2 lbs   1 lb = 0.45 kg

References

1. Tizard, *The Origins of Human Social Relations*, Academic Press, London, 1971, pp. 147-61.
2. Hornberger, *et al.*, *Health Supervision of Young Children in California*, Berkeley, Bureau of Maternal and Child Health, State of California Department of Public Health, 1960.

   Richman, *Journal of Child Psychology and Psychiatry*, vol. 16, 1975, pp. 277-87.

   Chess, *et al.*, *Behavioural Individuality in Early Childhood*, New York University Press, 1963.

   Chess, *Temperament and Development*, Brunner Mazel, New York, 1977.

   Chamberlin, *Paediatric Clinics of North America*, vol. 21, no. 1, February 1974.
3. Chess, *et al.*, See above.

   Chess, See above.
4. Chamberlin, See above.
5. Anders, *Paediatrics*, vol. 63, 1979, pp. 860-4.
6. Beltramini, *et al.*, *Paediatrics*, vol. 71, no. 2, 1973.
7. Chamberlin, See above.
8. Anders, See above.
9. Richman, See above.
10. Tizard, See above.
11. Green, *The Journal of Maternal and Child Health*, United Kingdom, February 1980.
12. Mason, *Veterinary Record*, vol. 86, 1970, pp. 612-16.
13. Green & Waters, 'Hyperactive Children', *The Australian Prescriber*, November 1986.
14. Egger *et al.*, *The Lancet*, 9 March 1985, pp. 540-5.
15., 16., 17. Connors, *Food Additives and Hyperactive Children*, Plenum Press, 1980.

   'New evidence on food additives in hyperkinesis', *American Journal of Diseases of Childhood*, vol. 134, December 1980.
18. Egger, *et al.*, See above.
19. Rutter, *Scientific Foundations of Developmental Psychiatry*, Heinemann, 1980.
20. Rutter, *Child Psychiatry—Modern Approaches*, Blackwell, 1985.
21. Green, *Medical Journal of Australia*, vol. 1, 1981, pp. 402-4.
22. Green, *The Practitioner*, vol. 223, 1979, pp. 690-5.

Index